9-18-63 (62-18303)

THE GREAT AMERICAN GENTLEMAN

THE GREAT AMERICAN GENTLEMAN

William Byrd

OF WESTOVER IN VIRGINIA

His Secret Diary for the Years
1709-1712

EDITED BY

Louis B. Wright and Marion Tinling

G. P. Putnam's Sons   New York

Library of Congress Catalog Card
Number: 62-18303
Manufactured in the United States of America

Preface

THE editors have selected those entries from *The Secret Diary of William Byrd of Westover 1709-1712* which best illustrate colonial life in this period and throw the most light on the writer of the diary, a fascinating and complex character. Limitations of space have made it necessary to delete many repetitive passages that are sometimes amusing by reason of their sheer repetition in Byrd's daily routine, but it is hoped that enough remains to give the flavor of day-to-day existence in the colony of Virginia in the early years of the eighteenth century. The editors have concentrated upon the earliest of the three sections of Byrd's diary in print because it gives a somewhat more comprehensive picture of life in Virginia than the later portions. Furthermore, to have attempted to give bits from all three portions would have required such drastic abridgment that the selections would have lost continuity and significance.

In making the selections and in the preparation of the copy the editors are indebted to Miss Ellen Eyler of the Folger Library staff.

L.B.W.
M.T.

December 24, 1961

Introduction

INTIMATE diaries, never intended for the eye of anyone except the writer, hold a fascination, sometimes a morbid fascination, for later generations. Because they are frank and revealing, they are not only useful for the information they provide about the individual who kept them, but they are also valuable for the light they throw upon the social history of a period. If the diary-keeper was someone prominent in his own time who moved in many spheres the document becomes all the more valuable. Such a diary is the one kept by William Byrd II, of Westover in the colony of Virginia, who lived between the years 1674 and 1744.

Byrd was the son of William Byrd I, who, as an Indian trader and planter, had established the family fortune in Virginia.[1] As a child of seven, young William was sent to relatives in England to be educated and was duly enrolled in Felsted Grammar School in Essex. Later he became a member of the Middle Temple and for a time went to Holland to learn business practices. When his father died in 1704, William inherited a substantial fortune and took his place as one of the leading members of the Virginia aristocracy. Few men of his time in Virginia had greater responsibilities and honors. As a youth he was elected to the House of Burgesses and later became a member of the all-important Council of State, of which he was president in the last year of his life. On several occasions he was sent to London to act as agent for the colony. At various times he served his county as colonel of the militia and in other official capacities. Early in his career he was elected a Fellow of the Royal Society and until the end of his life took pride in being member of that learned and august body. One of his most interesting duties was that of leader of the surveying party which in 1728 established the boundary between Virginia and North Carolina. That experience resulted in

3

Byrd's writing *The History of the Dividing Line Betwixt Virginia and North Carolina Run in the Year of Our Lord 1728,* a work which circulated in manuscript in Byrd's own lifetime and was first published in 1841. This document gave Byrd a reputation as one of the most urbane of Southern writers in the colonial period. He also wrote two or three shorter pieces, including *A Journey to the Land of Eden* and *A Progress to the Mines.*

Byrd became known as a diarist when the first section of his secret shorthand diary turned up in the Huntington Library and was edited by Louis B. Wright and Marion Tinling as *The Secret Diary of William Byrd of Westover 1709-1712* (Richmond, Va., the Dietz Press, 1941). In the meantime, Miss Maude Woodfin had discovered another portion of the diary at the University of North Carolina, which Mrs. Tinling transcribed. This was edited by Miss Woodfin and Mrs. Tinling as *Another Secret Diary of William Byrd of Westover 1739-1741 with Letters and Literary Exercises 1696-1726* (Richmond, Va., Dietz Press, 1942). Still a third portion was discovered in the Virginia Historical Society and was edited by Louis B. Wright and Marion Tinling as *William Byrd of Virginia. The London Diary (1717-1721) and Other Writings* (New York, Oxford University Press, 1958). All three volumes are still in print.

It is reasonable to suppose that Byrd kept a shorthand diary through most of his adult life. The three known portions are widely separated in date but they all are similar in physical appearance. They were written in small notebooks, and they begin and end abruptly as if they were parts of a series of notebooks. It is to be hoped that other portions may come to light.

The Huntington Library notebook has several preliminary leaves containing translations which Byrd had made from a law-French version of Sir Edward Coke's *Reports.* These are in longhand except for a few phrases. By comparing these shorthand phrases with the original, the present editors managed to build up a shorthand alphabet and read Byrd's shorthand entries. Later they discovered that Byrd had used a textbook on shorthand prepared by William Mason and first published in 1672 as *A Pen Pluckt from an Eagle's Wing* which was later revised and published in 1707 as *La Plume Volante.* Byrd apparently used this later revision, but, like many shorthand writers, he modified the system that he had learned to suit his own purposes.

The abridgment printed here is taken from the section covering the years 1709-1712 when Byrd was establishing himself as a leading planter in Virginia. This section contains fuller entries than are to be found in the later sections and is particularly important for the information that it gives about social life in the colony. Unlike the Puritans in the North, Southern colonists were not given to keeping extensive journals, and Byrd's is by far the fullest diary that has yet come to light for this period in the South. Rather than try to give a skeleton abridgment of all three portions of the diary, the editors have concentrated on the earliest section.

At the time Byrd was keeping this section of the diary, he was married to Lucy Parke, the spoiled daughter of Colonel Daniel Parke. Passionate as was their love at times, they quarreled with equal vehemence and their life together was tempestuous. The diary frequently mentions both moments of intimate tenderness and violent outbursts of anger. Byrd complacently asserts that in all their quarrels he was in the right and she was in the wrong. With the utmost self-satisfaction, he remarks on his efficacy as his wife's lover. At times Lucy must have found him hard to endure.

Unlike the Virginia cavalier of romantic fiction, Byrd was extraordinarily hard-working, whether about plantation affairs, the affairs of the colony, or the training of his own mind.[2] Despite the temptations of the flesh to which he often succumbed, he was genuinely pious and was a consistent reader of the sermons of the Reverend John Tillotson, or some other popular preacher whose works were in print. Over a long period of his life he read every day selections from Greek, Hebrew, or Latin. Nearly every entry in the diary closes with the formula: "I said my prayers. I had good health, good thoughts, and good humor, thanks be to God Almighty." This was a formula, to be sure, but it was indicative of one side of his complex character.

The section of the diary recounting his experiences in London covers the years 1717 to 1721 when Byrd had returned to England to serve as agent for the colony, a diplomatic post that required him to know everyone who mattered in the government, particularly members of the Board of Trade which dealt with colonial affairs. This part of the diary describes his daily routine in London and gives to the modern reader an impression of the triviality that occupied so much of fashionable life in eighteenth-century England. He frequented the coffeehouses; he often visited the Spanish ambassador, who seems to have run one of the more elaborate gambling resorts where Byrd lost more than he won; he attended countless balls and other social affairs; he went to horse races; and he took the waters at Tunbridge Wells.

5

Now a widower (for Lucy Parke had contracted smallpox and died in London), Byrd was determined to marry a rich heiress. To that end he pursued relentlessly a certain Mary Smith, daughter of John Smith, Esq., of Beaufort Buildings, a wealthy Commissioner of the Excise. The London diary recounts the ups and downs of this love affair until the prospective father-in-law demanded to see a balance sheet of Byrd's affairs and summarily rejected his because his income was not sufficient.

Byrd comforted himself all during his wooing of Mary Smith with the charms of a long list of women on all levels of society. On one occasion when a lady of fashion was not at home when he called, he improved the opportunity by seducing her maid. When the lady returned, he seduced her, and, after describing this afternoon of love, comments that he went home and ate a plum cake. Byrd, like Boswell, showed little discrimination in the women whom he chose to satisfy his lust and was not above picking up a wench in St. James's Park and having his way with her in the weeds nearby. All of this he sets down in the London diary, with an occasional expression of remorse and the note that he had been to St. Clement Danes in the morning to ask God to forgive him. His repentance too often did not last out the day.

The last section of the diary in print, that covering the years 1739-41, shows Byrd back in Virginia as an old man, still active in the affairs of the colony, still reading Greek, Hebrew, and Latin, and still amorous. He occasionally comments that he had "played the fool" last night with Sarah or Sally, or some other. This volume also contains many of his love letters, including those that he wrote to Miss Smith when he was pursuing her in London in 1717.

Byrd was no Samuel Pepys, but he was the nearest thing to Pepys that the colonial South produced. His diary provides the sort of day-to-day account of life that enables one to reconstruct the society of a past age. One could wish that he had told more about what he was thinking and said less about what he ate every day, or how often he took setting-up exercises ("danced my dance" or skipped rope), or what the state of the weather was, but these are the usual concomitants of a diary kept for one's personal use, and we must be thankful for the details that he does provide. Indeed, from such inconsequential details one is enabled to see clearly the routine of everyday life, something that is lacking in more formal writing. Byrd has given us a vast amount of the raw material of social history.

NOTES

[1] The fullest recent biography of Byrd is that contained in the introduction to *William Byrd of Virginia. The London Diary (1717-1721) and Other Writings* (New York, Oxford University Press, 1958).

The present editors have in preparation a full-length study of Byrd and an edition of his letters and other writings.

[2] For information about the quality of the Virginia aristocracy in this period, see Louis B. Wright, *The First Gentlemen of Virginia* (San Marino, Calif., the Huntington Library, 1940).

THE GREAT AMERICAN GENTLEMAN

February, 1709

. . .

8. I rose at 5 o'clock this morning and read a chapter in Hebrew and 200 verses in Homer's *Odyssey*. I ate milk for breakfast. I said my prayers. Jenny and Eugene were whipped. I danced my dance. I read law in the morning and Italian in the afternoon. . . .

9. . . . The people made an end of tarring the house. I ate nothing but pork for dinner. In the evening Mr. H-m brought me a letter from the President about the clerk of Prince George, and signifying that my Lord Lovelace, governor of New York, arrived the ninth of December at his government. . . .

10. . . . About 12 o'clock we went to the christening of Mr. Anderson's son, where we met abundance of company. There was a plentiful dinner but I ate nothing but bacon and fowl. Nothing happened particularly but there was dancing and evident mirth. Mr. Anderson was beyond measure pleased with the blessing God had sent him. . . . I desired Captain Llewellyn to send his godson to the College.

11. . . . Just at night Mr. Bland came on his way to Williamsburg, who told me that Prince George court had the third time refused the President's recommendation of Mr. Robin Bolling to be their clerk, without any reason, notwithstanding he had made all the submission that was fit for a gentleman to make. . . .

. . .

13. . . . In the evening I took a walk and met Dick Cocke's servant who in the absence of the Doctor sent to me for two or three purgatives. I sent him some blackroot sufficient for three doses but

refused to send him any laudanum because I think it is bad for the gripes. I said my prayers devoutly, having read a sermon in Dr. Tillotson. . . .

14. . . . Colonel Randolph dined with me and I ate chicken for dinner, and our chief business was concerning a ship for his son Isham. . . .

. . .

16. . . . [I] ate chocolate for breakfast with Mr. Isham Randolph, who went away immediately after. I promised him to be engaged of a quarter of a ship for him not exceeding a price of £1000. . . . I prepared a representation concerning the Indian trade to be presented to the Council, to meet on the eighteenth of this month. . . . Colonel Miles Cary died this day and was taken sick but yesterday. . . .

. . .

21. . . . In the afternoon the Doctor came from Williamsburg and brought me a letter from the President, who informed me that Mr. Burwell was by the Council made naval officer of York River in the place of Colonel Cary deceased. In the evening I had a letter from Mr. Parker who sent me a fat steer for a present. I gave the man a crown that brought it. . . .

22. . . . I threatened Anaka with a whipping if she did not confess the intrigue between Daniel and Nurse, but she prevented by a confession. I chided Nurse severely about it, but she denied, with an impudent face, protesting that Daniel only lay on the bed for the sake of the child. I ate nothing but beef for dinner. The Doctor went to Mr. Dick Cocke who was very dangerously sick. . . .

23. . . . I went to Colonel Randolph's. . . . The Colonel told me that two Nansemond Indians and two Meherrins were sent by the Tuscaroras to see if the English were alive. If they were, the Tuscaroras would send in the offenders. I went to visit Dick Cocke who was a little recovered of his gripes. . . .

. . .

25. . . . I gave the necessary orders, and after dinner went in the rain to Appomattox, where I found all things well. . . . Here I was told that several persons were sick with the gripes who had drunk of the rum brought over by L-n-n. Those that burned it found a substance at the bottom like lime. . . .

26. I rose at 6 in the morning. . . . It had rained so violently that Peterson's mill dam went away. In the afternoon it held up

and I went to Colonel Bolling's whom I found very ill of the dropsy. However he was cheerful and though he talked of dying it seemed to be in jest. The Colonel told me a man from North Carolina came to him to buy Indian goods but because he had no pay with him he let him have none. . . .

27. . . . Robin Bolling came over to see me to consult what was most proper to be done about the clerk's place. He wrote a letter to the President to desire him to appoint Mr. Mumford clerk since the justices would not admit him. I recommended the Colonel to God Almighty and returned home. When I came to the ferry I saw Mistress Mary Eppes, a pretty girl and capable of impression.[1] When I came home I found all things well. I ate roast beef for dinner. It rained again in the afternoon. I received a letter from my brother Duke to desire me to lend him £50. . . .

28. . . . I recommended my family to God Almighty and went the new way to Williamsburg, which seemed very tedious. I got to Mr. Bland's a little after sunset. I ate some rice milk and then went to visit the President where I found Colonel Rhett and Mr. Robinson. We played at cards till 10 o'clock. Then I went to lie at Mr. Bland's. . . . My sister Custis and Mrs. [Jeffrey] came about a week ago over the Bay and say the distemper continues still but not with the same violence it did, but that about [30?] people had died of it this winter in the two counties. It was infectious and killed chiefly poor people. The best remedy for it is sweating and the best way to prevent it is to vomit and purge. This distemper never comes but in winter and as the cold weather abates that abates also. Abundance of people in Appomattox and upper James River fell sick of the gripes occasioned by rum brought among them by the New England vessels. This is probably because most people that drink a little or much have the gripes unless they can bring it up again. So many people were never known in Virginia to have the gripes at one time. Several have died of it, several lost their limbs. I informed the President and Council of it but they took no notice of it.

March, 1709

1. I rose at 6 o'clock and said my prayers shortly. I ate rice milk for breakfast. Then I went to pay my court to the President. I could not persuade Mr. President to admit Mr. Mumford to be

clerk of Prince George. While I stayed there Colonel Carter, Colonel Duke, Mr. Commissary Colonel Digges, Mr. Lewis, Colonel Bassett, and Colonel Ludwell came over. They all went to Council and I presented a memorial to them, without effect. Mr. Burwell was sworn naval officer of York River and ordered a vessel to be fitted out with 10 guns and 80 men to guard the coast. We all went to dinner at 7 o'clock at night where I ate nothing but beef. Major Burwell dined with us and looked very well by the help of temperance. . . .

2. I rose at 6 o'clock and went to take my leave of the President. I ate custard for breakfast and then took leave of Mr. Bland and went to the Commissary's where I met my sister Custis and Mrs. [Jeffrey]. I was very much surprised to find Mrs. Blair drunk, which is growing pretty common with her, and her relations disguise it under the name of consolation. I ate nothing here but about 12 o'clock waited on the ladies to Green Spring where we found all in good health. I ate nothing but fowl for supper. Then we played cards till 11 o'clock. . . .

3. I rose at 6 o'clock and said my prayers and as soon as we had breakfasted we took our leave and went to Westover. By the way we called at the house of one [Wilkes] where we ate bacon and eggs which the people gave us very heartily. I would not give the woman money because it would have been spent in rum but I promised her six pounds of wool. From hence we got home a little after sunset where I found all in good health, thanks be to God. The ladies were not so weary but they ate their supper. . . .

4. . . . I sent Tom to Falling Creek to desire Grills[2] to lessen the number of the workmen and to forbid building the house at Westover. Mr. Mumford came to hear the success I had in the business of his being made clerk but he was disappointed. . . . Mr. Bland came on his way to Williamsburg and was persuaded to stay all night. The Doctor came drunk to dinner. He, Mr. Bland, and I played a pool at piquet and I lost all. . . .

. . .

25. . . . The Doctor went to Williamsburg. I wrote a letter to England. Parson Ware sent to me for a pint of canary, he being sick of the gripes with the New England rum, which I sent him, notwithstanding I have but a little, because I should be glad if I were in his condition to receive such a kindness from another. . . .

26. . . . Before we had dined Mr. Hardiman came to see me but would not eat. In the afternoon Peter Hamlin came also. We played at billiards. In the evening we took a walk about the plantation. I read Italian and some of my own work to the ladies. . . .

. . .

28. . . . I neglected to say my prayers this morning, notwithstanding it was my birthday, for which God forgive me. I ate milk for breakfast. About 10 o'clock I got on horseback and rode to Mr. Anderson's on my way to Falling Creek. I called at Colonel Eppes, but he was not at home. I went over the river and called at Dr. Bowman's where was a man sick of the gripes which he got by drinking New England rum. Then I proceeded to Falling Creek where I found Mr. Grills drunk and John full and the business not in so good order as I expected. I scolded at Mr. Grills till he cried and then was peevish. I ate nothing but milk. I said my prayers in bed. I had good health, good thoughts, but was out of humor in the evening.

29. I said my prayers in bed and then rose about 6 o'clock and ate milk for breakfast, and after I had been at the mill I rode with Mr. Grills to the Falls, where I found things not extraordinary. Here I went over the river with Mr. Grills and Tom Turpin to Shockoe and from thence to the other plantation on that side where matters were not very forward. We took John Blackman with us and went to try whether Captain Webb had not encroached on me and found that he had built his house on my land. We returned to John Blackman's and ate bacon and eggs and then went back to Falling Creek, very much tired. . . .

30. . . . [I] came home in the rain where I found all things in good order but only Jenny had run into the river last night but came out again of herself and was severely whipped for it. . . .

31. . . . Mr. Haynes came to see me and I appointed him to receive the President's tobacco. We made an end of sowing the oats. I ate nothing but boiled beef for dinner. My wife was out of humor for nothing. However I endeavored to please her again, having consideration for a woman's weakness. I played at billiards with the ladies. I read Italian. In the evening we walked about the plantation. My wife was out of order so we went to bed soon. . . .

13

April, 1709

1. . . . John West made an end of the two little houses and I settled the account with him. I ate some cold beef and then I waited on the ladies to Mr. Anderson's, where we got about 12 o'clock. About 3 o'clock we ate, and I ate nothing but dry beef, notwithstanding there were several other dishes. We returned home about sunset, and found the Doctor just come from Williamsburg. He brought a good deal of news from Europe and particularly that our last fleet was arrived in England. He told me likewise there was a report that my father Parke was killed by the lieutenant[?] of a man-of-war in the West Indies, which God grant may not be true. . . .

• • •

3. . . . We prepared to go to church, but the parson did not come, notwithstanding good weather, so I read a sermon in Dr. Tillotson at home. . . .

• • •

5. . . . The Doctor had a fever and ague. We played at billiards. I read more Italian. In the evening we took a walk about the plantation. The brickmaker came this evening. I scolded with John about managing the tobacco. I read to the ladies Dr. Lister's *Journey to Paris*. I was ill treated by my wife, at whom I was out of humor. . . .

6. . . . My wife and I disagreed about employing a gardener. I ate milk for breakfast. John made an end of trimming the boat, which he performed very well. I settled my accounts and read Italian. I ate nothing but fish for dinner and a little asparagus. We played at billiards. I read more Italian. In the evening we walked about the plantation after I read in Dr. Lister's book to the ladies. My wife and I continued very cool. . . .

7. . . . The men began to work this day to dig for brick. I settled my accounts and read Italian. I reproached my wife with ordering the old beef to be kept and the fresh beef used first, contrary to good management, on which she was pleased to be very angry and this put me out of humor. I ate nothing but boiled beef for dinner. I went away presently after dinner to look after my people. When I returned I read more Italian and then my wife came and begged my pardon and we were friends again. I read

14

in Dr. Lister again very late. I said my prayers. I had good health, good thoughts, and bad humor, unlike a philosopher.

8. . . . My wife and I had another foolish quarrel about my saying she listened on the top of the stairs, which I suspected, in jest. However, I bore it with patience and she came soon after and begged my pardon. I settled my accounts and read some Dutch. Just before dinner Mr. Custis came and dined with us. He told us that my father Parke instead of being killed was married to his housekeeper which is more improbable. He told us that the distemper continued to rage extremely on the other side the Bay and had destroyed abundance of people. I did not keep to my rule of eating but the one dish. . . . The Indian woman died this evening, according to a dream I had last night about her.

9. . . . My wife and I had another scold about mending my shoes but it was soon over by her submission. I settled my accounts and read Dutch. I ate nothing but cold roast beef and asparagus for dinner. In the afternoon Mr. Custis complained of a pain in his side for which he took a sweat of snakeroot. I read more Dutch and took a little nap. In the evening we took a walk about the plantation. My people made an end of planting the corn field. I had an account from Rappahannock that the same distemper began to rage there that had been so fatal on the Eastern Shore. . . .

10. . . . Our maid Jane began to cry out. I danced my dance. Jane was brought to bed of a boy. About 12 o'clock we went to my Cousin Harrison's, where we dined. . . .

11. . . . In the afternoon Ned Randolph came over in order to go to school at Mr. Harrison's. I proffered Colonel Randolph that he might be here for that purpose. . . .

· · ·

13. . . . In the evening Mr. Mumford came and told me the President had written to the court of Prince George not to sit until they would accept of Mr. Robin Bolling. . . .

14. . . . The Doctor came home. I paid the old wire man for what work he had done at Falling Creek. I ate only honey and bread for dinner and drank milk and water. Last night three moons were seen about 10 o'clock. We played at billiards. I read some Dutch. In the evening it rained very much. I ate milk for supper but in the night it made me a little feverish and my spirits

15

were strangely disturbed. Our daughter was taken ill at night of a fever. . . .

15. . . . I prepared my accounts against the General Court. I read some Dutch. My hoarseness was something better. The child continued to have her fever till about noon and then she fell into a sweat which drove out red spots. At noon I ate nothing but squirrel and asparagus for dinner. We played at billiards in the afternoon. Then I mended the locks of my closet and secretary. In the evening we took a walk to the bay to see the men fishing. We had a letter from my sister Custis by which we learned that Crapeau is come into our cape and taken a vessel. . . .

16. . . . The child was a great deal better and had no fever this day. I prepared my accounts for Williamsburg and read some Dutch. . . . In the evening I walked about the plantation and showed John what work I would have done when I was gone to Williamsburg. . . .

17. . . . The child had her fever again last night for which I gave her a vomit this morning, which worked very well. Anaka was whipped yesterday for stealing the rum and filling the bottle up with water. I went to church, where were abundance of people, among whom was Mrs. [Hamlin], a very handsome woman. Colonel Eppes and his wife, with Captain Worsham came to dine with me, who told me that Tom Haynes was gone out of his wits. . . .

18. I rose at 3 o'clock and after committing my family to the divine protection, I went in the boat to Mr. Harvey's, where I got by break of day. Mr. Harvey's mother met me on the shore and desired me to persuade her son to be more kind to her, which I promised I would. From thence I proceeded to Williamsburg, where I got about 10 o'clock. I waited on the President, where I saw Mr. Blair and Colonel Duke. Then I went to Mr. Bland's where I ate some custard. Then I went to court where I presented a petition to the General Court for Captain Webb's land as lapsed. When the court rose I went to dinner to [Kit Young's?] with the Council, where I ate nothing but boiled beef. Then we went to the President's where we played at cards till 10 o'clock. I won 25 shillings. I went and lay at my new lodgings. . . .

19. I rose at 5 o'clock and read in Homer and a chapter in Hebrew. I said my prayers and ate rice milk for breakfast. About

10 o'clock I went to court where I paid Mr. Conner 40 shillings instead of the note for £7 drawn by Daniel Wilkinson. He told me his sloop came the last of March from Barbados, and brings word that the King of France was dead and that my father Parke was well and not married. I read in Justin. In the afternoon I played at piquet with Mr. W-l-s. We dined very late and I ate nothing but fowl and bacon. When that was over we went to Mr. David Bray's where we danced till midnight. I had Mrs. Mary Thomson for my partner. I recommended myself to the divine protection. I had good thoughts, good health, and good humor, thanks to God Almighty. . . .

20. . . . We did not dine till 6 o'clock [when] I ate nothing but boiled beef. I was at a meeting of the College where we chose Colonel Randolph rector. We had Mr. Luke before us about his accounts, who could not justify them, nor say anything in his excuse. Afterwards we played at whist with the President. . . .

21. Rose at 6 o'clock and read three books of Homer. I said my prayers and ate milk for breakfast. I did a great deal of business this day. We dined about 3 o'clock and I ate fowl and bacon for dinner. Afterwards we went to whist £5.10 [sic] and then I played at dice and lost 50 shillings and John Bolling won £10. I wrote a letter to my wife to let her know my health. We sat up till 12 o'clock. I had good health, good thoughts, and good humor all day, thanks be to God Almighty.

22. I rose at 6 o'clock and read two books in Homer and said my prayers. I ate rice milk for breakfast and did some business. Then I went to church, it being Good Friday, where the Commissary preached. After church I went with abundance of company to dine at the Commissary's, where I ate with moderation. In the evening I returned into the town and played at whist and won 8:10 of Colonel Smith. We sat up till 12 o'clock and then separated. I had good health, good thoughts, and good humor, thanks be to God Almighty. Here we saw Mistress H-l-y who is a great instance of human decay.

23. . . . I went to the President's, where I learned that the Tuscarora Indians would not deliver up the men we demanded and Colonel Harrison now wrote that now it was his opinion the trade should be open, contrary to what he thought before. I did a great deal of business and dined with the President because it was St.

George his day. Then I went with Colonel Ludwell to Green Spring with Colonel Carter, where we danced and were very merry. I neglected to say my prayers. I had good thoughts, good humor, and good health, thanks be to God Almighty.

24. I rose at 6 o'clock and said my prayers very shortly. We breakfasted about 10 o'clock and I ate nothing but bread and butter and sack. We rode to Jamestown Church, where Mr. Commissary preached. When church was done I gave 10 shillings to the poor. Nothing could hinder me from sleeping at church, though I took a great deal of pains against it. We rode home to Colonel Ludwell's again where we dined and I ate fish and asparagus. In the afternoon we took a walk and saw the carcasses of 50 cows which had been burnt in a house belonging to Colonel Ludwell. Mr. W-l-s ran two races and beat John Custis and Mr. [Hawkins]. He likewise jumped over the fence which was a very great jump. Colonel Carter returned to town with Mr. Harrison and we stayed and ate syllabub for supper. . . .

25. I rose at 6 o'clock and said my prayers shortly. Mr. W-l-s and I fenced and I beat him. Then we played at cricket, Mr. W-l-s and John Custis against me and Mr. [Hawkins], but we were beaten. I ate nothing but milk for breakfast and then we returned to Williamsburg, where we received the news that the Governor was returned to France, not being able to get his exchange, and that he could not be here before the fall, and that tobacco was very low and that the Lord Somers was president of the Council. I did a great deal of business. About 5 o'clock we went to dinner and I ate nothing but boiled beef. In the evening I took a walk and then went to Mr. Bland's, where I examined my godson and Johnny Randolph and found the last well improved. . . .

26. . . . We went to the Council where it was agreed to open the Indian trade. . . . Then I took a walk and came to Mr. Bland's, from whence Mr. Will Randolph and I went to Colonel Bray's, where we found abundance of ladies and gentlemen dancing. We did not dance but got some kisses among them. . . .

27. . . . I wrote a letter to my wife by Will Randolph. I did abundance of business. My sister Custis came to town on her way to Major Burwell's. I went to wait on her at Mr. Bland's, where came abundance of other ladies. I stayed with them two hours. My brother and sister Custis went away. I paid several of the

Council their money. . . . After dinner we played at cricket and then went to whist and I lost 30 shillings. . . .

. . .

29. . . . About noon my spouse arrived and left all things well at home this morning, thanks be to God. We dined at Mr. Bland's and then rode to Mr. Commissary Blair's and were overtaken with a gust of thunder and rain. Mrs. Blair was sick and talked very simply. We were kindly entertained. About 10 o'clock we went to bed, where I lay in my wife's arms. . . .

30. . . . When the ladies had put their things in order we went into the vault and drank a glass of Rhenish wine and sugar. Then we rode to Kings Creek to Major Burwell's. We found him at dinner with my brother and sister Custis and Mistress Betty Todd. We ate with them. I ate nothing but boiled beef. The Major had the gout in one foot, very moderately because of his temperance. We took a walk to the marsh lately drained by a dam and sluice. We went to bed about 9 o'clock. . . .

May, 1709

1. . . . I endeavored to learn all I could from Major Burwell who is a sensible man skilled in matters relating to tobacco. In the evening we talked about religion and my wife and her sister had a fierce dispute about the infallibility of the Bible. . . .

2. . . . The women went to romping and I and my brother romped with them. About 12 o'clock my brother and sister Custis went on board their frigate in order to sail to Accomac. Then we went over the river to Carter's Creek and found Mr. Burwell indisposed with a cold and his lady ready to lie in. . . .

3. . . . I went to see Mr. Burwell's tobacco, which seemed to be very heavy. I ate fish for dinner, which they called trout. In the afternoon we went to see my cousin Berkeley. We found her big with child. Their house was very neat. We stayed about two hours and then returned to Mr. Burwell's, where we found Mr. Evans. Mrs. Burwell is a very pretty, good-humored woman but seemed to be a little melancholy, as he did likewise, I know not for what reason. . . .

4. . . . Captain Berkeley came to see us, who is a very good-humored man. We walked in the garden about an hour; then we went to dinner and I ate boiled beef. In the afternoon we danced a minuet and then took our leave and returned over the river again to Major Burwell's where we found Colonel Bassett and his lady who are very good people. In the evening we saw a great ship sail up the river. The Major sent on board for his letters which brought no news. . . .

5. . . . About 11 o'clock I ate some bread and butter and sack, and then took leave of Major Burwell and rode to Williamsburg with Colonel Bassett. On the way we met Mr. Ingles with his wife and daughter who were going to see us. When we came to Williamsburg, I delivered to Mr. Bland £600 in money to pay for the use of the vessel to guard the country. I gave Colonel Bassett a bottle of wine and then took our leave of him and Mr. Bland and proceeded to Green Spring where we found Nat Harrison and his wife and Mr. Edwards. I ate mutton and sallet for supper. . . .

6. . . . In the afternoon Colonel Ludwell . . . brought us the bad news that Captain Morgan had lost his ship in Margate Roads by a storm as likewise had several others. My loss was very great in this ship where I had seven hogsheads of skins and 60 hogsheads of heavy tobacco. The Lord gives and the Lord has taken away—blessed be the name of the Lord. In the evening Mr. Clayton and Mr. Robinson came and confirmed the same bad news. However I ate a good supper of mutton and asparagus. Then we went to dance away sorrow. I had good health, good thoughts, and good humor, notwithstanding my misfortune, thanks be to God Almighty.

7. We rose at break of day and were on horseback before sunrise to return home, after taking leave of our friends. We had nothing extraordinary happen in our journey but only that my wife had a pain in her belly which made me afraid she would miscarry. However we made shift to get her home and after some rest she recovered. We found all things well, thanks be to God, and the servants in good order. Mr. Salle had been here four days to speak with me about the disorder of Manakin Town[3] occasioned by the parson. I ate bacon and pigeon for dinner. In the afternoon Mr. Salle returned toward home and I took a walk to [M-n-s] and ate some cherries, which began to be ripe. In the evening I ate some strawberries and milk. . . .

8. . . . Mr. Mumford . . . told me Mr. Bolling had agreed with Mr. Goodrich that he be clerk on the consideration he should have half the profit for three years. I ate bacon and chicken for dinner. In the afternoon I wrote a letter to the President to recommend Mr. Mumford to be clerk of Prince George. . . .

9. I rose at 5 o'clock and read two chapters in Hebrew and two leaves in Plutarch's *Morals*. . . . I had an express from Falling Creek to tell me my uncle Byrd was dangerously sick and that Mr. Grills continued bad. . . .

10. . . . In the afternoon I wrote a petition for Mr. Salle that the clerk of the vestry might return the books. In the evening I walked about the plantation. I ate abundance of cherries. . . .

11. . . . Mr. Mumford brought me a letter from the President in which he was pleased to compliment me with the name of the clerk of Prince George. Mr. Cary came to see me. About 11 o'clock I went to Falling Creek, and called at Mr. Anderson's by the way but he was not at home, but his lady was, with whom I stayed about an hour; then I went over the river and at the Hundred met Will Randolph who gave me an account of the court business. About 4 o'clock I got to Falling Creek and the Doctor was got there before me and had given Mr. Grills some physic that passed through him and gave him some ease. . . . The Doctor refused to go to my uncle Byrd on pretense of much business. I ate roast pig for supper. The Doctor and I lay together. . . .

12. . . . Mr. Grills was something better. I went to see the tannery which was in a good forwardness. I viewed everything and went to see the sick negroes, who were both a little better. Then I proceeded to the Falls and went to see my uncle who was much better than he had been. I gave him the best advice I could and then went to view my plantation. The people were all planting because it was a rainy day. Everything was in good order but because I would not hinder the people's planting I returned to Falling Creek, and by the way called on my uncle and there ate bacon and eggs. I likewise called on the Dutchman who I understood was sick, but I found him not at home. But I saw his wife, who was mad again. When I came to Falling Creek I had some complaints against Robin Easely which seemed to be the effect of quarrelling. However I desired Mr. Grills to keep a watch on him. About 4 o'clock I returned home but did not find Mr.

21

Anderson, who was gone to Tom the tailor's wedding. I found all well at home, thank God. I had good health, good thoughts, but was out of humor. When I came home I ate some strawberries and wine.

13. I rose at 6 o'clock and read a chapter in Hebrew and some Greek in Josephus. I said my prayers and ate milk for breakfast. I danced my dance and settled my accounts. I ate red herring and sallet for dinner. In the afternoon I settled my accounts again. Nurse came home from the wedding where she had stayed all night, contrary to her mistress' orders, for which I was in too great a passion with her, but she gave me as good as I brought and she was so impudent to her mistress that she could not forbear beating her. . . . I had good health and good thoughts but was out of humor with Nurse.

· · ·

15. . . . We went to church, where the congregation was very small because it was like to rain. Mr. Anderson came from church to dine with us and complained he was out of order but by the symptoms he found the disorder to be nothing but hunger. I ate gammon and chicken for dinner. My river sloop came from Appomattox with 26 hogsheads of tobacco. Mr. Anderson went away in the evening and we took a walk about the plantation. . . .

· · ·

17. . . . I put my man Jack into a tub to sweat him but he found no service by it. . . . In the afternoon Mr. Mumford came to tell me that the justices of Prince George had resolved to accept of Mr. Bolling for their clerk on condition he would allow Mr. Goodrich half the profit and that Mr. Harrison had advised them to this because the President would not grant a commission to Mr. Goodrich according to Mr. Bolling's recommendation. Upon this I gave Mr. Mumford the commission which the President had sent me and he went away with it immediately. I played at billiards with the Doctor and won 15 pence. . . .

18. . . . This was fast day[4] to pray to God to remove the fatal sickness with which this country has been of late afflicted. There was the most people at church I ever saw there. Mr. Harrison was in deep consultation with Colonel Hardiman and Mr. Anderson, I suppose about the clerk's place of Prince George. Isham Eppes and his wife and Robin Bolling's wife came home and dined with us. . . .

22

19. . . . The nurse was in great haste to go and complain to Mr. Harrison that I should call her whore but was commanded not to go. I wrote to Mr. Mumford not to come to any terms with Mr. Goodrich about the clerk's place of Prince George. . . . My man Jack's knee began to swell which makes it look like the gout. I gave him some oil. I sent John to foment it, which gave him some ease. . . .

20. . . . The nurse went to Mr. Harrison to complain but met with no comfort there. . . .

21. . . . About 12 o'clock Mr. Bland came from Williamsburg and brought me some letters from England and an account from Mr. Perry of £7 a hogshead. He gave me the comfort that the skins and 350 hogsheads of tobacco were saved out of the *Perry and Lane* and some tobacco out of the other ships that were lost in the storm that happened in January last in England. The hatter brought some [hats] from Appomattox. They both dined with us. I ate mutton and sallet for dinner. In the afternoon we played at billiards. In the evening they went away and I took a walk about the plantation. I was out of humor at my wife's climbing over the pales of the garden, now she is with child. I recommended my all to God. I had good health, good thoughts, and good humor, thanks be to God Almighty.

• • •

23. . . . My horse died this morning. John Woodson came in the rain about paying me some money and left his papers at home; so he returned as wise as he came. My man Jack continued lame in his foot. I ate nothing for dinner but mutton boiled with turnips. In the afternoon we played at billiards. I read news till the evening and then I took a walk about the plantation. Moll was whipped for a hundred faults. . . .

24. . . . Mr. Mumford came and let me know the justices of Prince George had resolved to admit nobody except he would give Mr. Goodrich half the profit which showed almost unreasonable partiality and not according to the oath a justice takes to distribute equal justice to all men. Mr. Bland called here on his way to Williamsburg. He told me that Mr. Bolling had had the humility to agree to give half the profit to Goodrich as long as this secretary continues in place and then to surrender on condition the justices would admit him in opposition to Mr.

Mumford. I ate mutton and green peas for dinner. In the afternoon we played at billiards and in the evening I walked about the plantation. . . .

. . .

26. I rose at 5 o'clock and read a chapter in Hebrew and some Greek in Josephus. I said my prayers and ate milk for breakfast. I danced my dance, and then went to see Jack and found that he had slept very well without pain, for which reason I caused him to be let blood again and continued the same medicine. About 12 o'clock Mr. Parker came to see me and dined with us. I ate nothing but beans and bacon for dinner. Mr. Parker told me he lost a negro by salivating him for the rheumatism and Mr. Harrison lost another by applying a hot dressing and stupe[5] to the part affected. . . . He went away in the evening and I walked about the plantation. I said my prayers and had good health, good thoughts, but was out of humor with Tom for the disorder of the garden.

27. . . . When we were at dinner Mr. Will Randolph came from Williamsburg and brought me two letters from England, one of which told me a sad story of the misfortune of our last fleet by the storm but there are some hopes that the *Perry and Lane* is not lost as we had been informed, though she was in great danger. . . .

. . .

30. . . . I ate beans and bacon for dinner. While we were at dinner Colonel Harrison came to see me and told me there was a privateer at the Cape of 16 guns. He would not eat with us but stayed till about 4 o'clock and then went over the river again because his son was not at home. We played at billiards. In the evening I read in Homer and went to walk about the plantation. My wife was out of order all day with a headache. I recommended myself to heaven. I had good health, good thoughts, and good humor, thanks be God Almighty.

31. . . . This day we sheared the sheep. My man Jack was better and the swelling of his foot abated. We began to shear the sheep but the rain interrupted us. I read some Latin. I ate roast chicken for dinner and green peas. . . . I read more Latin and Greek and wrote on articles of faith. In the evening I walked about the plantation and went to see them hang the tobacco. . . .

June, 1709

1. . . . My man Jack was better today. Our people made an end of shearing the sheep. I read some Latin and Greek in Homer. I ate boiled beef for dinner. I was out of humor about Mrs. [Jeffrey] so that I would not let my wife go abroad. In the evening I took a walk about the plantation and went to the brick house where the people hung tobacco and some of it was extremely bad. . . .

2. . . . I was out of humor with my wife for trusting Anaka with rum to steal when she was so given to drinking, but it was soon over. My man Jack grew better and better, thanks be to God Almighty. He took a purge today that worked very well. . . .

3. . . . Mr. Parker came to tell me there was a petition against me for stopping the way against the people on the other side the creek. . . . About 4 o'clock Mr. Randolph came and told me the jury above had given me a shilling damages against Phil Pursell. . . .

4. . . . We made some wine of the common cherry for an experiment. It was extremely hot this day. I was out of humor with my wife for not minding her business. . . . In the evening Mr. C-s came to see me, who is a man of good understanding, and Ned Randolph brought me a letter from Mr. Bland in which he told me that the Lord Lovelace was dead at New York. . . .

· · ·

6. I rose at 5 o'clock and read two chapters in Hebrew and some Greek in Josephus. I said my prayers and ate milk for breakfast, and raspberries. I danced my dance. It thundered and rained this morning violently till 8 o'clock. I read some Latin and Greek in Homer and wrote a prayer. I ate pork and turnips for dinner. Just after dinner Mr. Mumford came with the Doctor and he told me that five justices of Prince George had written to the President in behalf of Mr. Bolling, contrary to their former resolution and the President upon that wrote a letter in favor of Mr. Bolling, notwithstanding the commission he had granted to Mumford by which Mr. Bolling's commission was made void. He likewise told me that Mr. Bolling did not stick to speak things very much to my disadvantage, against all truth and reason. I wrote to Mr. Bolling to let him know I did resent it. . . .

7. . . . I had a quarrel with Ned Randolph about his complaining that he was starved and because he ran about without my knowing anything of it and would not come to me when I sent to him, of all which I told his father who threatened him if he should dare to do so again. The Colonel and I made up accounts. Mr. Blackamore came to meet the Colonel here because he did not dare to come by himself, for I had reprimanded him for his being drunk. . . .

8. . . . About 10 o'clock we rode to see Colonel Eppes and Mrs. Anderson met us there. We were entertained very courteously. I ate bacon and fowl for dinner. The Colonel and I balanced accounts. In the evening as we returned home we met Mr. Anderson, who came that morning from Williamsburg. He brought news that there were 13 men of war arrived at New England with design to attempt the taking of Canada. We likewise met Mr. Randolph who came from Prince George Court and said the court had sworn Mr. Bolling, contrary to their first and repeated resolves, notwithstanding Mr. Mumford had a commission and Bolling only a letter. . . .

9. . . . I received a very foolish letter from Robin Bolling which contained many ridiculous arguments to justify his late foolish proceedings, to which I sent him a full answer. I ate mutton and sallet for dinner. My Eugene ran away this morning for no reason but because he had not done anything yesterday. I sent my people after him but in vain. The sloop came from Falling Creek with copper, timber, and planks. In the evening Captain Keeling came to see us to account with me for the quitrents of New Kent. . . .

10. . . . George B-th brought home my boy Eugene. . . . The Captain and I had some discourse about the philosopher's stone which he is following with great diligence. . . . Eugene was whipped for running away and had the bit put on him. . . .

. . .

12. . . . I received a letter from my dear friend Admiral Wager from Jamaica which signified his health and the continuance of his friendship. We went to church and heard a sermon. Nobody came home with us but Mr. Gee. I ate mutton pie for dinner. Mr. Gee stayed here till the evening and according to his custom spoke against several people like any woman. . . .

13. I rose at 5 o'clock and read two chapters in Hebrew but no

Greek by reason that Captain Collins came to see me, who came out of England about seven weeks ago and says the fleet came out 13 days before him and may be every day expected because they had been above nine weeks out of England. He brought me some letters from England. I had a great deal of discourse with him and drank chocolate for breakfast. . . . About 11 o'clock we rode to Drury Stith's where we met Mr. Anderson and his wife and Mr. Eppes. I ate pork and turnips for dinner. Then we played at nine-pins. . . .

14. . . . We heard guns this morning, by which we understood that the fleet was come in and I learned the same from Mr. Anderson. I ate bacon and chicken for dinner. I began to have the piles. I read some Greek in Homer. I heard guns from Swinyard's and sent my boat for my letters. In the meanwhile I walked about the plantation. In the evening the boat returned and brought some letters for me from England, with an invoice of things sent for by my wife which are enough to make a man mad. It put me out of humor very much. . . .

15. . . . While we were at dinner Captain M-r-n came with some more letters. He brought me a coaler recommended by Colonel Blakiston. He brought me also some goods for my wife, to an extravagant value. My letters gave me a sad prospect of the tobacco trade in England. My wife continued very ill. I sent Tommy to Williamsburg to inquire for my letters. I took a walk about the plantation. I said my prayers and had good thoughts, good humor and good health, thanks be to God Almighty, only I feared I was going to have the piles.

16. . . . Mr. Bland's boy brought me abundance of letters from Williamsburg, out of the men-of-war. I spent all the morning in reading them. My orders for being of the Council arrived among the rest. By these letters I learned that tobacco was good for nothing, that protested bills would ruin the country, that our trade with the Carolina Indians was adjusted in England, that my sister Braynes was in prison by the cruelty of C-r-l-y, that my salary was in a fair way of being increased, that the College was like to be rebuilt by the Queen's bounty, that there was a probability of a peace next winter. . . .

17. . . . In the afternoon we rode to my neighbor Harrison's where we stayed till the evening with Mr. [Gee]. Here I ate

some apple pie. Mr. Harrison had the same bad account of tobacco in England and advised me to ship none by this ship. I promised to give no more than £12 per ton. He told me that several gentlemen were extremely in debt with Mr. Perry. . . .

. . .

19. . . . Mr. Mumford came to see me and let me know that Jack Bolling did all he could to persuade people not to pay their debts and several low contrivances against me and my wife which were false. I ate boiled mutton and turnips for dinner. Soon after dinner Captain S-t-k came from below to let me understand he intended to sail in three days and gave me to understand that he wanted more money, but I was deaf. . . .

20. I rose at 3 o'clock and went in my boat to Weyanoke where I arrived at 5 o'clock and got on my horse and rode to Williamsburg, where I got by 9 o'clock. I went to Mr. Bland's where I found Dick Cocke and Isham Randolph. Here I ate some milk and then went to my chambers, where I slept sweetly for two hours. I dined at Mr. Bland's and ate beans and bacon for dinner. In the evening I sent for Mr. Clayton from the coffeehouse, to whom I gave a bottle of white wine. I did not go to see the President but sent for some letters he had of mine by Johnny Blair. By my letters I learned that the Governor was released and that the Queen had granted £500 to the College. I had a letter from Mr. Southwell that told me Lady Betty was like to die of a consumption. I neglected to say my prayers. . . .

21. I rose at 5 o'clock and while I was dressing of me, the President had the humility to come and visit me. I thanked him for the exact performance of his promise about the clerk's place. He had very little to say for himself, but told me Robin Bolling had written him word that he never employed me to get the commission for Mr. Mumford, which is a cursed lie. The President courted me to pass it by, but I continued out of humor. I neglected to say my prayers and ate milk for breakfast. Then I went to the capitol about my business. Then I went to the President's where I met several of the Council. They met about 12 o'clock, and I was before them concerning my accounts. They expected I would produce the Queen's letter for my being of the Council but I was not in haste. I went and dined with Mr. Bland and then returned to the Council at the President's, where I met the captains of the men-of-war, who were pretty gentlemen. We played at piquet till midnight and I went to my lodgings. . . .

28

22. I rose at 4 o'clock and got on horseback and rode to Mr. Harvey's and was courteously entertained by Mrs. Harvey till my boat came and then I came home, where I found all well, thanks be to God. I ate dry beef for dinner, though with the heat I ate but little. I slept in the afternoon. I wrote several letters to England. . . . When I was at town I ended my disagreement with Mr. Robinson. I had good health, good thoughts, and good humor, thanks be to God Almighty.

23. . . . In the evening Captain [. . .] came with several flats to fetch 36 hogsheads of tobacco, which he was content to take at £12 per ton. The seamen told John they did not come to roll tobacco, which made me give them a good scolding and I would not let them have the tobacco that night. The Captain returned to Mr. Harrison's, to whom I told the rudeness of his men. He promised to make them roll it tomorrow and went away. . . .

24. . . . Mr. Blackamore came to see me with Johnny Randolph. He told me that Mr. Will Randolph was to bring up his wife to Captain Stith's this night. He was married on Tuesday last. . . .

* * *

27. . . . I made an invoice of the things that my wife could spare to be sold. I settled the accounts of protested bills. I ate mutton for dinner. My wife was in tears about her cargo but I gave her some comfort after dinner. . . . Tom was whipped for not telling me that he was sick.

* * *

29. I rose at 5 o'clock and read only some Greek in Josephus, because I was hindered by Daniel who came last night from Williamsburg where the sea sloop is safe arrived, thanks be to God Almighty. Two of her men were pressed by the men-of-war, notwithstanding the proclamation. Wheat sold for about six shillings a bushel in Madeira and wine for £8 a pipe with the exchange. Captain Browne and Captain Collins came to see me. I said my prayers and ate milk for breakfast. I began to reap my wheat. I ate bacon and pork for dinner. In the afternoon Mr. Bland came to counsel the proper measures to be taken with the sloop and it was agreed he should go down to take care of the cargo and he went accordingly and was caught in a great shower of rain. Daniel behaved himself very foolishly. . . .

* * *

July, 1709

1. I rose at 5 o'clock and read two chapters in Hebrew and some Greek in Josephus. I said my prayers and ate milk for breakfast. I danced my dance. I wrote a letter to England. George began to plaster the house. I read some Latin. I ate broiled pork for dinner. In the afternoon I wrote more letters to England and read more Latin and some Greek in Homer. Then I took a walk about the plantation. I said my prayers and had good health, good thoughts, and good humor, thanks be to God Almighty.

. . .

3. . . . I wrote a letter to England, notwithstanding it was Sunday. About 12 o'clock we went in the coach to Mr. Harrison's where we dined and Mrs. L—was there. I ate boiled shoat for dinner. We were very friendly together. . . .

4. . . . I went to court to answer the petition against me about the landing of the people on the other side the creek and prevailed with the court to order their landing at Major Marshall's. The two captains and Frank Eppes dined with me and several others came after dinner. I ate fricassee of chicken for dinner. In the afternoon we played at billiards. Robin Bolling was at court but had not the confidence to look toward me. . . .

5. . . . In the afternoon Indian Peter brought me a letter from the President in which he desired me to send him his account and my bill for the balance, which I did accordingly and also sent several letters which I desired him to convey by the men-of-war. . . .

6. . . . Mrs. [Jeffrey] went away by moonshine to Williamsburg and my wife was very much concerned at her going. . . .

7. . . . In the afternoon it began to rain and blow very violently so that it blew down my fence. It likewise thundered. In all the time I have been in Virginia I never heard it blow harder. . . .

. . .

10. . . . I received a letter from poor Captain C-l-v who gave me to understand that he had been run down by another ship and that all the tobacco was lost. My part of this misfortune was

36 hogsheads. God gives and God takes away—blessed be the name of the Lord. Mr. Bland and Daniel came and told me they had lost a whole pipe of wine in getting it into the vat. We went to church, from whence only Captain Wilcox and Mr. Bland came home with me. . . . Captain Wilcox was so kind as to offer his pinnace to go down to see if anything was saved of the Captain C-l-v lading. He likewise offered me to set a new mast in the "Evelyn." . . .

11. . . . I was very angry with Bannister for letting Daniel have the key of the store, because he went away with it so that George could not get paint that he wanted. In the evening all the company went away except Mr. Mumford. I was extremely out of humor and scolded with Bannister before the company, and my wife thought me angry with her, which made her very melancholy. I had good health and indifferent thoughts and very bad humor.

12. . . . I ate pig for dinner and ate too much. I took a nap and was out of order over it. My wife was very melancholy, but I comforted her as well as I could and was troubled to see her so. . . .

. . .

14. . . . In the evening I rode out with my new horse and he had like to have broken my neck by running away and raising up an end, but I did not fall, thank God. . . .

15. . . . I was very sore with my ride last night which hindered my activity. I had a bad dream this morning which seemed to foretell the death of some of my family. I thought I saw my yard full of people and when I came into the house I could not find my wife. God avert her death. I read some Latin. I gave Ben O-d-s-n a vomit which worked very well. . . .

16. . . . This day my daughter Evelyn is two years old. Pray God send his blessing on her. Old Ben was extremely sick. I gave him a sweat that worked abundantly, which made him something better. . . .

17. . . . I sent back Mr. Mumford's fine horse because it is dangerous to ride him. Colonel Bolling died this morning after a long sickness. I read a sermon of Dr. Tillotson's. I ate roast pigeon for dinner. . . .

18. . . . I sent the boatmaker to Falling Creek to build me a little boat for my sea sloop. I read some Latin. Tom returned from Falling Creek and brought me word all was well there and that the coaler found the coal mine very good and sufficient to furnish several generations. . . .

19. . . . Robin Hix came over this morning, with whom I had some discourse about the Indian trade. I said my prayers and ate milk for breakfast. I read some geometry. I ate roast mutton for dinner. In the afternoon I read more geometry and some Greek in Homer. . . .

. . .

23. . . . Captain Wilcox went down with his ship and was so gallant as to give us five guns at parting. I ate dry beef for dinner. Robin Jones came from above and told me all was spoiled at my plantation for want of rain. I read some Greek in Homer and walked about the plantation. It was exceedingly hot. I neglected to say my prayers again. I had good health, good thoughts, but indifferent bad humor. Old Ben was very ill.

24. . . . Abundance of the N-t-s Indians came here this evening.

25. . . . The Indians went away this morning and I set them over the river in my boat. I was invited to Colonel Bolling's funeral who is to be buried tomorrow. I read some geometry. . . .

26. . . . Mr. Harrison came home and sent me two letters from England which informed of the likelihood of peace. . . .

27. . . . My wife was not well all day which made me send for Mrs. B-t-s [or P-t-s]. . . . In the afternoon I played at piquet with my wife. . . .

28. . . . Daniel came this morning and brought me a letter from Mr. Bland who told me the news that poor Captain Harrison was dead. I wrote a letter to England. About 12 o'clock Mrs. B-t-s came over. I ate no good dinner because our mutton was spoiled; however I ate some of it. In the afternoon we played at piquet. I read some geometry and a little Greek in Homer. . . .

. . .

30. . . . My wife continued well. We loaded the sloop. I ate fish for dinner. In the afternoon my wife and I played at piquet. I

32

read and wrote more geometry. I took a walk about the plantation. I had old Ben taken up and cleaned and he sat up an
hour. . . .

31. . . . I threatened Moll with a good whipping again tomorrow
for her many faults. Old Ben grew better and better. I read a
sermon in Dr. Tillotson. I took a little nap before dinner. I ate
roast pork for dinner. In the afternoon I read some geometry.
In the evening Mr. C-s came to see me and we drank a syllabub.
We walked in the garden till late. . . .

August, 1709

1. . . . I said my prayers and went to see old Ben and found
him much better. I read some geometry. I ate fish for dinner. In
the afternoon the Doctor and my wife played at piquet. Joe
Wilkinson came and gave me an account of the tobacco that he
raised this year and I agreed with him to be my overseer at
Burkland the next year. . . .

2. . . . I wrote a letter to the Governor of Barbados, to whom I
intend to consign my sloop and cargo. The old Ben was still
better and began to complain he was hungry. . . .

3. . . . Colonel Randolph came to see me, as did Mr. Anderson
and several others. It rained a little; however we resolved to go
to town tomorrow to the meeting of the College. . . .

4. We rose at 2 o'clock this morning and went in the sloop's
boat to Mr. Harvey's, where we arrived by break of day and
our horses were ready for us. We rode to town and got there
before 10 o'clock, notwithstanding we called at Green Spring,
but Colonel Ludwell was not at home. At Mr. Bland's I ate some
milk and then went to see the President, who persuaded me to
be sworn in Council but I refused. From hence we went to the
school house where we at last determined to build the college on
the old walls and appointed workmen to view them and compute
the charge. From hence we went to the Commissary's to dinner
where we found Mrs. Ludwell. In the evening we rode to Green
Spring and lay there all night. But this hurry made me neglect
to say my prayers, for which God forgive me. . . .

5. We rose at break of day and without ceremony rode away and got to the ferry before sunrise, and to Mr. Harvey's before 8 o'clock where we found the boat and got home before 10 o'clock, where we found Dr. Blair. He had been sent for to set a negro boy's leg which was broken this morning by the fall of the door in the brick house. He and Mr. Anderson dined with us and went away in the afternoon to see Mr. Harrison and his wife, that were both sick. I wrote letters to Barbados. . . .

. . .

7. . . . One of my fawns died of poison. In the evening . . . I took a walk about the plantation. It grew much cooler with a northwest wind. . . .

8. . . . I walked out to see my people at work at the ditch. I read a little geometry. I ate mutton for dinner. In the evening I took a little nap, and I read Mr. Woodson's pretense against me. . . .

. . .

13. . . . Twelve Pamunkey Indians came over. We gave them some victuals and some rum and put them over the river. I danced my dance. I removed more books into the library. I read some geometry and walked to see the people at work. I ate fish for dinner. I was almost the whole afternoon in putting up my books. In the evening John Blackman came from the Falls and brought me word some of my people were sick and that my coaler was sick at the coal mine. I scolded with him about the little work he had done this summer. I took a walk about the plantation. I had a little scold with the Doctor about his boy. . . .

14. . . . My cousin Betty Harrison came over and stayed till the evening. I took a walk about the plantation with my wife who has not quarrelled with me a great while. . . .

15. . . . In the afternoon I put my books into the cases in the library, notwithstanding Mr. Randolph was here. He said Captain Webb was very bad. In the evening I took a walk about the plantation. . . .

16. . . . I said no prayers this morning because my cousin Harrison came and hindered me. I ate milk for breakfast. I removed the rest of my books into the library. My cousin Harrison dined with us, and I ate mutton for dinner. In the afternoon I set up

all my books and then came in to the rest of the company. In the evening my cousin Harrison went home. . . .

17. . . . In the evening I took a walk about the plantation and found that some of my good neighbors had dug down the bank of my ditch to let their hogs into my pasture, for which I was out of humor. . . .

18. . . . About 8 o'clock got on my horse and rode to Will Randolph's where I saw his wife and gave her joy. She seems to be a good-humored woman and is handsome. Here I dined and ate boiled beef for dinner. In the afternoon I took my leave and walked to Colonel Randolph's where I only saw Mrs. Randolph because the Colonel was gone to see Captain Webb who was recovered. Mrs. Randolph and I talked of the debt which the Colonel owes to Mr. Perry. From hence Isham Randolph and I proceeded to Falling Creek, where I found all well and had the pleasure to hear that my coaler was recovered. . . .

19. I rose at 6 o'clock and Mr. Randolph and I walked to the tannery, with which we were both pleased. Then we went and viewed all the work at the dam. Then we ate milk for breakfast and rode to the Falls where we found a good crop considering the great drought. From hence we rode to Kensington where there is a very poor crop. Here we waded over the river, stepping from one rock to the other and so got to Burkland where John Blackman had little to show for his year's work. Here we ate bacon and eggs. From hence we proceeded to walk to Byrd Park where was the worst crop of all. Then we walked on to Shockoe where the crop was something better. Here we crossed the river in a canoe and rode to Falling Creek where we ate chicken pie for supper. I recommended myself to heaven in a short prayer and had good health, good thoughts, but indifferent humor.

20. I rose at 6 o'clock and said a short prayer and then we ate milk for breakfast and I gave audience to some of the workmen and then rode towards the Hundred. We called on board Captain Collins but we could not meet with the Captain. Then we crossed the river to Colonel Hill's where we found nobody at home. Then we rode to Colonel Eppes but we found only his wife. After staying a little there we rode to each of our homes. I found all well, thanks be to God Almighty. I ate fish for dinner. In the afternoon I enjoyed my wife. I read some Greek in Homer and took a walk about the plantation. . . .

27. . . . I denied my man Grills to go to a horse race because there was nothing but swearing and drinking there. I ate roast mutton for dinner. In the afternoon I played at piquet with my own wife and made her out of humor by cheating her. . . .

· · ·

31. . . . In the afternoon I read some news that came to hand, by which I found there is a great likelihood of peace. I read some Greek in Homer and in the evening took a walk about the plantation. I said my prayers shortly. I had good health, good thoughts, and good humor, thanks be to God Almighty. My letters from England tell me tobacco is sold for nothing there and skins for very little, that hardly any bills are paid, and very little goods will come by the next fleet. It is time there should be peace to remedy these misfortunes. Mrs. B-t-s taught me to reckon 20 weeks from the time a women is quick when she will seldom fail to be brought to bed. In this reckoning there are seven days in a week.

September, 1709

· · ·

2. . . . Notwithstanding the rain Mrs. Ware came to desire me to take tobacco for her debt to me but I refused because tobacco was good for nothing. I ate hashed pork for dinner. In the afternoon Mr. Taylor came from Surry about his bill of exchange. He told me there was news by way of Barbados that the peace was expected there to be already concluded. The rain kept him here all night but Mrs. Ware went away. . . .

3. . . . I said my prayers and ate chocolate with Mr. Taylor for breakfast. Then he went away. I read some geometry. We had no court this day. My wife was indisposed again but not to much purpose. I ate roast chicken for dinner. In the afternoon I beat Jenny for throwing water on the couch. I took a walk to Mr. Harrison's who told me he heard the peace was concluded in the last month. After I had been courteously entertained with wine and cake I returned home, where I found all well, thank God. . . .

· · ·

5. . . . My wife was much out of order and had frequent returns of her pains. I read some geometry. . . . In the evening I took a walk about the plantation and when I returned I found my wife very bad. I sent for Mrs. Hamlin and my cousin Harrison about 9 o'clock and I said my prayers heartily for my wife's happy delivery, and had good health, good thoughts, and good humor, thanks be to God Almighty. I went to bed about 10 o'clock and left the women full of expectation with my wife.

6. About one o'clock this morning my wife was happily delivered of a son, thanks be to God Almighty. I was awake in a blink and rose and my cousin Harrison met me on the stairs and told me it was a boy. We drank some French wine and went to bed again and rose at 7 o'clock. I read a chapter in Hebrew and then drank chocolate with the women for breakfast. I returned God humble thanks for so great a blessing and recommended my young son to His divine protection. My cousin Harrison and Mrs. Hamlin went away about 9 o'clock and I made my satisfaction to them for that kindness. I sent Peter away who brought me a summons to the Council. I read some geometry. The Doctor brought me two letters from England from Captain Stith. I ate roast mutton for dinner. In the afternoon I wrote a letter to England and took a walk about the plantation. I said my prayers and had good health and good thoughts, thanks be to God Almighty.

7. . . . My wife grew much better. I danced my dance. It rained in the night and likewise this day. I broached another pipe of wine, the other having lasted about half a year. I wrote a letter to England and read a little geometry. I ate roast pigeon for dinner. Just as we had dined Joe Wilkinson came to justify himself against some accusation he thought had been brought against him. Captain Collins came over for his protested bills of my endorsement and I renewed them. In the evening Mr. Clayton came and brought me a letter from my father Parke in which he signified he received all my letters and expressed himself well satisfied with us. We drank a bottle of wine. . . .

8. . . . Mr. Clayton and the Doctor and myself went to Mr. Anderson's where we stayed till the evening. I ate bacon and chicken for dinner. We talked politics abundantly and returned in the evening. Then we played at cards till 12 o'clock at night. My wife was very well, thank God. . . .

9. . . . Mr. Clayton told me the Governor of Maryland died about a month ago very suddenly. Mr. Dennis also came, as likewise did Mr. Anderson and they all dined with us. I ate fricassee for dinner. In the afternoon we talked politics till the evening, when all the company but Mr. Clayton went away. Then we went again to cards and I had bad luck. . . .

10. . . . Captain Collins came over this evening, to whom I delivered a letter to my uncle Rand. I gave him some physic for some of his men that were sick. . . .

11. . . . My wife and child were extremely well, thanks to God Almighty, who I hope will please to keep them so. I recommended my family to the divine protection and passed over the creek and then rode to my brother Duke's whom I found just recovered of the ague by means of my physic. Here I ate some roast beef for dinner, and then proceeded to Colonel Duke's, whom I found indisposed. He entertained me very courteously. . . .

12. I rose at 5 o'clock and said my prayers and then the Colonel and I discoursed about his debt to Mr. Perry in which I promised to be the mediator. I ate milk for dinner [*sic*] and then I met Colonel Bassett and with him rode to Williamsburg. We called at Mr. Blair's but nobody was at home. Then went to Mr. Bland's where I found all well. Then I went to Mr. President's, where I found several of the Council. The President persuaded me to be sworn, which I agreed to, and accordingly went to Council where I was sworn a member of the Council. God grant I may distinguish myself with honor and good conscience. We dined together and I ate beef for dinner. In the evening we went to the President's where I drank too much French wine and played at cards and I lost 20 shillings. I went home about 12 o'clock at night. . . .

13. . . . Several people came to see me and Mr. Commissary desired me to frame a letter to the Lord Treasurer which I did and then went to the meeting of the College where after some debate the majority were for building on the old wall; I was against this and was for a new one for several reasons. We heard that my sister Custis was brought to bed of a daughter and that Mrs. [Jeffrey] was married to Parson Dunn. I ate bacon and chicken for dinner. I received some protested bills and then we went to the President's and played at cards and I lost £4 about 10 o'clock and went home. . . .

14. I rose at 5 o'clock and Colonel Randolph came to see me to discourse about his debt to Mr. Perry. Then I went to take leave of the President and Mr. Bland and rode to Colonel Ludwell's, whom I overtook on the road. I ate rice milk for breakfast. I presented Mrs. Bland with a keg of sweetmeats. Colonel Ludwell and I discoursed about my father Parke's business. I ate bacon and chicken for dinner. About 3 o'clock I rode towards home, where I got about 8 o'clock and found all well, thanks be to God Almighty. By the way every time my horse went through the water he was lame for a little time. I said my prayers shortly, and had good health, good thoughts, and good humor, thanks be to God Almighty.

15. . . . I neglected to say my prayers because Mr. John Bolling came to see me. I ate milk for breakfast. I received him very coldly because he is a sharper. However, we played at billiards. I ate blue wing for dinner. In the afternoon Will Randolph brought me Mrs. Ware's debt and Mr. Salle came likewise to see me and we all played at billiards. In the evening all except Mr. Salle went away. Mr. Salle came about the contest with the parson, who is a pestilent fellow. I took a walk about the plantation. . . .

16. . . . I wrote a letter to England to make interest for the government of Maryland; God send good success. Jenny was whipped for abundance of faults. I ate fresh beef for dinner. In the afternoon I played at cards with my wife who was something indisposed. . . .

. . .

19. . . . I beat Anaka for letting the child piss in bed. I wrote a letter to England for the government of Maryland. I read some law. I ate blue wing for dinner. In the afternoon I wrote another letter to England and then took a walk about the plantation. . . .

20. . . . In the afternoon I played at cards with my own wife and then wrote another letter to England. I agreed with John L—to let him shoot in the marsh provided he brings me the eat and keeps the feathers for himself. . . .

21. . . . My boat went down to Green Spring for Colonel Ludwell and his lady and Major Burwell and I went in it as far

as Mr. Parker's, who was very sick. I stayed with him most all day and ate fish for dinner. He lent me a horse back again and in the evening I got home where I found all well, thanks be to God Almighty. . . .

22. . . . Phil Pursell came to speak with me and I treated him as he deserved. It rained very hard all day. I had another quarrel with my maid Anaka. Mr. Will Eppes came to see me and stayed to dinner. I ate roast mutton for dinner. In the afternoon Mr. Eppes went away in the rain though I persuaded him to stay. In the evening the rain hindered me from walking. . . .

23. . . . Last night my boat returned without the company I expected because both my Aunt Ludwell and Major Burwell were indisposed. I danced my dance. I wrote a letter to England. I read some law. I ate blue wing for dinner. In the afternoon I was angry with Grills for being sick and not telling me of it and with Tom for not doing well in the garden. . . .

24. . . . About 11 o'clock Colonel Randolph came and brought me an answer to Mr. Perry's claim against him, by which it appeared that the interest was twice as much as the principal. . . .

• • •

26. . . . I took a walk about the plantation and when I returned Captain R-b-n, Captain Cook and Mr. Robinson arrived from Williamsburg. I gave them some blue wing and partridge for supper. . . .

27. I rose at 6 o'clock but could read nothing because of my company. I said my prayers shortly and ate milk for breakfast. The company drank chocolate. Then we played at billiards and I showed them a rattlesnake. After this we played at cards. I played at piquet till dinner. We had a very handsome dinner, and particularly a fine dessert which the company admired. After dinner we played at piquet again till 12 o'clock at night. I had a cold which troubled me. Mr. Isham Randolph came over. I asked the captains to be godfathers, which they kindly accepted. . . .

28. . . . It rained much in the night and also this morning, for which reason my company went to cards again. About 11 o'clock Mr. Anderson came and soon after Mr. Harrison, his wife, and daughter. About 12 o'clock our son was christened and his name

40

was Parke. God grant him grace to be a good man. The two captains of the men-of-war were godfathers. . . . Mrs. Betty Harrison was godmother.

. . .

October, 1709

1. I rose at 6 o'clock and read nothing because I got ready to go see the quarters. I ate milk for breakfast and said my prayers shortly. I went to see Westminster who had a pain in his back, to which I ordered to apply some cold water. About 9 o'clock I rode to [Warwick] where I found Tom Turpin and Joe Wilkinson. I took the last with me to the Falls where things were in good order. We went over the river and found that Blackman left everything in a sad condition for which reason I refused to pay him. I stayed on this side till 5 o'clock and returned by the Falls to Falling Creek. Frank Eppes came to us but too late to survey the land in dispute between Captain Webb and me. We ate beef for supper. Frank Eppes lay with me. . . .

2. I rose at 6 o'clock and prepared to return home. I ate milk for breakfast and about 8 o'clock I rode towards the Hundred. By the way I met Will Bass who gave me a sad account of Robin Easely, who is a lazy fellow. I said my prayers on my horse. I called at Doctor Bowman's who gave me some apples. I got home about noon, where I found all well, thanks be to God Almighty. I ate beef for dinner. In the afternoon I took a nap and then went to see the Doctor, who had an ague. . . .

3. . . . The Frenchman came to demand some tools which I detained for a debt he owes me and so I refused to deliver it to him. I went to see the Doctor, who was something better. Mr. Salle and his wife came over, as did John Woodson, while we were at dinner. I ate blue wing for dinner. In the afternoon Mr. Salle and I played at billiards. In the evening we got some supper for our company and I ate some myself. . . .

. . .

5. I rose at 6 o'clock and prepared to go to Williamsburg. I said my prayers and ate milk and potatoes for breakfast. The Doctor

was something better this morning. I was set over the creek and from thence rode to Green Spring where I found Mr. Ludwell sick and Mrs. Wormeley not well recovered. The Colonel had been at general muster and brought home two of his captains with him. . . .

6. I rose at 6 o'clock and said my prayers and ate milk for breakfast. Then I proceeded to Williamsburg, where I found all well. I went to the capitol where I sent for the wench to clean my room and when I came I kissed her and felt her, for which God forgive me. Then I went to see the President, whom I found indisposed in his ears. I dined with him on beef. Then we went to his house and played at piquet where Mr. Clayton came to us. We had much to do to get a bottle of French wine. . . .

7. I rose at 6 o'clock and ate milk for breakfast. The President and Mr. Clayton came to see me. When they were gone I wrote several letters to England. I could get nobody to go with me to Kiquotan and therefore I forbore the journey. I went to the President's and dined with him again. Then took my leave and rode to Green Spring where I found Mr. Ludwell worse. I wrote a letter to England and received one from Mrs. Dunn directed to my wife by which I found out some handy dealings which put me out of humor. . . .

8. I rose at 6 o'clock and said my prayers and ate milk for breakfast. I took my leave and rode towards home where I got about noon and found all things well. . . . The Doctor had been very sick and continued so. In the afternoon Daniel came to see the Doctor who had taken a great quantity of laudanum. I thanked God for my safe return home. . . .

9. . . . The Doctor was very ill so that I thought he would die. . . . In the afternoon I sent for the parson and Mr. Harrison to see the Doctor and they were both of opinion he would die. Mr. Anderson stayed all night and about 7 o'clock his fever began to go off. We prayed by him. We gave him Dr. Goddard's Drops, which seemed to do him great service. We had sent for Dr. Blair but he could not come because of Mrs. Ludwell who was very ill. . . .

10. . . . Captain Stith came again and found the Doctor well enough to make a codicil to give B-l-n-m to his son, which he persuaded him with great importunity to do. . . .

11. . . . Daniel went back to Williamsburg much out of humor with the Doctor because he would not lend him a book notwithstanding the care he had taken with him. About noon Colonel Randolph came to visit the Doctor, and dined with me. I ate roast beef for dinner. He went away in the afternoon and I played at piquet with my own wife. . . .

12. . . . The Doctor was much better but honed after strong drink very much. . . .

. . .

14. . . . I put up my things with design to go very early to Williamsburg. . . .

15. I rose at 3 o'clock and recommended my family to the divine protection. Then I was set over the creek and proceeded towards Williamsburg by moonshine. I got as far as C-ler before the rising of the sun and to Williamsburg by 10 o'clock. I waited on the President and found five of the Council there. A letter came from Colonel Parke that informed us that he had like to have been assassinated by a negro hired for that purpose who shot at him and broke his arm. I was sworn a judge of the General Court and took my place on the bench. . . .

16. . . . I went to the President's and waited on him to church where we heard Mr. Gray preach, who did not attack his sermon well. It rained much in the night and good part of the day. I dined with the President and ate roast chicken for dinner and then ran through the rain home. . . .

17. . . . I went to court and discoursed Mr. Holloway about my law affairs. About 10 o'clock the court sat. There was little business for want of a jury because it rained almost all day and blew very hard. About noon I returned to my chambers and ate some biscuits and butter. Then I returned again to the court and we rose about 3 o'clock and went to dinner. I ate boiled beef for dinner. Then we went to whisk[6] and I won 4 pounds 10 shillings. . . .

. . .

19. . . . About ten o'clock we went to court where a man was tried for ravishing a very homely woman. There were abundance of women in the gallery. I recommended myself to God before I went into court. About one o'clock I went to my chambers for

a little refreshment. The court rose about 4 o'clock and I dined with the Council. I ate boiled beef for dinner. I gave myself the liberty to talk very lewdly, for which God forgive me. . . .

20. . . . I went to court, where I sat almost all day without anything remarkable. About 4 o'clock the court rose and we went to dinner. I ate boiled beef for dinner. In the evening we played at cards at Mr. President's, and I won 35 shillings. . . .

21. . . . About 3 o'clock we went to Council about the Indians. About 4 I went home with Mr. Blair where I found abundance of ladies. I ate boiled pork for dinner. We stayed here till 7 o'clock when I returned to Mr. Bland's. . . .

22. . . . About 10 o'clock we went to Council and heard the dispute between Parson Slater and his parish and between the parson and vestry of Manakin Town, but nothing was decided. Several of the Council went home. We just went to adjourn the court and then went to dinner. I ate beef for dinner. In the evening I went to Mr. Bland's where the President came likewise and we played at cards. . . .

23. . . . Daniel came and shaved my head. About 11 o'clock I waited on the President and Colonel Harrison to church, where Mr. Cargill preached a good sermon. After church Colonel Harrison asked me to go to Mr. Blair's to dinner. I ate fish and goose for dinner. I went in the evening to Colonel Bray's where we found abundance of company and agreed to meet there the next day and have a dance. About 10 o'clock I came home and neglected to say my prayers and for that reason was guilty of uncleanness. I had bad thoughts, good health and good humor, thanks be to God Almighty.

24. I rose at 6 o'clock and read nothing because Mr. Bland came and gave in his accounts. I said my prayers and ate milk for breakfast. I had a letter from Colonel Lee with his accounts. I went to court where I sat till noon and then returned to my chambers and ate some biscuits and neat's tongue. I did some business and about 4 o'clock went to Mr. Bland's and from thence to Colonel Bray's where we found abundance of company. We danced till 2 o'clock in the morning. . . .

• • •

27. . . . The President was so kind to offer to put off passing the accounts till my order came for increasing my salary. We went

to court and sat till 4 o'clock. Then we went to dinner and I ate boiled beef for my dinner. In the evening we played at cards and I won £5. We drank some of Will Robinson's cider till we were very merry and then went to the coffeehouse and pulled poor Colonel Churchill out of bed. I went home about one o'clock in the morning. . . .

28. . . . Colonel Harrison's vessel came in from Madeira and brought abundance of letters and among the rest I had ten from Mr. Perry with a sad account of tobacco. We went to court but much time was taken up in reading our letters and not much business was done. About 3 we rose and had a meeting of the College in which it was agreed to turn Mr. Blackamore out from being master of the school for being so great a sot. . . .

29. I rose at 6 o'clock and read nothing because the governors of the College were to meet again. However I said my prayers and ate milk for breakfast. When we met Mr. Blackamore presented a petition in which he set forth that if the governors of the College would forgive him what was past, he would for the time to come mend his conduct. On which the governors at last agreed to keep him on, on trial, some time longer. Then we went to court where we sat till about 3 o'clock and then I learned that my sister Custis was at Mr. Bland's. I went to her and there was also Mrs. Chiswell. . . .

30. I rose at 6 o'clock but read nothing because by the time I was dressed Mr. Holloway, Mrs. Chiswell, and Mrs. Custis came to see me. However I said my prayers and ate milk for breakfast. I gave them a bottle of sack and as soon as they went away I waited on the President to church where Mr. Goodwin preached a good sermon. After church I went to Mr. Blair's to dinner with all the Council in attendance. . . .

31. . . . About 10 o'clock we went to court. The committee met to receive proposals for the building the College and Mr. Tullitt undertook it for £2,000 provided he might wood off the College land and all assistants from England to come at the College's risk. We sat in court till about 4 o'clock and then I rode to Green Spring to meet my wife. I found her there and had the pleasure to learn that all was well at home, thanks be to God. There was likewise Mrs. Chiswell. I ate boiled beef for supper. Then we danced and were merry till about 10 o'clock. . . .

November, 1709

1. I rose at 8 o'clock because I could not leave my wife sooner. Then I ate milk for breakfast. I neglected to say my prayers nor could I read anything. About 11 o'clock I went to Williamsburg and about 12 took my place in court. I sat there till about 4 and could not go out of town because I had accounts to settle with several people. About 5 o'clock we went to dinner and I ate boiled beef. Then the President took us home to his house, where I played at cards and won 35 shillings. We were very merry and in that condition went to the coffeehouse and again disturbed Colonel Churchill. About 11 o'clock I went home and said a short prayer. . . .

2. . . . In the evening I went to Dr. [Barret's] where my wife came this afternoon. Here I found Mrs. Chiswell, my sister Custis, and other ladies. We sat and talked till about 11 o'clock and then retired to our chambers. I played at [r-m] with Mrs. Chiswell and kissed her on the bed till she was angry and my wife also was uneasy about it, and cried as soon as the company was gone. I neglected to say my prayers, which I should not have done, because I ought to beg pardon for the lust I had for another man's wife. However I had good health, good thoughts, and good humor, thanks be to God Almighty.

3. I rose at 6 o'clock and without ceremony went away to court to hear the orders read. However I ate my breakfast in milk first. We had likewise a short Council. I settled accounts with Colonel Digges and Mr. President. Then I took leave of the Council and returned to Dr. [Barret's], from whence I waited on the ladies to Queen's Creek where my mother Parke's things were divided between my wife and her sister. My uncle Ludwell was there with us. . . .

4. I rose at 6 o'clock but neglected to say my prayers because Mr. Commissary kept me to hear a verse he had made for the College. I ate chocolate for breakfast. Mr. Holloway and Mr. Clayton came over this morning. We went to dinner about 12 o'clock and I ate some hash. Then we went to Mr. Bland's where we found letters from England but no news. Then we rode to Major Burwell's where we found turkey for supper. We sat and talked till 10 o'clock and then went to bed. . . .

5. I rose at 7 o'clock and read a little in my common-place, but I neglected to say my prayers. I drank posset for breakfast. Then I took a walk about the plantation. About one o'clock we went to dinner. I ate boiled beef and pudding. About 3 o'clock we went over the river to Mr. Burwell's where we arrived about 5. In the evening we drank two bottles of French claret. I was so sleepy I could not keep my eyes open. However we did not go to bed before 10 o'clock. . . .

6. . . . About 11 o'clock we rode to the church of Abingdon Parish which is the best church I have seen in the country. We heard a sermon of Parson Smith. After church we returned to Mr. Burwell's and Mr. Berkeley and his wife with us. We dined late and I ate boiled beef and pudding. In the evening we sat and talked till 10 o'clock and I told abundance of lies by way of diversion. . . .

7. I rose at 7 o'clock and said my prayers. I ate chocolate for breakfast. We walked about till dinner and then I ate roast beef. We had intended to go over the river again but my sister Custis asked me to move her over the Bay and I said I would if Mr. Burwell would. He said he would if his wife would, and she agreed to go and drew us all into the frolic. In the afternoon we rode to my Cousin Berkeley's with design to take him and his wife with us but he escaped by being from home. His wife was at home and gave us a good supper. I ate boiled beef. Then we had some cherries which had been scalded in hot water which did not boil and then put in bottles without water in them. They were exceedingly good. . . .

8. I rose at 7 o'clock and said a short prayer. I ate chocolate for breakfast. Then we took our leave of Mrs. Berkeley and went in a boat to York where there is a stone church. Then we went over the river to Gloucester Town and about noon went aboard the shallop and sailed down the river with a fair wind. When we came to the mouth of the river it grew calm so that we came to anchor but soon after the wind began to blow again. We saw a [c-l-n] sloop in the bay which soon put aboard us and the men were so rude we kept them off because we took them for privateers. I ate roast beef for dinner, but the women were frightened with the boat that they could not eat. We lay in the shallop all night but about 5 o'clock in the morning we dropped anchor in Pigot's Hole. . . .

9. I turned out about 7 o'clock and Mr. Burwell and I rowed ourselves ashore because the men were all gone for horses. We went to Mr. Littleton's where I ate milk for breakfast. About 10 o'clock the horses came from my brother Custis and we rode to Arlington which is a great house within sight of the Bay and really a pleasant plantation but not kept very nicely. We walked all over the plantation in which the hogs had done great damage. My brother Custis received us kindly. I ate goose for dinner. In the afternoon we walked again and in the evening Mr. Dunn and his wife came to see us. We ate oysters and were merry together till about 11 o'clock. . . .

10. I rose about 7 o'clock and read some Greek in Anacreon. I said my prayers shortly and ate roasted potatoes for breakfast. About 10 o'clock we rode to the Cape with design to go to Smith Island but it blew too hard. Among the [. . .] here and everywhere on this shore is a tree called [p-l] tree, a suffusion of whose bark will cause salivation. The leaves and berries smell of spice. We were kindly treated at George Freshwater's where I ate beef and potatoes for dinner. Parson Dunn was sick here, who is a man of no polite conversation, notwithstanding he be a good Latin scholar. From hence we rode to Mr. [Harris] who gave us a bottle of good wine, of which he was very generous. Then we went home, where we were merry till 11 o'clock. . . .

11. . . . In the afternoon we went to visit Colonel Waters, a very honest man, who lives about six miles off. He gave us some good wine called [Saint George's] wine. We took a walk by the side of the Bay and then went to supper and I ate some roast beef. Then we returned in the dark to Arlington where we found some of the women sick and some out of humor and particularly my wife quarreled with Mr. Dunn and me for talking Latin and called it bad manners. This put me out of humor with her which set her to crying. I wholly made the reconciliation. The parson was more affronted than I, and went to bed. . . .

12. . . . We rode on bad horses to Hungars to visit Colonel Custis who is 20 miles off Arlington. It began to rain before we got there. We were very kindly received by all the family. The Colonel is an honest well-meaning man. About 3 o'clock we went to dinner and I ate boiled beef. Then we took a walk about the plantation. Colonel Waters met us here. In the evening we danced and were very merry till about 10 o'clock. . . .

48

13. I rose about 7 o'clock but could read nothing because we were in haste to go to church. I ate milk for breakfast notwithstanding it was here not very good. About 10 o'clock we rode to church which is six miles off. There was the biggest congregation I ever saw in the country. The people look half dead since the sickness which they had last year. Mr. Dunn preached a good sermon. After church we returned to Colonel Custis' again. About 3 o'clock we dined and I ate boiled beef. In the evening we drank a bottle of wine pretty freely and were full of mirth and good humor and particularly Colonel Waters. However we were merry and wise and went to bed in good time by my means. I neglected to say my prayers but had good health, good thoughts, and good humor, thanks be to God Almighty.

14. . . . About 12 o'clock we went to dinner and I ate goose, which are very good and in great plenty here. In the afternoon we paid a visit to Mr. Hamilton who lives across the creek. He is a man of bad character and he got the estate nobody knows how. We walked about his plantation and saw a pretty shallop he was building. He was very courteous to us and provided a supper but we could not stay to eat it because it grew dark and it was dangerous to stay late for fear of the dogs which are fierce at Colonel Custis'. In the evening we all designed to be merry but were all out of humor by consent and would neither dance nor drink. About 8 o'clock we went to supper and I ate some mince pie. . . .

15. I rose about 7 o'clock with design to return to Arlington but the rain prevented. I said my prayers and read a great deal in Anacreon. About 10 o'clock we went to breakfast and I ate some goose, of which they have great plenty here. The rain did not hold up till towards evening when I took a walk in the garden. Then we went to a play called [burning coals][7] at which we ran much and were very merry. However some of the women were out of humor, as was natural among so many. About 7 o'clock we went to supper and I ate mutton. Colonel Waters stayed with us to the last. . . .

16. I rose about 7 o'clock and said my prayers. I read a little in Anacreon. About 9 o'clock we went to breakfast and I ate goose again. It rained a little but that did not discourage us from going; but we took leave of the good company. Then we rode very hard because it rained. Colonel Custis lent me the only good horse I

met with on this shore. About 2 o'clock we came to Arlington. I got a pain in my loins I suppose by cold and my brother Custis had a [remembrance] of the gripes. In the evening we were all very dull and therefore we went to bed early. . . .

17. I rose about 8 o'clock and read in Anacreon. The wind was directly contrary so that we could not think of embarking to return over the Bay. I neglected to say my prayers. I ate milk for breakfast, which is hard to be got here. We took a walk about the plantation. About 3 o'clock we went to dinner and I ate goose again. In the afternoon we took a walk of about three miles. In the evening I read some Latin in Horace. We were very merry till about 10 o'clock, notwithstanding my wife was much incommoded with her term which came away in great abundance. . . .

18. . . . The contrary wind continued, at which my sister Custis was very uneasy and quarrelled with Mrs. Dunn for persuading my wife to stay so long at Hungars. Here are the worst servants that ever I saw in my life. My wife continued indisposed with a great flux of blood. I took a walk about the plantation. About 3 o'clock we went to dinner. Wine was very scarce here so that we were very moderate. I ate boiled beef. In the afternoon we walked very fast to the church and almost killed Parson Dunn, who was forced to run all the way to keep up with us. In the evening we were as merry as we could till about 9 o'clock. . . .

19. I rose at [. . .] o'clock on the news the wind was fair, but it soon came contrary again. I said my prayers and ate milk for breakfast. I read some Greek in Anacreon and some Latin in Horace. My sister continued out of humor with us and especially with Mrs. Dunn. About 11 o'clock I took a walk about the plantation, notwithstanding it was very cold. About 2 o'clock we went to dinner and I ate roast beef. The wind blew very cold at northwest. In the afternoon I took a walk again with my friend Horace. In the evening we were as merry as we could. . . .

. . .

25. I rose about 6 o'clock because the wind was come fair again. I said a short prayer, gave the servants money, and we all rode away to the Hole with expedition. About 8 we took leave of Mr. Custis and went on board the shallop, notwithstanding the wind was very scanty and blew hard. This made us all very sick and

particularly the women. In about five hours we made a shift to reach Back River, for the wind would not permit us to reach York. We went ashore at Mr. Wallace's who was not at home himself, but his wife was very kind to us and gave us a good supper. I ate roast beef. In the evening Mr. Wallace came home and gave us some excellent cider. I said a short prayer and had good health, good thoughts, and good humor, thank God Almighty.

26. I rose about 7 o'clock and because we were in haste to go I neglected to say my prayers. I [ate] toast and cider for breakfast. The parson was so kind as to provide us with six horses and would hardly part with us so that it was noon before we could get away. He lives very neatly and is very kind to all that come to his house. At 12 we mounted and it was my fortune to have a horse that would not run away with me. We all got safe in the evening to Major Burwell's, where we found abundance of company. I was grieved to hear my daughter had received a fall and hurt her forehead but I was comforted again with a letter from Bannister that told me she and all the family was well. . . .

27. I rose about 7 o'clock but neglected to say my prayers. I could read nothing but wrote some notes for Major Burwell. So soon as Mr. Burwell sent my [papers] over the river I thought to go away, but I ate milk for breakfast and likewise stayed to dinner and I ate mutton. About 4 o'clock we took leave of Major Burwell and Mrs. Burwell, who is a well-humored woman that I had not seen once out of humor since our voyage. We rode to Williamsburg and had a little rain by the way. Mr. [?] nor his wife were at home so that we were forced to tarry till it was dark, when they came. Here I saw honest Mr. Clayton, Mr. Jones, and Mr. Robinson. Mr. Clayton was so kind as to lend me his horse to Green Spring, because mine was lame. We got there about 7 o'clock. . . .

28. . . . We stayed till noon and then took our leave of all the company. My wife was uneasy and much out of humor by the way. We got home by 5 o'clock where we found all well, thanks be to God. Poor old Ben died ten days ago and I learned that Mr. Isham Eppes died likewise about the same time. I examined into all my business and was well satisfied with it. . . .

29. . . . I thought to go to Falling Creek but I learned that Grills had laid a wager that he would saw 1,000 feet of planks in ten

hours with two saws and by way of [. . .] afterwards performed it in six hours, to the confusion of Webb and Woodson, that had laid with him. I ate fish for dinner. In the afternoon I walked about the plantation to see what my negroes had done and was not displeased. . . .

30. I rose at 3 o'clock and read two chapters in Hebrew and some Greek in Cassius. I went to bed again and lay till 7. I said my prayers, danced my dance, and ate milk for breakfast. Eugene was whipped for pissing in bed and Jenny for concealing it. I settled several accounts. I ate boiled beef for dinner. In the afternoon I played at billiards with my wife and then took a walk about the plantation to look over my affairs. I said my prayers. In the evening I read some Italian. About 8 o'clock we went to bed and I had good health, good thoughts, and good humor, thanks be to God Almighty.

December, 1709

1. . . . Eugene was whipped again for pissing in bed and Jenny for concealing it. About 11 o'clock came Captain Stith and his wife, not on a visit but Mrs. Stith came to desire me justify her to Mrs. Harrison that she had not told me that Mrs. Harrison was delivered of two children before her time. I wrote to Mrs. Harrison to assure her that Mrs. Stith had never told me any such thing. But my wife could not deny but she had told that Mrs. Stith told her so. Thus women will be [p-r-t]. I denied her and so did Mrs. Mallory and Bannister's sister. In the afternoon the company went away. . . .

2. . . . My wife was very much vexed with the conversation she had yesterday with Mrs. Stith. I ate fish for dinner which we catch in great quantity. It rained a little in the afternoon. I settled more accounts and played at billiards with my wife. In the evening I read more Italian and washed my feet. . . .

3. . . . Eugene pissed abed again for which I made him drink a pint of piss. I settled some accounts and read some news. About 12 o'clock I went to court where I found little good company. However I persuaded Mr. Anderson and Colonel Eppes to come and dine with me. I ate a venison pasty for dinner. In the evening

Mr. Anderson and I walked to Mr. Harrison's where we found Frank W-l-s and James Burwell and Isham Randolph. Here I ate custard and was merry. I stayed till 9 o'clock and when I came home my wife was in bed. . . .

4. . . . I danced my dance, and then took a walk in the garden because the weather was very tempting for so late in the year. God continue it for the service of those that have but little corn. I ate boiled beef for dinner. In the afternoon I ate an apple and then took a long walk about the great pasture with my wife and I found they finished stacking. . . .

5. . . . About 10 o'clock Mrs. Harrison and her daughter came and soon after Mr. Harrison, Frank W-l-s and James Burwell and Isham Randolph. I gave them some strong water. Then we went and played at billiards and I won half a crown. About one we went to dinner and I ate fish. Mrs. [Ware] managed with great [order]. In the afternoon we shot in a bow[s] but none of us could hit the mark. My wife was guilty in reproaching Frank W-l-s for swearing and he was out of humor for it. They went away just as it was dark. . . .

· · ·

7. . . . About 10 o'clock I rode to Captain Stith's to see the Doctor who lay there very ill. Here I met Colonel Randolph who was going to Williamsburg. I ate some roast beef here and then proceeded with Colonel Randolph over S-n-s Bridge to Colonel Duke's. It was exceedingly cold. We did not get over till after sunset. We found the Colonel under great fear of the distemper, which he said was very violent in the neighborhood. . . .

8. . . . About 9 o'clock we proceeded to Williamsburg and by the way called at Mr. Blair's, who was already gone. Then we went to Mr. Bland's, who was sick. From hence I went to the President's where a council was held concerning the loss of the man-of-war which ran ashore near Coratuck Inlet on the 29th of the last month about one o'clock in the morning. All the men were saved except 12 who had been overset in a yawl. Orders had been sent to Colonel Wilson to press a sloop to go to the assistance of the men to save the stores and rigging. The Council also considered about taking off the protection of corn but agreed not to do it. They also agreed to give directions to the Attorney General to prosecute the vestry of Charles Parish for disturbing divine services, and then a general fast was appointed on account

of the sickness. Then we went to dinner and I ate boiled beef. In the afternoon we had a meeting of the College to confirm the agreement with John Tullitt to build the College. The President received a letter from Colonel Wilson which said that several of the men belonging to the unfortunate man-of-war had left the captain and were come to Kiquotan and were [distressed] for victuals. The Council sat till 8 o'clock when I went to Queen's Creek, notwithstanding the great cold. . . .

• • •

14. . . . I sent Tom to know how the Doctor did and he brought word he died about 5 o'clock last night. His distemper was first a fever, of which he recovered but went too soon to Major Allen's and was sick again there but made a shift to get back again and recovered again, and then he went to Captain Stith's where he got what strong drink he pleased . . . and got cold and that brought intermittent fever and short breath which killed him. He was a good natured man but too much addicted to drink. . . .

15. . . . About 10 o'clock Mr. Harrison, Dr. Blair, and Jimmy Burwell came over to see some of the Doctor's things and took some account of them, but they went away about 12 and I and my wife went to Mr. Harrison's, where we dined. I ate boiled mutton for dinner. We were very merry and stayed till about 4 o'clock and then returned home where we found all well, thanks be to God. In the evening I read nothing but only wrote two letters to Williamsburg. . . .

16. . . . My wife had a great pain in her belly and so took a purge which worked very well. Eugene was whipped for doing nothing yesterday. I danced my dance. I settled several accounts. I ate roast mutton for dinner. My [wife] was better after her physic, which worked 12 times. In the afternoon I played at piquet with my wife to divert her. . . .

17. . . . About 10 o'clock I ate some hashed mutton in order to go to Dr. Oastler's funeral. Accordingly about 11 o'clock we went to Captain Stith's and there heard a sermon on the occasion preached by Mr. Anderson and then followed him to his grave. About 3 o'clock we returned and found that one of my negro women had broken her leg and another had sprained herself. But thank God Daniel came home with us and did great service in setting the broken leg and dressing the other. In the evening

54

my cousin [Pye], lieutenant of the lost man-of-war, came over. I made him very welcome. . . .

18. . . . My cousin and I played at billiards because there seemed to be no more harm in it than in talk. Then we took a walk about the plantation. I ate roast goose for dinner. In the afternoon we walked again about the plantation. My cousin [Pye] is a good humored man and has seen abundance of the world. . . .

. . .

21. I rose about 8 o'clock but neglected to say my prayers because Mr. [Pye] lay with me. He is a merry good humored man as can be. About 10 o'clock we went to breakfast and I ate sausage and chocolate. Then we took our leave and went to Colonel Randolph's but there it began to rain so that we went to cards again. About one we went to dinner and I ate roast beef. In the afternoon we played at cards again because the rain prevented our departure. . . .

22. I rose about 8 o'clock but continued to neglect my prayers because Mr. [Pye] lay with me. About 10 o'clock we went to breakfast. I ate pickled oysters and chocolate. Then we thought to take our leave, but the rain prevented us again. However we sent for John Pleasants with whom Mr. [Pye] had some business. We played at cards again and about 3 o'clock went to dinner. I ate broiled pork. In the afternoon because the rain continued we played at cards again. In the evening Mrs. Randolph gave us some apples. We played at cards till 10 o'clock and then went to bed. . . .

23. I rose at 7 o'clock and said my prayers shortly. I ate milk for breakfast. About 8 o'clock we took leave and proceeded with Mr. [Pye] and Isham Randolph to Falling Creek. Here I found matters in good order. Mr. [Pye] was well pleased with the sawmill and other matters at Falling Creek. We stayed here about two hours and ate some milk and then rode away to the Hundred where we were forced to wait above an hour because the boat was not at home, for which Captain Worsham came and made an excuse. However, we got over the river in Isham Eppes' boat and about 5 o'clock were at Colonel Hill's, where we found Mr. Anderson and all the family. In less than an hour we went to supper over a turkey pie. We sat and were merry till 9 o'clock. . . .

24. I rose about 8 o'clock and read in my commonplace and said

my prayers. I cast water over a negro maid that was passing under the window. I ate custard for breakfast. Then we took a walk about the pasture and about 11 o'clock went to dinner. I ate [sh-ler]. Then we took our leave and got home about 2 o'clock where I found all well, thanks be to God. About 3 o'clock came Dick Randolph and Mr. Jackson from Williamsburg and brought me a letter from Mr. Bland who was much better. . . .

25. . . . We went to church, notwithstanding it rained a little, where Mr. Anderson preached a good sermon for the occasion. I received the Sacrament with great devoutness. After church the same company went to dine with me and I ate roast beef for dinner. In the afternoon Dick Randolph and Mr. Jackson went away and Mr. Jackson rode sidelong like a woman. Then we took a walk about the plantation, but a great fog soon drove us into the house again. In the evening we were merry with nonsense and so were my servants. . . .

26. . . . I wrote several letters to Falling Creek which I sent by Dick. It rained very hard all night. We played at billiards till about 12 o'clock when Mr. Harrison and his wife came to dine with us. I ate boiled beef for dinner. We were not very merry because the weather had some effect over us. . . .

27. . . . About 12 o'clock we went to Mr. Harrison's, notwithstanding it was extremely cold and the wind blew very hard. About 2 o'clock we went to dinner and I ate some goose. In the afternoon we were very merry by a good fire till 5 o'clock. Then we returned home, where I found all well, thank God. . . .

28. . . . In the afternoon we played again at billiards till we lost one of the balls. Then we walked about the plantation and took a slide on the ice. In the evening we played at cards till about 10 o'clock. . . .

29. . . . About 9 o'clock I ate again some chocolate with the company. Then we took a walk and I slid on skates, notwithstanding there was a thaw. Then we returned and played at billiards till dinner. I ate boiled beef for dinner. In the afternoon we played at billiards again and in the evening took another walk and gave Mr. Isham Randolph two bits to venture on the ice. He ventured and the ice broke with him and took him up to the

mid-leg. Then we came home and played a little at whisk but I was so sleepy we soon left off. . . .

[There are no entries for December 30 and 31.]

January, 1710

1. . . . In the afternoon we took a walk about the plantation. The weather was very warm. In the evening we drank a bottle of wine and were merry. I said my prayers and had good health, good thoughts, and good humor, thanks be to God Almighty. I gave my wife a flourish this morning.

2. I rose at 6 o'clock and wrote several letters to recommend my Cousin [Pye] to a ship. I said my prayers and ate milk for breakfast. News was brought that Colonel Hill was come from England and came to his house last night. He came in a ship by way of Bristol. . . . In the afternoon I sent Mr. Mumford to compliment Colonel Hill on his return from England and by him I learned that our Governor Colonel Hunter has quit this government for that of New York, and that there is no likelihood of a peace or of the fleet's coming over. . . .

3. I gave my wife a flourish and then rose at 7 o'clock. I read nothing because my Cousin [Pye] went away and I sent my man Tom to Williamsburg. News was brought that the distemper was at Captain Stith's where he had ten negroes sick of it. God of his excessive goodness deliver from it! Mr. Mumford and I played at billiards till dinner after we had settled our accounts. My wife was very sick. I ate hashed turkey. My son began to breed teeth which disordered him. In the afternoon Mr. Mumford went away and I took a walk about the plantation and when I came home I gave a vomit to six of my people by way of prevention. God send it may succeed. . . .

4. . . . About 10 o'clock I went to bid Colonel Hill welcome to Virginia. There was abundance of company, on the same account, and among the rest Parson Robertson. The Colonel was very courteous and complaisant. About 3 o'clock we went to dinner and I ate boiled beef. I could stay but a little while after dinner and then took leave and returned home and found all well, thanks

be to God. One from the Falls brought me some venison and told me all was well and Tom returned from Williamsburg and brought me a letter from Mr. Bland by which I learned that he was recovered. Mrs. Ware sent her daughter over to live with my wife. In the evening I read some French. . . .

• • •

10. . . . My sloop returned from Chickahominy with shingles which I caused to be unloaded. My wife continued indisposed in her head. I wrote a letter to England and read some Latin in Terence. I ate chicken and hashed mutton for dinner. In the afternoon I played at piquet with my wife and she fell down which increased the pain in her head. I took a walk and endeavored to kill a partridge for my wife but could not. In the evening Mr. Salle came down and told me all was well at Falling Creek and put me out of humor by putting stories into my head of several people, I cannot tell with what design. However I discouraged him as much as I could. I said my prayers shortly and had good health, good thoughts, but ill humor, for which God forgive me.

11. . . . This day was appointed for a fast and notwithstanding it rained, abundance of people came to church and when I came there I was surprised to find Mr. Clayton and Mr. Robinson there, who had laid at Mr. Harrison's that night. Mr. Anderson gave us a good sermon on the occasion. These two gentlemen went home with me. They knew no news at all. . . .

12. . . . My daughter Evelyn was indisposed and took a purge which did not work very well. My wife was better, thank God, but did not come out to the company. . . .

13. . . . My daughter was not well and took a purge which did not work much. My wife was severe to her because she was fretful. In the afternoon I danced more dances, and then took a walk again about the plantation with my bow and arrow. In the evening I [reproached] Bannister for his pride. . . .

• • •

15. . . . Mrs. Ware's daughter got up in the night and went away without any cause in the world. . . . I sent my English letters over the river to Peter Hamlin who will go on Tuesday next to England. In the evening I took a walk about the plantation. I read some French about the [experience] of some people in the [savannahs]. . . .

• • •

19. . . . Dick Randolph came and brought me a letter from England by which I learned the Queen's letter was sent to Carolina to forbid them from meddling with our traders. I ordered my people to set him up to Mr. Bland's. . . .

20. . . . An express came from my brother Custis with the news that they had lost four negroes of the distemper and desired me to send more ipecac. In the evening I wrote a letter to my brother Custis. . . .

21. . . . I danced my dance and then sent away my brother Custis' boy with the things he came for. I settled some accounts and then took a walk. I ate pork and peas for dinner. In the afternoon I read some Latin. About 3 o'clock my cousin Betty Harrison came to see us and told us they had lost a negro man. . . .

22. . . . About 11 o'clock we went to church and before we went in Mr. Harrison's horse ran away with his coach and broke down my mother's tombstone. Mr. Anderson gave us a good sermon and after church he and Colonel Hill and Mrs. Anderson and Mrs. B-k-r came and dined with us and so did Mr. C-s. I ate beef for dinner but ate too much. They went away about 4 o'clock and then Mr. C-s and I took a walk about the plantation. My daughter was indisposed and had a fever, for which I gave her a vomit of the tincture of ipecac. . . .

23. . . . My daughter slept very well this night and was well this morning, thank God. . . .

24. I could not sleep all night for the disturbance my daughter gave me. . . . I had my father's grave opened to see him but he was so wasted there was not anything to be distinguished. . . . In the evening I read nothing by my wife's desire. I had good health, good thoughts, and good humor, thanks be to God Almighty.

• • •

28. . . . In the afternoon I played at cards with my wife but we quarrelled and she cried. About 3 o'clock Mrs. Harrison and Mr. Gee came to see us and stayed about two hours. George made an end of setting up my father's tomb. In the evening my river sloop came from Falling Creek, loaded with pales. . . .

• • •

31. I rose at 7 o'clock by reason of my cold. I said my prayers and ate milk for breakfast. I read nothing because I rode to Colonel Randolph's, where I arrived about 12 o'clock. The Colonel had the gout severely but the rest of the family were well. Here I stayed till the evening and then I went to Will Randolph's and Isham Randolph with us. There I ate some beef for supper. We sat and talked about my case in Henrico court and of other things till about 9 o'clock and then retired to bed. I proffered Isham Randolph to teach him French if he would come to our house, which he promised he would very thankfully. I said my prayers shortly. My cold continued bad. I had in other respects good health, good thoughts, and good humor, thanks be to God Almighty. Generally this month the wind was from the south and the weather extraordinarily warm for the time of year, which was very happy considering the distemper is worse in cold weather and considering the great want of corn in the country.

February, 1710

1. . . . I said my prayers shortly and found my cold bad, which made me resolve not to go to court but I recommended my business to Will Randolph and wrote to Mr. Grills. Then we went to breakfast with Colonel Randolph and stayed till 11 o'clock, and then Isham Randolph and I rode to Colonel Hill's. The Colonel and Mr. Harrison were just going to court but I stayed with Mr. Anderson and he and Colonel Eppes played with Isham Randolph and me at cricket but we beat them. About 4 o'clock I returned home, where I found all well, thanks be to God. . . .

2. . . . I gave Bannister leave to visit his father-in-law who was sick and sent him some physic. It was very warm weather. I took a walk about the plantation. I ate boiled beef for dinner, and was out of humor with my wife about stewed cherries. . . .

3. . . . About 10 o'clock Mr. Parker came to see me and told me that George Carter had left some shoes and nails at his quarters which he thought might have been stolen from me. Soon after Colonel Hill and Mr. Anderson and Captain Llewelyn came. When we had drunk a glass of wine we went to court, where we stayed about an hour and then came home to dinner and Isham Randolph with us. Here I found Captain Keeling to buy

quitrents. I ate roast beef for dinner. Then we went to the vestry where we ordered the church yard to be paled in for 8,000 pounds of tobacco by Mr. Parker. Then my boat set Colonel Hill and Mr. Anderson to Mrs. Taylor's. I took a walk about the plantation. My man Tony brought me an Indian boy called Harry. . . .

4. . . . The sheriff of Isle of Wight was here about the quitrents which I ordered him to sell by inch of candle.[9] . . .

• • •

8. . . . I settled some accounts and then Mr. Harrison and Dr. Blair came, the first to sell me the Doctor's things and the last to buy some of the medicine. About 11 o'clock they went away again. Then I surveyed the Doctor's things and found them not so many as I expected. I ate boiled beef for dinner. In the afternoon I played at billiards with my wife and then removed some of the Doctor's books. Then I took a walk about the plantation to overlook my people. . . .

9. . . . I settled some accounts and removed the Doctor's books. Then Captain Eppes came to make up his accounts. He stayed at dinner. I ate some roast pig. In the afternoon my uncle Byrd came to speculate about [seizing] his things to secure himself in case the hour should come. Mr. Eppes went away and I took a walk about the plantation to overlook my people. When I returned I found Mr. C-s here. I ate roast beef for supper with my uncle. Then I said my prayers and had good health, good thoughts, and good humor, thanks be to God Almighty. My wife found herself very much out of order because I forgot to give her a glass of physic when she desired it.

10. . . . I settled some accounts. I desired my uncle to stay this day, which he agreed to. I gave a poor man some physic for his sick child. I ate boiled beef for dinner. In the afternoon Mr. [Henry] Goodrich and Bannister came over and Mr. Isham Randolph came over to [. . .] with me to learn French. He and I took a walk about the plantation. . . .

11. . . . I settled some accounts and Mr. Randolph began his French. My uncle went away pretty well satisfied because I told him he might come and live with me. I ate hashed beef for dinner. Mr. Bland called here on his way to Williamsburg with his shallop. In the afternoon I settled some of the Doctor's affairs and then Mr. Randolph and I took a long walk about the planta-

61

tion. In the evening I read some Latin and taught Mr. Randolph his lesson. . . .

12. . . . I took a walk with my wife and daughter and Mr. Randolph. I ate boiled beef for dinner. In the afternoon I read about an hour, then Mr. C-s came to see us and we drank a bottle of white wine. He stayed till 9 o'clock, then I said my prayers and had good thoughts, good humor, and good health, thanks be to God Almighty.

13. . . . I settled some of the Doctor's affairs and amended my [creed]. I wrote a letter to Colonel Duke and another to my brother Duke in answer to a letter I received from them. I ate roast beef for dinner. In the afternoon I played at billiards with Mr. Randolph and then removed several of the Doctor's things into my closet. Then we went to take a walk and were taken in the rain but were not very wet. In the evening I instructed Mr. Randolph in his French. I said my prayers and had good health, good thoughts, and good humor, thanks be to God Almighty. As soon as we were in bed my wife complained of great pains in her belly. I persuaded her to be bled and I rose to call Grills to let her blood. She refused a long time; at last she agreed, but there was no one appeared. However, she was more at ease and we went to bed again and she was easy all night, thank God.

14. I rose at 7 o'clock and read the Psalms and some Greek in Cassius. My wife miscarried this morning. I said my prayers and ate milk for breakfast. I danced my dance. My cousin Harrison and Mrs. Anderson came to see my wife to comfort her in her affliction. They stayed and dined with me. I ate roast shoat. In the afternoon they went away and Mr. Randolph and I walked to Mr. Harrison's where we found Colonel Hill extremely troubled with a headache. We stayed about two hours and then Colonel Hill and Mrs. Anderson went over the river and Mr. Randolph and I took a walk. In the evening my spouse was better. . . .

15. . . . My wife was indisposed again today so that I sent for Mrs. Hamlin. I danced my dance. About 10 o'clock Mrs. Hamlin came and soon after her Mrs. Bolling, the widow. She came for some physic which the Doctor had prepared for her and would have paid me for it but I would not take it. They both stayed and dined with me. I ate boiled beef for dinner. In the afternoon I read some Latin and put the Doctor's medicines in order. . . .

16. . . . My wife was better, thank God. I removed several things out of the Doctor's closet. I taught Mr. Randolph French in which he made good improvement. I ate roast beef for dinner. In the afternoon Mr. Randolph and I played at billiards and then Captain Cook came from Williamsburg to see me, where there was no news. He ate some roast beef and then we took a walk about the plantation. He is a very good-humored man and has been very unfortunate. . . .

· · ·

20. I rose at 6 o'clock and read the Psalms and some Greek in Cassius. I said my prayers and ate milk for breakfast. My maid Anaka was taken sick yesterday but I gave her a vomit that worked very much and she was better this day. Then I had her sweated and bled which gave her some ease. However her fever continued violently. We rode to Colonel Hill's where we were kindly received. We played at cricket and I sprained my backside. I ate bacon and fowl for dinner. In the afternoon we played at the same sport again but I could not run. When we came away I was forced to get on my horse by a chair. We found my wife not very well. . . .

21. . . . The Captain received letters from a gentleman of North Carolina about the man-of-war that was lost. I ate pork and rice for dinner. In the afternoon we shot with bow and arrow and I hit the mark. Mr. C-s came to see us. We took a walk in the evening. When we returned we drank two bottles of wine and I was very merry. . . .

· · ·

23. . . . My maid Anaka was better, thank God. The Captain's bitch killed a lamb yesterday, for which we put her into a house with a ram that beat her violently to break her of that bad custom. We played at billiards. It rained with a northeast wind. I ate roast beef for dinner. In the afternoon we played at cards and were very merry. The pool lasted so long that we played till 11 o'clock at night. . . .

24. . . . Mr. Harrison invited us to dinner and we went, notwithstanding it was bad weather and snowed a little. Colonel Hill had been sick very much. We found Mrs. John Stith at Mr. Harrison's, who dined with us. . . .

25. . . . Mr. Grills put up the pales round my father's and

mother's tombs and the others. Tom went away after breakfast. We played at billiards till 12 o'clock; then Mr. Harrison, his wife, and Mrs. Stith came and soon after them Robin Mumford and Captain Hamlin who all dined with us. I ate boiled beef for dinner. In the afternoon they played at cricket, at which the Captain sprained his thigh. About 5 o'clock the company went away and Mr. Harrison seemed to be very gallant to Mrs. Stith. . . .

26. . . . In the afternoon we saw a good battle between a stallion and Robin about the mare, but at last the stallion had the advantage and covered the mare three times. The Captain's bitch killed another lamb for which she was beat very much. We took another walk about the plantation. My maid Anaka was very well again, thank God, and so was Moll at the quarters. My wife was out of humor with us for going to see so filthy a sight as the horse to cover the mare. In the evening we drank a bottle of wine and were very merry till 9 o'clock. . . .

27. . . . It was no good weather to go abroad; however, for fear of disappointing the Colonel we agreed to go with him to his ship. Accordingly about 10 o'clock we went, notwithstanding it snowed. Just before we went into the boat Captain John Bolling and Tom Randolph came but did not stop us. When we got over the river we walked to Mrs. Taylor's to see Colonel Hill's ship and then dined with Mrs. Taylor. In the afternoon we stayed till 4 o'clock and then returned the same way we came and got home before dark, where I found all well, thank God. We had roast pigeon for supper and then were merry till about 10 o'clock. . . .

28. . . . I took a walk about the plantation. The weather was very cold. My horse Robin was melancholy because the mare was shut up with the stone horse[10] and would not eat but stood at the fence all day to look at her. I ate duck for dinner and in the afternoon in pure pity let the mare come out to Robin who was glad to have her again though he could do nothing to her but keep her company as a Platonic lover. I set some of the Doctor's things in order in my closet and then took a walk with Mr. Randolph, but it was very cold. In the evening I read some Latin and ate some milk with my wife. I said my prayers and had good health, good thoughts, and good humor, thanks be to God Almighty. The weather has been warm the greatest part of this month and the sickness is favorable in this neighborhood, thank God. Mr. Drury Stith lost a very good slave and some others have

died for want of using remedies in time. I received a summons to Council the 8th of next month.

March, 1710

1. . . . I wrote a letter to my father Parke to be sent by way of Barbados. Then I took a little walk before dinner. I ate hashed mutton for dinner. In the afternoon set some things in order in the Doctor's closet. About 4 o'clock Tom H-n-s came for some physic for his father who has a cancer in his lip, which I gave him. . . .

2. . . . About 12 o'clock we rode to Colonel Hill's where we dined. Then we went over the river in the ferry boat though the Colonel proffered to set us over in his boat. In the afternoon we rode up to Falling Creek where we found all things well, thank God. In the evening we ate some milk for supper. I was better satisfied than I used to be with the affairs of this place. . . .

3. I rose at 7 o'clock and read a little in my commonplace. I said a short prayer and ate milk for breakfast. We took a walk to the mill and then proceeded to the Falls where we ate some milk and pone. From hence we rode to Kensington where I reprimanded Robin for not looking after the cattle better. Here we went over the river to Burkland where things were in good order. Then we walked to Byrd Park where I had several of the negroes whipped for stealing the hogs [or hogsheads]. From hence we walked to Shockoe where things were in good condition. Then we went over the river again to the Falls and from thence to Falling Creek, where we ate venison for supper. . . .

4. I rose at 7 o'clock and said a short prayer. Then I discoursed Mr. Grills about several things and likewise Tom Turpin. Then we walked to the mill where we looked over everything. Then we ate milk for breakfast. Then we rode to Dr. Bowman's who showed me some of his physic. From thence we rode to the Hundred and went over the river to Colonel Hill's where we dined. I ate boiled bacon for dinner. In the afternoon we played at cricket and then rode home where I found all well, thank God, and my sister Custis come from Queen's Creek. In the evening we talked till 10 o'clock. . . .

. . .

14. . . . I received a letter by Captain Posford from Mr. Bland by which I learned that my sloop was taken into Martinique. Captain Ned Bolling died of the smallpox at sea and so did Ch-s-t-r, both pretty young men. The death of this last makes way for Isham Randolph to command Colonel Hill's ship, for which he shall have my recommendation. My wife was melancholy, which made me weep. . . .

15. . . . George made an end of painting the library and gave in his account, which was a very reasonable one. The boatwright was here to mend the boat. Mr. Harrison invited us to dinner but my wife had a cold and could not go. But I went about 12 o'clock with Colonel Eppes who came over for some physic which I gave him. I found Colonel Hill, Mr. Anderson, his wife, and Mr. Gee. Mrs. Harrison was better but he was not very well. I ate fish for dinner. In the afternoon we played at cricket but Mr. Harrison was soon tired. Then we drank a bottle of wine and about 5 o'clock the company parted and I walked home with Mr. C-s who stayed with me till 8 o'clock. I said my prayers and had good health, good thoughts, and good humor, thanks be to God Almighty.

16. I rose at 6 o'clock and read the Psalms and some Greek in Anacreon. I said my prayers and ate chocolate with Colonel Hill who came this morning to see me. I put him in mind of his promise to Isham Randolph concerning his ship, for which he promised to use his interest but he thought Mr. Platt would be against it. I danced my dance. Colonel Hill went away over the river about 9 o'clock. My wife was out of order and melancholy. I ate hashed mutton for dinner. In the afternoon I wrote a letter to Barbados and then took a walk about the plantation. In the evening I had an express from Falling Creek to let me know Mrs. Byrd[11] was dead. I said my prayers and had good health, good thoughts, and good humor, thank God Almighty.

17. . . . About 12 o'clock Mr. Isham Randolph came. I ate boiled beef for dinner. In the afternoon Mr. Will Randolph and Robin Mumford came. We played at cricket. I committed my business concerning my uncle Byrd to Will Randolph. In the evening they went away and Colonel Hill came. I applied to him again in behalf of Isham Randolph and he expressed himself very kindly. . . .

18. . . . I wrote a letter to Barbados, while Mr. Randolph and Mr. Mumford played at billiards. About 11 o'clock we ate some duck and then went over the river in my boat to visit Mr. Platt and his wife to give them joy, and to recommend Mr. Randolph. Mr. Platt was not at home but his wife was. . . .

19. . . . About 11 o'clock I went to church, where I heard that Captain B-r-k was dead suddenly. It rained a little before church. After sermon I invited Colonel Eppes and his wife and the sheriff and Mr. C-s to dinner. I ate fish. In the afternoon the company went away and soon after there came a great gust of wind and rain to punish them for not staying. It likewise thundered a little. . . .

20. . . . My wife was indisposed and took a sweat and so did Nurse and it did them both service. I ate fish for dinner. In the afternoon Mr. Randolph and I played at billiards. I was amicable with my wife in her sickness. In the evening I took a short walk and when it was dark Mr. Randolph and my wife played at piquet. . . .

21. . . . In the afternoon Captain Posford came and presented us with 12 bottles of wine. He bespoke some planks of me and I agreed to give him £12 a ton. I set the Doctor's closet to rights. In the evening we took a walk about the plantation. Then I had a messenger from above with news that the gust on Sunday last blew down three houses, which I bore with a submission to God Almighty who knows best what to do for us. . . .

22. . . . We rode to Colonel Hill's where we found abundance of company, more than we expected and among the rest Mr. Harrison who was not well. About 2 o'clock we went to dinner and I ate bacon and fowl. In the afternoon played at cricket, four of a side, and Mr. Harrison among us, who looked exceedingly red a great while after it. In the evening most of the company went away and we recommended Mr. Randolph to Mr. Platt who was very equable and suave. He made, however, some difficulty of the matter but with the air of consent. About 10 o'clock we went to bed. . . .

. . .

27. . . . I began to say my prayers but was interrupted. About 10 o'clock Dr. Blair, Mrs. James Burwell and Major and Captain Harrison came to see us. After I had given them a glass of sack

we played at cricket and after that at billiards till dinner. I ate boiled beef for my dinner. In the afternoon we played at billiards. John Bolling and young Woodson came. Then we played at shooting with arrows till about 4 o'clock when we went all to Mr. Harrison's, whom we found better. Here we went to cricket again till dark; then we returned home where I [found] Jenny sick. . . .

28. . . . About 10 o'clock Major Harrison, Hal Harrison, James Burwell and Mr. Doyley came to play at cricket. Isham Randolph, Mr. Doyley, and I played with them three for a crown. We won one game, they won two. Then we played at billiards till dinner, before which Colonel Ludwell came on his way to Mr. Harrison's. They all dined with us and I ate boiled pork. Soon after dinner the company went away and I took a nap. Then we walked to Mr. Harrison's, whom we found better. We played a game at cricket again. I took leave about 8 and returned home where I found Jenny better. I caused her to be cupped and then gave her [m-t-y] pills. This was my birthday, on which I am 36 years old, and I bless God for granting me so many years. I wish I had spent them better. . . .

29. . . . I settled my matters to go to Falling Creek, but first we ate our dinner and then after recommending my family to the protection of Almighty, we rode to Colonel Hill's. With him and Mr. Anderson we talked and were merry all the afternoon and all the evening, but on our way over I met one of Mr. Harrison's people that told me his master was much better. We went to bed soon because I rose early the next morning. . . .

30. I rose at 3 o'clock and ate milk about 4 and then we went over the river and were a-horseback by 5 and so rode to Falling Creek, where we got about 7, and we found Mr. Grills getting ready the mill for a wager and a little after 8 o'clock the mill began to saw and sawed 2,000 feet in five hours and finished the rest in four hours more by which we won a wager of £40 of John Woodson, who laid that the mill could not saw 3,000 feet of planks in ten hours. There was abundance of company there, the best of which I treated with wine. About 5 o'clock we returned to Colonel Hill's where we were told that Mr. Harrison was relapsed again and in great danger. . . .

31. I rose at 7 o'clock and read some Greek in bed. I said my prayers and ate milk for breakfast. Then about 8 o'clock we got

a-horseback and rode to Mr. Harrison's and found him very ill but sensible. Here I met Mr. Bland, who brought me several letters from England and among the rest two from Colonel Blakiston who had endeavored to procure the government of Virginia for me at the price of £1,000 of my Lady Orkney and that my Lord [agreed] but the Duke of Marlborough declared that no one but soldiers should have the government of a plantation, so I was disappointed. God's will be done. From hence I came home where I found all well, thank God. I ate fish for dinner. In the afternoon I went again with my wife to Mr. Harrison's who continued very bad so that I resolved to stay with him all night, which I did with Mr. Anderson and Nat Burwell. He was in the same bad condition till he vomited and then he was more easy. In the morning early I returned home and went to bed. It is remarkable that Mrs. Burwell dreamed this night that she saw a person that with money scales weighed time and declared that there was no more than 18 pennies worth of time to come, which seems to be a dream with some significance either concerning the world or a sick person. In my letters from England I learned that the Bishop of Worcester was of opinion that in the year 1715 the city of Rome would be burnt to the ground, that before the year 1745 the popish religion would be routed out of the world, that before the year 1790 the Jews and Gentiles would be converted to the Christianity and then would begin the millenium.

April, 1710

1. Before sunrise I returned home and after recommending myself and the sick man to the divine protection, I went to bed and lay till 12 o'clock at noon. . . .

2. . . . About 11 o'clock I went to church and heard a sermon of Mr. Anderson. After church I invited Nat Burwell and his wife and several others to dinner and treated them very well. I ate boiled beef for dinner. They stayed till the evening and then I went to see Mr. Harrison, who seemed to be better but his fever still on him. I stayed about an hour and then returned home. We sat up with my Cousin Burwell till about 11 o'clock. . . .

3. . . . Colonel Eppes came about 11 o'clock and said Mr. Harrison was very bad. Mr. Parker came likewise; then came Mr.

Burwell, Colonel Hill, and Nat Harrison and they all gave a bad account of Mr. Harrison. We played at billiards till dinner. I ate roast beef for dinner. In the afternoon we shot with a bow and then played at cricket. In the evening we walked to Mr. Harrison's, with whom I had intended to watch but there were several that came for that purpose. He was very ill. . . .

4. . . . I sent to inquire how Mr. Harrison did and received word that he was no better notwithstanding he had slept much in the night by the help of laudanum. My wife was indisposed this morning and I took a walk with her. I ate fish for dinner. In the afternoon I settled the Doctor's closet and then read some news. Mr. C-s came and told me Mr. Harrison continued extremely bad. About 5 I walked there with him and found him in a bad condition, sometimes dozing then waking with groaning and frenzy. I found Mrs. Hamlin and Mrs. Stith there and likewise Colonel Hill. I ate milk about 8 o'clock and then went into the chamber and sat up with him all night. His fever was very high and he began to break out in pimples but was very restless all night. We gave him tea with ten drops of spirits of saffron. I stayed till 5 o'clock in the morning and then returned home and went to bed. . . .

5. I rose about 10 o'clock and read only a chapter in Hebrew, being interrupted by Mr. Bland who brought word my cousin Harrison continued bad and that Dr. Blair was with him and despaired of his life. I settled accounts with Mr. Bland. My wife took a vomit which worked very well but did not remove the pain in her side. I ate milk for breakfast. I had abundance of discourse with Mr. Bland concerning our store at Williamsburg. . . .

6. . . . I sent to know how Mr. Harrison did and received word that he seemed to be a little better, which was confirmed by Mr. Anderson whom I sent for to let me blood because of a little pain I found in my side. He sucked about a pint of blood from me which gave me ease, but my wife would not be let blood notwithstanding the pain in her breast. . . .

7. . . . I said my prayers and then took a purge of laxative salts, as did also my wife who was much indisposed with her breast. I sent to inquire how Mr. Harrison did and received word that he was still worse. I sent him some spirits of saffron. My purge

did not work much but made me hot and out of order. I set my closet in order. My godson John Stith came to see me and I examined him and found he had made a good progress. I ate chicken for dinner. In the afternoon I played at cards with my wife and then ordered the coach to go visit Mr. Harrison. I found him better in appearance and everybody full of hope. . . .

. . .

9. . . . Went to church. We heard a good sermon from Mr. Anderson and after received the Sacrament with great devoutness. Mr. Harrison had a mind to partridge, which I sent him, and he ate one of them. We had nobody but our own family at dinner. I ate roast beef. As soon as we had dined we went to Mr. Harrison's, who we found past all hopes, and a very melancholy family. We stayed till the evening and then returned home. . . .

10. I rose at 6 o'clock and wrote several letters to my overseers. I sent early to inquire after Mr. Harrison and received word that he died about 4 o'clock this morning, which completed the 18th day of his sickness, according to Mrs. Burwell's dream exactly. Just before his death he was sensible and desired Mrs. L— with importunity to open the door because he wanted to go out and could not go till the door was open and as soon as the door was opened he died. The country has lost a very useful man and [one] who was both an advantage and an ornament to it, and I have lost a good neighbor, but God's will be done. I said my prayers and ate caudle for breakfast. I danced my dance. My wife rode to Mrs. Harrison's to comfort her and to assure her that I should be always ready to do her all manner of service. My wife returned before dinner. I ate tripe for dinner. In the afternoon we played at piquet. Then I prepared my matters for the General Court. It rained, with the wind at northeast, and it was very cold, and in the night it snowed. . . .

11. . . . I prepared my accounts against the General Court. I took a walk before dinner. Then I ate hashed beef. In the afternoon my wife went to visit the widow to comfort her and stayed with her all the afternoon. In the meantime I wrote out more accounts against the General Court. . . .

12. . . . My boat set Mr. Randolph and Mr. Rogers over the river because they could not get the ferryboat. Mr. C-s came over

to invite to Mr. Harrison's funeral. I invited him in case he left Mrs. Harrison to come and live with me. I settled my accounts against I go to Williamsburg. . . .

13. . . . Captain Posford came to see me and offered me his boat to carry my things to Williamsburg. Mr. Doyley came over to borrow some black wax but I had none. I was much troubled with wind since I took physic. In the evening we took a walk and in the meantime Mr. Clayton and Mr. Robinson came in order to go the next day to the funeral. . . .

14. . . . About 10 o'clock we walked to Mrs. Harrison's to the funeral, where we found abundance of company of all sorts. Wine and cake were served very plentifully. At one o'clock the corpse began to move and the ship "Harrison" fired a gun every half minute. When we came to church the prayers were first read; then we had a sermon which was an extravagant panegyric or [eulogy]. At every turn he called him "this great man," and not only covered his faults but gave him virtues which he never possessed as well as magnified those which he had. When [the] sermon was done the funeral service was read and the poor widow trembled extremely. When all was over I put the widow, her daughter, and two sisters into my coach and Colonel Randolph, his wife, Colonel Hill, Mrs. Anderson, and the two B-r-k-s went home with us and I invited several others who would not come. . . .

15. I rose at 6 o'clock but it rained and so I would not go to Williamsburg. . . .

• • •

17. I rose at 4 o'clock and sent my horses over the creek and followed them about 5 o'clock, after committing my wife and family to the protection of the Almighty. I likewise left orders with my family what to do. Nothing happened by the way extraordinary, so that I got to Williamsburg about 10 o'clock, where I found several letters from England, and among the rest one from Mr. Perry who told me that my father's accounts were passed and that my salary was increased to 5 per cent with one year's retrospect. I had also a letter from Lady Guise by which I learned how much I am obliged to her for endeavoring to get for me the governorship of Maryland. About 12 o'clock we went to court and finished the business of the day by 4 o'clock. I went to dinner soon after. I ate boiled beef for dinner. Then we went to the

President's where we drank some of his French wine. In the evening Captain Cook came and I ate some broiled beef with them. Then I went home. . . .

18. . . . I went to the capitol about 8 o'clock and settled my accounts till 9. Then I went to the President's where I found several of the Council and about 10 we went to Council where among other things we directed the negroes to be arraigned for high treason. We continued in Council till 4 o'clock and then went to court where we sat till 5. Then I went with my brother Custis to Dr. [Barret's] where my sister was, Mr. Dunn and his wife and Mrs. Chiswell. . . .

19. . . . I had abundance of company before I could get out of my chamber. I settled my accounts till about 11 o'clock and then went to court, where the negroes were arraigned for treason. About 3 o'clock we had news that the captain of the man-of-war called the "Enterprise" was come to town and soon after he came to the capitol and the Council was called about him where it was concluded that he should have orders to stay and cruise at the Cape to protect the country but he seemed resolved to sail to New York. . . .

20. . . . I went to the capitol where I wrote a letter to England and settled some accounts. Then I went to court where three persons were tried for felony and acquitted. I returned again to my chambers and settled more business. About 6 o'clock the court rose and went to dinner. Then Colonel Basset and I took a walk and then went and drank cider at Will Robinson's chambers. . . .

21. . . . About 8 o'clock I went to see the President and then went to court. I settled some accounts first. Two of the negroes were tried and convicted for treason. I wrote a letter to England and then went to court again. About 3 o'clock I returned to my chambers again and found above a girl who I persuaded to go with me into my chambers but she would not. I ate some cake and cheese and then went to Mr. Bland's where I ate some boiled beef. Then I went to the President's where we were merry till 11 o'clock. Then I stole away. I said a short prayer but notwithstanding committed uncleanness in bed. I had good health, bad thoughts, and good humor, thanks be to God Almighty.

22. . . . I went to the capitol where I settled some business. Then I went to court where I stayed a little and then returned again to my chambers where I wrote two letters to England. About 12 o'clock I ate some cake and cheese and about 5 o'clock I went to Mr. Bland's where I ate some fish. In the evening we went to the President's where we played at piquet till about 10 o'clock. Then I went to my chambers and read some news. . . .

. . .

27. . . . I went to Council where my warrants passed and several other matters of consequence were done. About 12 o'clock I ate some tongue and then we tried an unfortunate man who had against his will killed his nephew and he was found guilty of manslaughter. I was appointed commander in chief of two counties. I received a letter from my father Parke of an old date. About 5 o'clock we dined. I ate roast beef for dinner. Then we sat in Council again till 9 o'clock. I had good health, good thoughts, and good humor, thank God Almighty, and said my prayers.

28. . . . I went to the capitol and settled some accounts. Then I went to court where I sat till 12 o'clock. Then I went to my office and did more business and settled Captain Cook's account which was in very great confusion. Then we went to dinner and I ate boiled mutton. Several of the Council went out of town. In the evening I agreed with Mr. Ingles to lend him £200 on good security, for which he was very thankful. Then I went to the President's and stayed there till about 10 o'clock. . . .

29. . . . I went to court to hear the orders read, after which we went to Council and settled some affairs. Then I gave Captain Cook a certificate of the truth of his account and took leave of him and of the gentlemen of the Council. I settled some accounts with the President and Mr. Robinson. About 12 o'clock I ate some cake and cheese. About 3 o'clock my man brought my horse and a letter from home that told me all was well, thank God. Then Mr. Custis and I rode to Mr. Blair's where I ate some roast mutton for dinner. Then we went to Queen's Creek where I was received very kindly. I was much tired. . . .

30. . . . I read nothing because I had no books with me. I wrote a letter of excuse to Major Burwell for not going to see him as I ought to do. I also excused myself to my uncle Ludwell for the

same purpose. About 11 o'clock I took my leave and rode to Colonel Duke's where I came about 2 o'clock. There I found my brother Duke, who told me all was well at his house. I ate some cold beef and salad. In the afternoon it rained exceedingly and thundered terribly for about an hour. However it did not prevent me from proceeding to my brother Duke's, where we came before sunset. My sister and her child were very well. I ate milk for supper. I said a short prayer and had good health, good thoughts, and good humor, thanks be to God Almighty. Colonel Duke told me that Ben Goodrich died at night and was well that morning two days since. The distemper continues violent in some parts. This was a very backward spring, notwithstanding we had a favorable winter.

May, 1710

. . .

7. . . . I read a sermon of Dr. Tillotson's which affected me very much and made me shed some tears of repentance. The weather grew very hot. The sick boys were a little better. I ate [moderately] of roast beef for dinner. In the afternoon my wife and I took a long sleep which discomposed me. Then I read another sermon in Dr. Tillotson, after which we took a walk and met Mr. C-s who walked with us and told us several strangers were come to my cousin Harrison's. . . .

8. . . . I accounted with old [Higbee] and promised him my good word to be sexton. I settled some accounts. About 11 or 12 o'clock our cousins R-d, Betty Bassett, and Betty Harrison came to see us and were forced to be content with our own dinner. I ate bacon and pigeon for dinner. In the afternoon we played at billiards and diverted the company as well as we could. . . .

. . .

12. . . . It was very hot this day, and the first day of summer. I read some news. I ate boiled beef for dinner. In the afternoon I cut some [sage] and then read a sermon in Tillotson. I also read some news. Then my wife and I took a walk about the plantation; when we returned we found our son very sick of a fever and he began to break out terribly. We gave him some treacle water. . . .

13. . . . About 12 o'clock Mr. Parker came and told me his parish had agreed with Mr. Dunn and would give him [?]. I ate sallet and shad for dinner. Soon after dinner Mr. Parker went away and then my wife and I cut [sage]. Our child was a little better, thank God. . . .

14. . . . My wife had the headache very much this morning and our child continued bad. About 11 o'clock I went to church without my wife and heard a sermon from Mr. Anderson. . . . In the afternoon I persuaded Drury Stith to be a justice of peace. . . .

15. I rose at 5 o'clock and prepared to ride to Falling Creek, notwithstanding it rained a little. I said my prayers and ate milk and strawberries for breakfast. The child continued sick. I pray God restore him to his health again. About 7 o'clock I got on my horse but before I got four miles it rained very hard and I was wet to the skin, but when I came to Colonel Randolph's they gave me clothes. Here I had an opportunity to converse with Mr. Finney the minister, who is a sober, ingenuous man. About 12 o'clock we went to dinner and I ate some chicken fricassee. In the afternoon I proceeded with Will Randolph and Isham Randolph to Falling Creek. Mr. Grills was not returned from Carolina, nor was his brother there as he promised. It rained violently in the evening and all night. We went and looked about and all things were in order except the dam, in which there was a leak. We ate some milk. I neglected to say my prayers and had good thoughts, good health, and good humor, thanks be to God Almighty.

16. We lay in bed till 9 o'clock because it rained and we knew not what to do up. We ate milk for breakfast. I said a short prayer; then we walked to the mill and about 12 o'clock departed. Will Randolph went home and Isham and I rode to Colonel Hill's where I ate some broiled chicken. After dinner we ate cherries and talked till about 6 o'clock and then I took leave and rode home, where I found all my family well except my son, who had still a fever. It had rained very much till about 2 o'clock. . . .

17. . . . My son was a little worse, which made me send for Mr. Anderson. My express met him on the road and he came about 10 o'clock. He advised some oil of juniper which did him good. I ate some sack and toast with him. About 12 o'clock he

went away. I danced my dance. I ate fish for dinner. In the afternoon my wife and I cut some [sage]. In the evening took a walk to Mrs. Harrison's to inquire if they had any service for me. . . .

18. . . . Mrs. Hamlin came to see the child, whose fever continued. I sent my sloop to Falling Creek. I read some Italian. A little before dinner Mr. Randolph came and dined with us. I ate hashed mutton for dinner. The company stayed almost all the afternoon. I read more Italian and then with my wife took a walk about the plantation. My little boy was a little better, thank God. I gave a poor woman some physic for her daughter. . . .

19. . . . My little boy was better, thank God Almighty. I read some Italian and ate abundance of cherries. I ate fish for dinner. In the afternoon my wife and I cut a little [sage] but were interrupted by a visit we had from Colonel Hill, Mr. Anderson, and his wife, who stayed with us all the afternoon. The Colonel was out of order and I gave him some physic. . . .

20. . . . I received letters from above that gave an account of the appraisal of my uncle's estate and that Mr. Grills was not returned from Carolina and that the dam was out of order. . . .

21. . . . The child continued indisposed. I read two sermons in Tillotson, which edified me very much. I ate roast shoat for dinner, and Miss Sarah Taylor dined with us. I was out of humor with my wife for forcing Evie to eat against her will. In the afternoon we went in the coach to Mrs. Harrison's and found her very disconsolate. Mr. Anderson came there likewise. We ate some cherries. I comforted my cousin as well as I could. In the evening we walked home and found Evie in a great fever and to increase [it] they had given her milk. I remembered both my children in my prayers and had good health, good thoughts, and good humor, thanks be to God Almighty.

22. I rose by 5 o'clock and sent our excuses to Colonel Hill for not going with him to Colonel Harrison's because our children were both sick. However, they came to see us in our affliction. I read two chapters in Hebrew but no Greek because the company hindered me. We ate milk and strawberries for breakfast. Then we played at billiards till about 11 o'clock when Mr. Woodson came to see me. We ate cherries and talked of many things. I ate beef for dinner but ate too much. In the afternoon we drank

some tea and ate more cherries. Tom Randolph came and brought me word that Colonel Randolph had the gout in his stomach for which I sent him some [b-v-r mineral]. . . .

23. . . . My daughter was very ill, but the boy had lost his fever, thank God. I settled some accounts and wrote some commonplace. I ate hashed shoat for dinner. In the afternoon Evie had a sweat that worked pretty well but not long enough, for which I was out of humor with my wife. I read some Italian and some news and then took a walk about the plantation. When I returned I had a great quarrel with my wife, in which she was to blame altogether; however I made the first step to a reconciliation, to [which] she with much difficulty consented. . . .

24. . . . I sent for my cousin Harrison to let Evie blood who was ill. When she came she took away about four ounces. We put on blisters and gave her a glyster which worked very well. Her blood was extremely thick, which is common in distemper of this constitution. About 12 o'clock she began to sweat of herself, which we prompted by tincture of saffron and sage and snake-root. This made her sweat extremely, in which she continued little or more all night. I ate some fish for dinner. In the afternoon Mr. Anderson whom I had sent for came and approved of what I had done. I persuaded him to stay all night which he agreed to. It rained in the evening. We stayed up till 12 o'clock and Bannister sat up with the child till 12 o'clock and Grills till break of day. . . .

25. . . . Evie was much better, thank God Almighty, and had lost her fever. The boy was better likewise but was restless. It was very hot today. . . . I never was more incommoded with heat in my whole life. . . .

26. . . . I said my prayers and ate milk and strawberries with Captain Posford for breakfast. He told me that a ship was arrived with negroes and offered his service to fetch my wine from Williamsburg. Evie was better but the boy was worse, with a cold and fever for which we gave him a sweat which worked very well and continued all day. About 9 o'clock Mr. J— came to buy some glass and stayed here about an hour. . . .

• • •

28. . . . We went to church and heard a sermon and received the Sacrament. I heard at church that Colonel Ludwell had lost 3

or 4 negroes more. I invited nobody home this day. I ate beans and bacon for dinner. In the afternoon I discoursed with Joe Wilkinson about my affairs and learned that all went well. In the evening Mr. Grills came with a heavy heart and cried on my reproaching him for staying so long in Carolina and not leaving his brother in his stead as he promised me, and offered to make me any reparation. He told me of the breaking of the dam, which was like my fortune. It put me very much out of humor. . . .

29. . . . I agreed with Joe Wilkinson to be my overseer four years. I ordered Mr. Grills to repair the break in the dam as soon as possible. Then they both went away. The boy continued very ill of the fever. . . . My belly ached exceedingly. . . . My boy appeared to be a little better this evening, blessed be God for it.

· · ·

31. . . . In the afternoon I played at billiards with my wife and was exceedingly griped in my belly. I ate as many cherries as I could get for it, but they did no good. I read more Italian, and in the evening took a walk to my cousin Harrison's, whom I found very melancholy. She told me she was much alone and little company came near her. When I returned I found the child a little better. I said my prayers and had good health, good thoughts, and good humor, thanks be to God Almighty. The weather of this month was generally cold, notwithstanding for about a week of it, it was very hot. The wind was often east and northeast and northwest, which did much injury to the fruit trees and made the weather unseasonable and the people sickly.

June, 1710

1. . . . In the evening I took a walk and met the new negroes which Mr. Bland had bought for me to the number of 26 for £23 apiece. This evening the sloop likewise came from above where all was well. . . .

2. . . . I sent away the sloop to Appomattox. The child was worse and his nurse was very ill. I gave her a vomit which worked very well. Colonel Eppes called here. I ate cold mutton for dinner. In the afternoon I read some English. About 5 o'clock Robin Hix and Robin Mumford came to discourse about the skin trade. We gave them some mutton and sallet for supper. In the evening

I did not walk because of my company. Robin Hix asked me to pay £70 for two negroes which he intended to buy of John [Evans] which I agreed to in hope of gaining the trade. I neglected to say my prayers but was griped in my belly and had indifferent bad humor.

3. I rose at 6 o'clock and as soon as I came out news was brought that the child was very ill. We went out and found him just ready to die and he died about 8 o'clock in the morning. God gives and God takes away; blessed be the name of God. Mrs. Harrison and Mr. Anderson and his wife and some other company came to see us in our affliction. My wife was much afflicted but I submitted to His judgment better, notwithstanding I was very sensible of my loss, but God's will be done. Mr. Anderson and his wife with Mrs. B-k-r dined here. I ate roast mutton. In the afternoon I was griped in my belly very much but it grew better towards the night. In the afternoon it rained and was fair again in the evening. My poor wife and I walked in the garden. . . .

4. I rose at 6 o'clock and read nothing because I took physic which did not work. I said my prayers and ate water gruel. I had no more than two stools but was a little griped. I was so indisposed that I could not settle to anything. My wife had several fits of tears for our dear son but kept within the bounds of sub-mission. I ate hashed mutton for dinner. In the afternoon we walked a little abroad but it was so hot we soon returned. My dinner griped me again but not so much as it did. My man Tom returned from Williamsburg and brought me letters from Green Spring and Queen's Creek. Jimmy brought a coffin from Falling Creek made of walnut tree. . . .

5. . . . About 12 o'clock my brother Custis came without my sister who could not come because she was big with child. . . . My wife continued very melancholy, notwithstanding I com-forted her as well as I could. . . .

6. I rose at 6 o'clock and read two chapters in Hebrew and no Greek because we prepared to receive company for the funeral. I said my prayers and ate cake and water gruel for breakfast. About 10 o'clock Colonel Hill, Mr. Anderson and his wife came. Half an hour after my sister Duke came without my brother who could not leave his business, and about 11 came my cousin

Harrison with her son and daughter, Mr. C-s and Mr. Doyley. We gave them burnt claret and cake. About 2 o'clock we went with the corpse to the churchyard and as soon as the service was begun it rained very hard so that we were forced to leave the parson and go into the church porch but Mr. Anderson stayed till the service was finished. About 3 o'clock we went to dinner and I ate boiled beef for dinner. The company stayed till the evening and then went away. Mr. Custis and I took a walk about the plantation. Two of the new negroes were taken sick and I gave each of them a vomit which worked well. . . .

7. I rose at 6 o'clock and read a chapter in Hebrew and some Greek in Pindar. My brother Custis went away before I was up. I said my prayers and ate cake for breakfast. I danced my dance. My gripes were better, thank God. I wrote a letter to England. My wife continued to be exceedingly afflicted for the loss of her child, notwithstanding I comforted her as well as I could. I ate calf's head for dinner. In the afternoon my gripes returned again and made me uneasy. I drank several strong things for them but they did no good. Robin Jones came from above where all was well, thank God. I took a walk in the evening and met Colonel Harrison and Nat Harrison going to my neighbor's. They told me that about eight weeks since our fleet was ready to sail with a Governor and that there was no sign of a peace. I took some [Lady Kent's] powders, which did me good. . . .

. . .

10. . . . Just before dinner Mr. Bland came from Williamsburg and told us that Colonel Parke was recalled from his Governorship. I ate minced veal for dinner. In afternoon I wrote more letters to England. In the evening Mr. C-s came and stayed till 9 o'clock and told me all was well at the next house. My belly was not quite well. . . .

11. . . . It continued to rain so that we could not go to church. My wife was still disconsolate. I was better, thank God. It rained almost all day. Colonel Hill sent his man to know if I had any service at Williamsburg. . . .

. . .

14. . . . My wife began to be comforted, thank God. and I lost my gripes. A poor woman brought her daughter over that was troubled with the vapors extremely. I let her know if her daughter would come and stay here for two months I would endeavor to

cure her. I ate cold chicken for dinner. In the afternoon I read some physics. About 4 o'clock Dick Cocke came from Prince George court where he saw Captain [Goodwin] just come from Barbados loaded at £9 per ton. The weather grew very hot again. In the evening I took a walk about the plantation and when I returned I found Mr. C-s here. I encouraged him to pursue the law without being discouraged and he resolved he would. . . .

15. . . . In the afternoon my gripes returned on me and continued till the evening with some violence. Hot things did it no good but in the evening I drank some warm milk from the cow which eased me immediately. It rained this afternoon very hard with a little wind and thunder. This hindered my walking anywhere but in the garden. I foretold by my cellar stinking that it would rain. I impute my gripes to cherry wine, or else pulling my coat off. . . .

16. . . . About 10 o'clock Captain Drury Stith and his wife came to make us a visit, notwithstanding it was very hot. I was glad to see them because I think them excellent people. We played at billiards till dinner. I ate boiled pork. In the afternoon we passed away the time pleasantly till about 6 o'clock and then they went home. In the evening I took a walk with my wife. We made a little cider of the G-n-t-n apples, which yielded but little juice. . . .

17. . . . About 8 o'clock Mr. Anderson came on his way over the river. He told me the quarrel was made up between Parson Slater and his vestry without coming to trial. He stayed about half an hour. Colonel Hill sent his man with a basket of apricots, of which my wife ate twelve immediately and I ate eight which however did not make my gripes return. I set my closet right. I ate tongue and chicken for dinner. In the afternoon I caused L-s-n to be whipped for beating his wife and Jenny was whipped for being his whore. . . .

18. . . . I read a sermon in Dr. Tillotson about angels. I wrote a letter to Williamsburg to send by my sloop which I sent for rum, wine, and sugar from thence and that this might come safely I resolved to send Bannister with the sloop. I ate chicken for dinner but very little because I had no appetite. In the afternoon my wife told me a dream she had two nights. She thought she saw

a scroll in the sky in form of a light cloud with writing on it. It ran extremely fast from west to east with great swiftness. The writing she could not read but there was a woman before her that told her there would be a great dearth because of want of rain and after that a pestilence for that the seasons were changed and time inverted. Mr. James Burwell and Charles Doyley came and in the evening I took a walk with them. Our nurse went away in the sloop. . . .

19. . . . About 10 o'clock came Isham Randolph and Mr. Finney to see us. They told me Colonel Randolph was very ill and very melancholy. We played at billiards till dinner. I ate fish for dinner. In the afternoon Mr. Stith came over with my cousin Berkeley, who all stayed here till the evening and then they all went away but Mr. Finney. In the evening we took a walk. Mr. Finney is a sensible man and good natured. He told me that Major Allen died on Thursday last. . . .

20. . . . Mr. Finney returned home without any breakfast but I gave him some strong water. Colonel Hill sent us another present of apricots. I wrote a letter to England. I ate five apricots which put my belly out of order. I ate roast mutton for dinner. In the afternoon my belly was griped. I played with my wife at piquet and then I ordered the boat to carry us to my cousin Harrison's where we found my cousin Berkeley and Jimmy Burwell. I was out of order in my belly. About 8 o'clock we returned home where we found all well, thank God. . . .

21. . . . I sent Tom to Appomattox to desire Mr. Mumford to go to the outcry of my uncle's estate. About five nights since I dreamed I saw a flaming star in the air at which I was much frightened and called some others to see it but when they came it disappeared. I fear this portends some judgment to this country or at least to myself. I ate roast mutton for dinner. In the afternoon I settled the closet. About 5 o'clock I received an express from Mr. Clayton that the Governor, Colonel Spotswood, with two men-of-war arrived last night at Kiquotan with several other ships. I sent word of this to Mrs. Harrison and then prepared to go to Williamsburg tomorrow. . . .

22. I rose at 6 o'clock because it rained in the morning which I thought would hinder my voyage. But when I was up I resolved to go. I ate milk for breakfast and about 8 o'clock got on my

horse on the other side the creek. I neglected to say my prayers before I came out but afterwards I committed my family to God Almighty. About 12 o'clock I got to the ferry, where I heard the Governor was at Green Spring. Just before I came there I changed my clothes and about one o'clock arrived at Green Spring where I found abundance of company. I complimented the Governor who seemed to be a very good man and was very courteous to me and told me I had been recommended to him by several of my friends in England. I met likewise with Dr. Cocke, my old school-fellow. The Governor brought with him a niece, a pretty woman. I ate boiled [. . .] for dinner. In the evening I danced a minuet. The mosquitoes bit me extremely. . . .

23. I rose at 7 o'clock and got the Governor's man to shave me. I neglected to say my prayers because I was never alone. I read some of my letters, by which I found a sad account of tobacco and abundance of protested bills. I ate nothing but bread and butter and drank tea and milk for breakfast. About 10 o'clock we waited on the Governor to Williamsburg and he was met out of town by the President and abundance of people. From thence we went to town and then to Council where I found I was left out of the instructions; however after a dispute I was allowed to be sworn among the rest till further news from England, which nobody seemed to oppose but the President. The Governor was [r-n-s-t] for my [seat]. The Governor made a courteous speech and told the Council that he was come with a full disposition to do the Queen and country service and hoped we should all concur with him in that good design. Then we went to dinner at C-t where the President treated us. I ate calf's head for dinner. In the afternoon we retired to the President's to drink the Queen's health, where I drank some French wine that did not agree with me but gave me the gripes. In the evening we returned to Green Spring with the Governor but I could not enjoy him because of my indisposition. However he always distinguished me with his courtesy. I took leave of the Governor this night, because I resolved to go early in the morning. I neglected to say my prayers but had good health, good thoughts, and good humor, thank God Almighty.

24. I rose at 3 o'clock and Major Harrison with me and away we went and got to the ferry at four o'clock and the Major and I parted a little after we got over. I proceeded, however, and got home about 8 o'clock in the morning, where I found all well

except that a negro woman and seven cattle were gone away. . . . In the afternoon Mr. Mumford came and gave me an account of the outcry. My sloop came from Williamsburg with the wine and rum and she was unloaded in the evening, when Mr. C-s came over and gave me an account of the rencounter with Charles Doyley. We took a walk and drank some new milk. I neglected to say my prayers and was out of humor extremely and had indifferent health and thoughts, but God send me better if it please his good will.

25. I rose at 6 o'clock and found myself a little hot and therefore I took a vomit of infused ipecac, which worked but moderately. I neglected to say my prayers. I ate some toast and canary for breakfast. I could not go to church nor would my wife leave me but I sent several letters to people there. After church Will Randolph came over and told me his father was better. I ate poached eggs for dinner. In the afternoon I found myself a little better and then Will Randolph went away and my wife and I took a walk and met Mr. C-s who came home with us and told us of the unkindness of Mrs. Harrison. I was so tired with walking that I could not hold open my eyes. My people could not find the negro woman but found her hoe by the church land. I neglected to say my prayers but had indifferent health, humor, and thoughts; God send me better. This morning the hogshead of molasses looked above half out.

26. I rose about 6 o'clock and took a purge [of p-l-c-ch] which worked very extremely. I neglected to say my prayers, for which God forgive me. I had eight stools and my fundament was swelled with a sharp humor and very sore. I drank some water gruel. They began to reap this day. I read a chapter in Hebrew. I ate some boiled chicken for dinner. In the afternoon I took a nap which refreshed me a little. The violence of the purge gave me the piles extremely. . . . Mr. Gee came to see me and in the evening Mr. Bland came up in his shallop from Williamsburg and expected to find cargo but I told him it was not come. . . .

27. I lay in bed till 9 o'clock because of the piles, and read a chapter in Hebrew and some Greek in the Testament. I said my prayers and ate milk and [m-l-y] for breakfast. My wife anointed my fundament with tobacco oil and balsam of saltpeter mixed together. It was very much swelled and very painful so that I could not sit nor stand. I settled my closet.[12] . . . About 4 o'clock

Mrs. Anderson, Colonel Hill, and Mr. Anderson came to see me and condoled my sore backside and advised me to use linseed oil made hot. As soon as they were gone I tried their medicine and soon after went to bed, but was in exceeding pain so that I was forced to take an opiate and could hardly sleep with that. . . .

28. I lay abed till 10 o'clock and read some letters which Mr. Mumford brought me. Then I read some news. I said a short prayer and ate boiled milk and [m-l-y] for breakfast. My wife anointed my bum with hot linseed oil which had done it some good. However it was not easy yet. Captain Broadwater brought over my sister Brayne's two children who were much below my expectation, being very ordinary. I thanked him for his kindness to the children. About 12 o'clock came Captain Burbydge and Mr. J—, who both dined here. I ate fish for dinner. In the afternoon the company went away. I went to bed early and had my breech anointed. The negro woman was found again that they thought had drowned herself. I said a short prayer. . . .

. . .

30. . . . I wrote a letter to Mr. Perry to desire him to send Mr. Bland's goods by the fall fleet. My bum was better, thank God, and I was well again. I ate roast mutton for dinner. In the afternoon the sloop came from Appomattox with tobacco and the other sloop from the ship with my goods and Mr. Bland and Mr. Mumford went aboard to part them between them and in the evening they made an end. I ate some bread and butter for supper. In the evening I said a short prayer and had good health, good thoughts, and good humor, thank God. I gave my wife a flourish. My cousin Betty Harrison was here this evening and told us Colonel Harrison was very ill of a fever.

July, 1710

. . .

3. . . . About nine Captain Burbydge came with another master and after that Colonel Hill and Mr. Anderson with many others because it was court day. Some of us played at billiards. We had abundance of people dine with me and I ate some mutton hash as good as ever I ate in my life. We did not settle the freight.

The company all went away in the evening, when my cousin Harrison came over to inquire if I would buy any goods, for which I thanked her and walked home with her, as did also my wife. . . .

4. I rose at 4 o'clock, and dressed me because I expected Colonel Hill and Captain Burbydge in his boat to carry us to Colonel Ludwell's bay, where I said a short prayer and then we went about 6 o'clock. We called aboard his ship and took some bread and cheese and wine in the boat and then went to breakfast. About 11 o'clock we called at Major Tooker's where we stayed about half an hour and then proceeded to Major Harrison's, but neither he nor his lady were at home. However, we went in and had some victuals. About 5 o'clock Mrs. Harrison came home and we had just [time] to take leave of her and proceed to Green Spring, where we arrived as soon as it was dark. The Colonel was melancholy because his daughter was sick. I ate cold veal for supper. I recommended myself to heaven and had good health, good thoughts, and good humor, thank God Almighty.

5. I rose about 6 o'clock and read nothing but said a short prayer and got ready to go to Williamsburg, but it was necessary to eat milk for breakfast. About 9 o'clock we took leave of the Colonel and rode to town and when we came to Mr. Bland's he told us my chest of linen sent to his store had been plundered before it came to him. This was according to my whole fortune, which I must try to bear with patience till God shall please to better it. Then we waited on the Governor and drank coffee with him. Then the rest of the Council came and we went to Council, where the Governor's instructions were read, one of which was to suffer the people have the settlement of the habeas corpus act. Many things were debated and Major Harrison was appointed naval officer and I and Colonel Hill were his securities. About 3 o'clock we dined with the Governor where everything was very polite and well served. . . .

6. I rose at 4 o'clock and settled some bills of exchange. Mr. Randolph came to introduce him to the Governor and recommend him to be clerk of the House of Burgesses, which I did in the best manner and the Governor promised him. Mr. Bland and Mr. Clayton also came to my chambers. When I went to wait on the Governor I found most of the Council there. Then I drank some coffee and ate bread and butter. Then we went to Council where we stayed till about 2 o'clock in the afternoon. Then we

went to dine with the Governor where everything was extremely polite and I ate fish and then we took leave of the Governor and rode to Green Spring where we found Hannah Ludwell very ill and the family melancholy. We stayed about half an hour and then went in the boat to Major Harrison's where we arrived about 8 o'clock and the Major soon after. I ate some apple pie for supper and then said my prayers and had good health, good thoughts, and good humor, thanks be to God Almighty.

7. I rose about 6 o'clock and read some of the *Tatler*. I said my prayers and drank chocolate for breakfast. We had a long debate with the captains about freight and at last I generously offered them £10 per ton, which they received with negation but I believe must submit to it. We dined about 11 o'clock and I ate boiled mutton for dinner. About 2 o'clock the Major and I rode to Colonel Harrison's to make him a visit in his sickness and found him abroad in his store but very weak. I stayed there about two hours therefore and then rode home, where I found all well, thank God. . . .

8. . . . I unpacked several things in the afternoon [*sic*] and then gave my wife a flourish and then read in the *Tatler*. Two negroes of mine brought five of the cows that strayed away from hence and told me all was well above, but that Joe Wilkinson was very often absent from his business. It rained all the afternoon, that I could not walk. The negro woman was found and tied but ran away again in the night. . . .

9. . . . About 11 o'clock we went to church and had a good sermon. After church I invited nobody home because I design to break that custom that my people may go to church. I ate boiled pork for dinner. In the afternoon my wife and I had a terrible quarrel about the things she had come in but at length she submitted because she was in the wrong. For my part I kept my temper very well. In the evening Mr. C-s and I took a walk about the plantation and on our return Mr. M-r-s-l overtook us and told me all was well at Falling Creek. He told me that my two overseers above fought and that Joe Wilkinson was to blame for desiring Mr. Grills to bid for some things at the outcry and before anybody could bid above him Joe gave him the goods. Tom Turpin told him this was not fair, which made the quarrel between them. . . .

10. . . . More goods came up from the ship. About 10 o'clock, Mr. Anderson and his wife came to help me and my wife work. About 12 o'clock Mrs. Betty Todd and Betty Harrison came and so did Colonel Eppes and the captain of the Plymouth ship. They all dined with us, and I ate pigeon for dinner. In the afternoon we went to work again and finished about 4. . . .

11. . . . In the afternoon we went to work again till the evening, when Mr. Clayton, Dr. Cocke, and Mr. Bland came over. We took a walk together about the plantation and the Doctor seemed to be well pleased with the place. . . .

12. . . . The Doctor, who is a man of learning, was pleased with the library. Mr. Clayton and Mr. Bland went to Prince George court, but the Doctor stayed here. About 10 o'clock Captain Broadwater came over about his freight but I could resolve nothing but advised him to take the common freight. He went likewise to court. . . .

13. . . . It rained almost the whole day; however it did not hinder Mr. Clayton from going to Mrs. Harrison's and the Doctor and me from going to Colonel Hill's. When we came there nobody was at home but the ladies but about 2 o'clock the Colonel came home and we went to dinner and I ate sheep's head and bacon for dinner. . . .

14. . . . The gentlemen took their leave and I went with them to Mrs. Harrison's where we ate again. Then they all went away and I looked into the library and bought as many books as cost £10. About 2 o'clock I returned home and found Mr. Parker there. He came to pay me interest for the money he owes me. About 4 o'clock he went away. Billy Brayne and I had a quarrel because he would not learn his books and I whipped him extremely. In the evening we took a walk and I drank some milk warm from the cow. . . .

15. . . . My wife against my will caused little Jenny to be burned with a hot iron, for which I quarreled with her. It was so hot today that I did not intend to go to the launching of Colonel Hill's ship but about 9 o'clock the Colonel was so kind as to come and call us. My wife would not go at first but with much entreaty she at last consented. About 12 o'clock we went and found abundance of company at the ship and about one she was

launched and went off very well, notwithstanding several had believed the contrary. When this was over we went to Mr. Platt's to dinner and I ate boiled beef. We stayed till about 5 o'clock and then returned home, where all was well. I found an express from above with a letter from Joe Wilkinson desiring to be discharged from my service when his year was out. . . .

. . .

18. I rose at 5 o'clock and wrote a letter to the Governor to beg him to intercede with the men-of-war to let Colonel Hill's ship have men. I read a chapter in Hebrew and some Greek in Thucydides. I said my prayers and ate milk and pears for breakfast. I settled my cases in the library till about 11 o'clock when Major Chamberlayne came to see me, who is one of the biggest men in Virginia. I ate dry beef for dinner. In the afternoon I caused some of the goods to be unpacked. About 4 o'clock Isham Randolph came to see me. I gave him a letter to the Governor in his favor and sent a squirrel to Mrs. Russell. In the evening Mr. C-s and I went into the river. Then I drank some warm milk. . . .

. . .

21. . . . About eight nights ago I dreamed that several of my negroes lay sick on the floor and one Indian among the rest and now it came exactly to pass. I ate roast chicken for dinner. In the afternoon I settled my books again till the evening and then took a walk with Mr. C-s about the plantation. I drank some milk and water after I came out of the river where I had been to swim. . . .

22. . . . The Indian continued very ill. I settled my books till about 12 o'clock, when Captain Burbydge came to see us. I gave him a bottle of cider. I ate lamb for dinner. In the afternoon while the Captain smoked his pipe I settled my books again and then came in again. About 6 o'clock he went away and I walked along with him to the Point. He and the rest of the masters agreed at last to go at £10 per ton. A negro came from Falling Creek to tell me all was well. . . .

23. . . . About 11 o'clock we went to church and heard Mr. Anderson preach. We invited nobody home because we would not make our people work too much of a Sunday. . . .

24. . . . My wife was also better, notwithstanding the impression

90

she had that she should die. I sent this morning 15 hogsheads of tobacco on board Captain Burbydge. I settled my books. I wrote a letter to England. I ate roast shoat for dinner. In the afternoon I settled my books again. In the evening I quarreled with my wife for not taking care of the sick woman, which she took very ill of me and was out of humor over it. . . .

25. . . . My wife was out of humor this evening for nothing, which I bore very well and was willing to be reconciled. . . .

26. . . . In the evening my wife and I took a walk about the plantation and were good friends. Mr. C-s went to Mrs. Harrison's. I said my prayers and had good health, good thoughts, and good humor, thanks be to God Almighty. I gave my wife a flourish.

27. . . . Colonel Hill came this morning and stayed about an hour. Then came Colonel Randolph who was just recovered of a dangerous sickness. My sloop came from Sandy Point and I sent more tobacco on board Captain Bradby. . . .

28. . . . In the afternoon my wife and I had a little quarrel because she moved my letters. Captain Burbydge came to see us and told me my great sloop was come round. I sent ten hogsheads more on board him. I walked with him some part of the way towards Mrs. Harrison's. When we came home my wife was pleased to be out of humor. . . .

. . .

30. . . . I read a sermon in Dr. Tillotson and then took a little [nap]. I ate fish for dinner. In the afternoon my wife and I had a little quarrel which I reconciled with a flourish. Then she read a sermon in Dr. Tillotson to me. It is to be observed that the flourish was performed on the billiard table. I read a little Latin. In the evening we took a walk about the plantation. I neglected to say my prayers but had good health, good thoughts, and good humor, thanks be to God. This month there were many people sick of fever and pain in their heads; perhaps this might be caused by the cold weather which we had this month, which was indeed the coldest that ever was known in July in this country. Several of my people have been sick, but none died, thank God.

31. . . . My daughter was taken sick of a fever this morning

and I gave her a vomit which worked very well and brought away great curds out of her stomach and made her well again. My people were all well again, thank God. I went to the store and unpacked some things. About 12 o'clock Captain Burbydge and Captain Broadwater came over. The first went away to Colonel Randolph's; the other stayed to dine with us. I ate hashed mutton for dinner. In the afternoon Dick Randolph came from Williamsburg and brought me the bad news that much of my wine was run out. God's will be done. In the evening Mrs. Harrison and her daughter came over. . . .

August, 1710

. . .

2. . . . My daughter was worse this morning and my wife gave her another vomit of tartar emetic which worked much both up and down. She continued very ill all day and was not sensible. . . .

. . .

4. I rose at 5 o'clock and found my daughter very ill, so that I sent for Dr. Cocke. I read a chapter in Hebrew and a little Greek in Thucydides. I said my prayers but ate no breakfast, I was so concerned for my daughter. I read French but could not keep my mind steady. Mr. Anderson came to the next house and would not be so kind as to call to see the child. I ate some minced veal for dinner. In the afternoon I took a little [nap] and then read more French. I sent for Dr. Cocke, but a gust hindered him from coming and me from taking a walk. In the evening my daughter began to be better and had a sort of a looseness which abated her distemper. . . .

5. . . . About 10 o'clock the Doctor came but found the child in no danger. Dr. Bowman came to tell me that my negro boy which he had was too big for him to manage, and therefore desired me to send for him, which I did. The Doctor ordered the child oil of bitters drunk three times a day. About 10 o'clock Mr. Anderson and his wife and Mrs. Harrison came to see us. I scolded at Mr. Anderson for not coming to see the child, but I was satisfied with his excuse. . . .

6. . . . Mrs. John Stith sent my wife some grapes. The Doctor

took part of them. The child was much better and [I] gave the Doctor four pieces of gold and desired him to accept of them. He went away about 9 o'clock. About 11 o'clock I went to church and heard a sermon from Mr. Anderson. . . . I gave my wife a flourish on the couch in the library.

. . .

8. . . . The child had rested very ill tonight and drank abundance of water. However she had little fever and was hungry. Colonel Hill and Mr. Anderson called here on their way over the river. About 10 o'clock Captain Burbydge came with his boat and I went with him over the river to choose burgesses for Prince George. When we came there we found abundance of people met together and about 2 o'clock they chose Colonel Hardiman and Robin Bolling. I stayed there till 5 o'clock and then went to Mrs. Harrison's where we found Major Burwell. . . .

9. . . . I paid the builder of my sloop £60 which was £10 more than I agreed for. I settled my public accounts. My daughter was better, thank God, but was a little bloated. I was very much out of humor for nothing by reason of the weather or my constitution. I ate boiled lamb for dinner. In the afternoon I read some French. Mr. Salle came and told me that my coaler had the ague and that my shoemaker was sick at his own house. I drank some syllabub and after that ate some beef with him for supper. . . .

. . .

11. . . . In the afternoon I received a letter from Williamsburg which told me the Governor's family began to be sick, and Mrs. Russell was the first of them and was sick of a fever. I wrote an answer and sent it by Indian Peter and sent it immediately. Then I settled my library. It rained very hard for an hour, so that I was forced to walk in the library. . . .

12. . . . I had a quarrel with my wife about her servants who did little work. I wrote a long and smart letter to Mr. Perry, wherein I found several faults with his management of the tobacco I sent him and with mistakes he had committed in my affairs. . . .

13. . . . I ate abundance of peaches and figs before dinner. I read in a good book. I ate boiled beef for dinner. In the afternoon I took a nap, which disordered me. Then I read more in my good book. I ate abundance more fruit but drank some

canary after it. About 6 o'clock we took a walk about the plantation. Henry brought me a letter from Falling Creek by which I learned that many of my folks were sick above, though without danger. . . .

14. . . . Walter Scott came to offer himself to be my overseer at Burkland but I could not give him any answer till I see Joe Wilkinson. The weather was hotter this day than it had been a good while. I ate some muskmelon before dinner and then I ate some hashed mutton. In the afternoon I settled my library. . . .

15. . . . About 12 o'clock we went to the courthouse where the freeholders were met to choose burgesses. After a great deal of persuading the choice fell on Colonel Eppes and Sam Harwood, notwithstanding Mr. Parker thought he should have carried it. But Colonel Hill used his endeavors to make the people vote for Colonel Eppes and he had it by one vote. Nothing remarkable happened but that the disappointment gave Mr. Parker a fever. We did not dine till 4 o'clock and then had so much company that there was no pleasure. I ate stewed eggs. In the evening the company went away. I walked to the courthouse, where the people were most of them drunk and Mr. Doyley gave me some letters which he brought from Williamsburg, among which was one from Colonel Parke which told us he was going to England but was not put out of his government and though he was dismissed he should not be put out if he could justify himself from the accusation against him. . . .

. . .

19. . . . About 1 o'clock we rode to Mr. Platt's, in whose field there was a race. There was Captain Burbydge and some other company. Here was another dinner provided but I could eat nothing but a little lamb. About 5 o'clock we went home in our boat, which came for us about 4 o'clock and Colonel took a passage with us. We found all well but old Jane who had a fever. We went into the river. . . .

20. . . . About 11 o'clock we went to church and had a good sermon from Mr. Anderson. Cope Doyley died yesterday morning at Mrs. Harrison's of an imposthume in his head. We had some watermelon in the churchyard and some cider to refresh the people. We asked nobody to go home with us, that our servants might have some leisure. I ate roast veal for dinner. In the afternoon I read in Grotius' *Truth of the Christian Religion*. About

4 o'clock there happened a small gust with little rain. I heard Mr. Drury Stith was sick and I gave a man some Jesuit's bark. . . .

. . .

25. . . . I went to the store about 10 o'clock with Bannister and was angry with him for letting the tar run out. We unpacked several things. I read some Latin. Captain Llewellyn came over but would not dine with us. I ate some dried beef. In the afternoon the Captain went away and I received a letter from Colonel Hunter. Mrs. Harrison sent to desire me to go see her in the evening, which I did and found her indisposed in her side. Her business was to speak with me concerning some iron which she had come in. I wrote a letter for her to George Walker about it. . . .

. . .

27. . . . I translated Solomon's Song. It was very hot again. I ate fish for dinner. In the afternoon Captain Burbydge came again and about 4 o'clock we went in his boat to see my cousin Harrison. On the way we took up Mr. Anderson, who [told] us Colonel Hill was very disconsolate for the loss of his wife. . . .

28. . . . About 10 o'clock the rain left off and Mr. C-s and I rode to see Mr. Drury Stith. We found him much better than when I saw him last and all the family were well likewise. After we had been there about an hour Mr. Stith and I went to look for some flowers in the wood and found several, which I brought home. About 3 o'clock we went to dinner and I ate some chicken. We stayed till about 6 o'clock and then returned home. . . .

29. . . . I dreamed last night that the lightning almost put out one of my eyes, that I won a tun full of money and might win more if I had ventured, that I was great with my Lord Marlborough. I settled my accounts and then translated out of Hebrew. I ate roast mutton for dinner. While we were at dinner Mr. Bland came and brought me some English letters, but without news of a peace. He stayed here till 5 o'clock and then went over the river. I read some news. In the evening I and my wife took a walk about the plantation. . . .

. . .

31. . . . The sick people were better, thank God. Eugene was whipped for cheating in his work and so was little Jenny. About 11 o'clock I went to see Colonel Hill to condole him over the

death of his wife, who died in England. I found him in great concern; however he came out to me and talked a little. . . .

September, 1710

1. . . . My wife and I had a quarrel because she neglected to give the child the bitter drink. . . . Colonel Randolph and Captain Bolling were chosen burgesses for the upper county. My wife and I took a long walk about the plantation. In the evening I read a sermon of Dr. Sacheverell, and had good health, good thoughts, and good humor, thank God Almighty.

. . .

3. . . . In the afternoon I read some divinity, and about 6 o'clock took a walk about the plantation. In the evening [I read] the speech of the Bishop of Sarum against Dr. Sacheverell. . . .

4. . . . About 10 o'clock Mr. Bland came and Captain Drury Stith and several other gentlemen, among the rest Parson Robinson who was charmed with my library. About one o'clock my cousin Harrison came and desired me to go with her to court, which I did and she there took letters of administration and was bound in £12,000 security. About 3 o'clock we came home and went to dinner and I ate calf's head. In the afternoon the company went away and my wife was taken with a violent colic which lasted till the evening. . . .

5. . . . My wife was still indisposed but not so much as to keep me from going to Falling Creek, because Mr. Grills was sick of the gripes and it was necessary to get my sloop dispatched. So about 11 o'clock I recommended my family to God Almighty and went to Falling Creek, where I arrived about 3 o'clock and found Mr. Grills very bad of the gripes. I found things in an indifferent condition. I went to the tannery, which is a very good one. . . .

6. I rose at 6 o'clock and said a short prayer and ate boiled milk for breakfast. Mr. Grills continued ill. About 8 o'clock I rode to the Falls where things were in good order and there seemed to be abundance of tobacco and corn but the tobacco is injured by too much rain. About 10 o'clock I rode from hence to Kensington where things were well. From thence we went over

the river to Burkland where I found Joe Wilkinson sick. However I scolded at him for neglecting his business. He excused all with the good crop which indeed he showed me everywhere. There I ate some potatoes and milk and then proceeded to Byrd Park where there was a very good crop. Then I went to Shockoe where there was a good crop likewise. I made [. . .] stay his year out and two months besides. From hence we went over the river to the Falls where I understood that my man Tom had an ague. I went by myself to Falling Creek where Mr. Grills continued bad. . . .

7. I rose at 6 o'clock and settled accounts with several men. I ate milk for breakfast but neglected to say my prayers. Captain Webb came to see me. I had some words with him but at last by his fair speaking we parted friends. Mr. Laforce came likewise but could not pay me the money he owes. Mr. Grills was still bad. I returned home about 9 o'clock and got to Colonel Hill's about 12, where I dined and ate boiled shoat for dinner. It rained all the afternoon. However I went home about 5 o'clock and found several of my family sick but without danger. I scolded at John for letting five of the cattle stray away. I prepared some physic for Mr. Grills. . . .

. . .

10. . . . In the afternoon I took a flourish with my wife and then read a sermon in Tillotson. In the evening we took a walk. Mr. C-s had the headache very badly but towards the evening was better. It was very hot again this day. . . .

11. . . . Tom the tailor came to alter the sleeves of my coat. . . .

. . .

16. . . . I left some directions concerning my house with Mr. Bland and then took my leave of him and his wife and about 8 o'clock rode to Colonel Ludwell's where I ate some fricassee of chicken. About 11 o'clock I went towards home and by the way called on Mr. Gee where I stayed about an hour and then proceeded home where·I arrived about 6 o'clock and found several of my family sick, and my daughter among them. I ate some milk and quince. Since I went Captain Lee, one of the captains of the men-of-war, was here and brought me a letter from my cousin H-s. . . .

17. . . . About 11 o'clock came Captain Burbydge to inquire what news. I desired him to let his boat be ready to receive the Governor on Wednesday next. He stayed. At dinner I ate roast beef. In the afternoon my sloop came over. We walked and talked till the evening when we drank a syllabub and then he went away. In the evening I wrote letters to the officers of the militia to be ready against the Governor's coming. . . .

18. . . . I sent John Grills with orders to Colonel Randolph and Colonel Eppes to summon the militia of the two counties for the Governor to review. I ate boiled beef for dinner. In the afternoon Mrs. Hamlin went away. We fired several pistols to teach my horse to stand fire. . . .

19. . . . The house and ground was made clean to receive the Governor. We gave the child the bark which put away her fit. Several of the negroes were sick. I ate roast beef for dinner. In the afternoon I caused all the rut to be cut away that lay at the woodpile and the pasture to be made clean. I caused a hogshead of punch to be made for the people when they should come to muster. Joe Wilkinson sent us some strawberries and peaches by little Peter who told me all the people were well and that Joe Wilkinson carried all the cider away. . . .

20. I rose at 6 o'clock and read nothing because I prepared for the Governor's coming in the evening. I neglected to say my prayers but ate milk for breakfast. I settled several things in my library. All the wood was removed from the place where it used to lay to a better place. I sent John to kill some blue wing and he had good luck. I ate some boiled beef for dinner. In the afternoon all things were put into the best order because Captain Burbydge sent word that the Governor would be here at 4 o'clock but he did not come till 5. Captain Burbydge sent his boat for him and fired as he came up the river. I received at the landing with Mr. C-s and gave him three guns. Mr. Clayton and Mr. Robinson came with him. After he had drunk some wine he walked in the garden and into the library till it was dark. Then we went to supper and ate some blue wing. After supper we sat and talked till 9 o'clock. I neglected to say my prayers but had good health, good thoughts, and good humor, thank God Almighty.

21. I rose at 6 o'clock and read nothing but got ready to receive the company. About 8 o'clock the Governor came down. I offered

him some of my [fine water]. Then we had milk tea and bread and butter for breakfast. The Governor was pleased with everything and very complaisant. About 10 o'clock Captain Stith came and soon after him Colonel Hill, Mr. Anderson, and several others of the militia officers. The Governor was extremely courteous to them. About 12 o'clock Mr. Clayton went to Mrs. Harrison's and then orders were given to bring all the men into the pasture to muster. Just as we got on our horses it began to rain hard; however, this did not discourage the Governor but away we rode to the men. It rained half an hour and the Governor mustered them all the while and he presented me to the people to be their colonel and commander-in-chief. About 3 o'clock we returned to the house and as many of the officers as could sit at the table stayed to dine with the Governor, and the rest went to take part of the hogshead in the churchyard. We had a good dinner, well served, with which the Governor seemed to be well pleased. I ate venison for dinner. In the evening all the company went away and we took a walk and found a comic freak of a man that was drunk that hung on the pales. Then we went home and played at piquet and I won the pool. About 9 the Governor went to bed. I had good health, good thoughts, and good humor, thank God, but neglected to say my prayers.

22. I rose at 6 o'clock but read nothing. About 8 the Governor appeared and we had nothing but milk tea for breakfast, and bread and butter. I neglected to say my prayers. About 10 o'clock we got on our horses and rode towards Henrico to see the militia. Colonel Randolph with a troop met us at Pleasant's mill and conducted us to his plantation, where all the men were drawn up in good order. The Governor was pleased with them and exercised them for two or three hours together. He presented me likewise to them to be their commander-in-chief [who] received me with an huzzah. About 3 o'clock we went to Colonel Randolph's house and had a dinner and several of the officers dined with us and my hogshead of punch entertained all the people and made them drunk and fighting all the evening, but without much mischief. Some of the French came to wait on the Governor and Mr. Salle made him a speech. We sat up till 10 o'clock. I neglected to say my prayers but had good health, good thoughts, and good humor, thank God Almighty.

23. I rose about 7 o'clock but read nothing. About 8 the Governor appeared and several of the French came to wait on the Governor.

He recommended to them, and particularly to Mr. Salle and to the parson, to live in peace and to be reconciled to one another. The parson [seemed] more difficult to be reconciled than anybody, which the Governor resented and told them if they put him to the trouble of hearing their disagreement he would never forgive them that were in fault. This frightened them into an agreement and they promised that they would forgive what was past and for the future live with kindness to one another. Mr. Anderson made them a speech to that purpose. We had breakfast about 10 o'clock and I ate blue wing. Then the French company was exercised and performed very well and the Governor made out of them a troop of dragoons with orders that Mr. Salle should command them as well as the foot. About 3 o'clock we went from hence to Colonel Hill's where we supped and I ate roast beef. We sat up till 9 o'clock but I was sleepy before that. I neglected to say my prayers but had good health, good thoughts, and good humor, thank God Almighty.

24. I rose at 6 o'clock and shaved myself and said a short prayer. The Governor's horses got away but Colonel Hill sent men after them and got them again. We had chocolate for breakfast and about 10 o'clock rode home to my house, where we refreshed ourselves and then the Governor and I went to church in the coach and my wife was terribly out of humor because she could not go likewise. Mr. Anderson preached very well and pleased the Governor. After church I invited abundance of gentlemen home where we had a good dinner. My wife after much persuasion came to dinner with us. The company went away in the evening and the Governor and I took a walk on the river side. The Governor was very willing to favor the iron works. We sat up till 9 o'clock. I neglected to say my prayers but had good health, good thoughts, and good humor, thank God Almighty.

25. I rose at 6 o'clock but read nothing. The Governor appeared about 8 o'clock and we had milk tea and bread and butter for breakfast. About 10 the Governor went away and I waited on him to Captain Stith's where several gentlemen came. About 12 o'clock we dined and I ate nothing but beef. About 2 o'clock we went from hence and I conducted the Governor as far as [Bridgewater's] mill, and so did Colonel Hill. On our return we called at Mr. Gee's but he was not at home. From thence I returned home where I found Jenny very sick. . . . About 8 o'clock we went to bed, where I gave my wife a flourish. . . .

26. . . . I danced my dance, and then wrote a letter to New England to Colonel Dudley. I settled some accounts. About 12 o'clock a man came to get some physic which I gave him. Then came the doctor of Captain Broadwater's ship, who is a sensible man. I asked him to stay to dinner. . . .

. . .

28. . . . About 10 o'clock Mrs. Harrison came to go with us to Colonel Harrison's but I ate some fish first. About 12 o'clock we got over the river and then proceeded to Colonel Harrison's where we got about 3 o'clock and found the Colonel pretty well. About 4 we went to dinner and I ate some boiled beef. . . .

29. I rose at 6 o'clock and read some Greek but nothing else. I shaved myself and about 8 o'clock I drank some chocolate. Then I went to the Colonel and he talked abundantly about the old affairs of Governor Nicholson, with whose successor he is already well pleased. Captain Harrison was gone to Gloucester but his lady was here. I presented my wife with some Indian goods to the value of 4 pounds 10 shillings. I ate some fricassee of chicken for dinner. In the afternoon we took our leave and returned home where we came about 6 o'clock and found all well, thank God. Then we had some blue wing for supper and Mrs. Harrison supped with us and then returned home. . . .

. . .

October, 1710

. . .

3. . . . Then came Captain Bolling with whom I accounted, and then Colonel Randolph and many more and I went to court with them. About 2 o'clock several gentlemen came home with me to dinner. I ate pork and peas. In the afternoon came Captain Broadwater with whom we all accounted and the poor Captain was arrested. About [. . .] o'clock they all went away. I neglected to say my prayers but had good health, good thoughts, and good humor, thank God Almighty.

4. . . . Mr. C-s came to me to complain of his bad fortune in getting any business and talked of going to England. My wife told me that she conceived this morning by the token that she voided

some blood. I wrote several letters to England. About 10 o'clock Mrs. Harrison came and we settled the disagreement between her and Mr. C-s and she went away soon after. . . .

5. . . . About 10 o'clock Drury Stith came over from the court martial, but I was so busy I could not go there. However I invited the commanders of the militia to dinner and they came accordingly. I ate boiled pork for dinner. Soon after dinner they went away and I went to write more letters to England. Then I went and took a walk about the plantation. I read a little in Dr. Sacheverell's trial. . . .

6. . . . In the afternoon my wife and I played at billiards. Then came Frank Eppes to give me a bill of exchange and he told me that Joe Wilkinson was willing to stay with me. I wrote more letters to England and Frank went away. In the evening I took a walk about the plantation. I sent Drury Stith some Madeira brandy and he sent me some peach brandy. I sealed up my letters. . . .

. . .

8. . . . In the afternoon I wrote more letters to England and in the evening prepared all my things for my journey to Williamsburg. Then I took a walk about the plantation with my wife. At night I settled accounts with Mr. C-s who [talks] of going to England with Captain Randolph. . . .

9. I rose about 5 o'clock and got myself ready for my journey, and about 6 o'clock [I] recommended my wife and my family to God's protection, and after my people had set me over the creek, I got on horseback about 7 and proceeded to Williamsburg where I arrived about 12. About one I went to wait on the Governor, where I found Colonel Digges and several other gentlemen. My wife sent a present of blue wing which were kindly accepted. I ate some roast beef for dinner. In the afternoon we drank a bottle of claret and then we took leave of the Governor and went to the coffeehouse where after we had settled some accounts of the naval officers we played at cards till 11 o'clock. Then I went to my lodgings but my man was gone to bed and I was shut out. However I called him and beat him for it. I neglected to say my prayers but had good thoughts, good health, and good humor, thank God Almighty.

10. I rose about 6 o'clock and read nothing because I prepared my matters against the Council. I neglected to say my prayers but ate boiled milk for breakfast. I settled accounts with several people and then went to the Governor's where several of the Council were. Here I drank chocolate and then we all went to Council, where several matters were debated, and particularly we had the journal of the commissioners for settling the bounds between this colony and Carolina, which made the business much in our favor. About 4 o'clock we went to dine with the Governor and I ate boiled beef and several other things. After dinner we went to cards and I won half a crown. About 9 o'clock we went home. I neglected to say my prayers but had good thoughts, good health, and good humor, thank God Almighty.

11. I rose about 6 o'clock and read nothing because Colonel Digges came to settle accounts with me. I neglected to say my prayers but ate boiled milk for breakfast about 9 o'clock, and went to the Governor's where I drank tea with him and then settled accounts with him and gave him bills. About 11 I took my leave and Dr. Cocke and I rode to visit my sister Custis, whom we found very well but Mr. Custis was not at home. Here we stayed about two hours and then proceeded to Green Spring. Mrs. Ludwell was gone to Surry but the Colonel was there. In the evening I ate some boiled beef for supper and then the Doctor and I played at cards and I lost half a crown. About 10 o'clock we went to bed. . . .

12. I rose at 7 o'clock but read nothing. I neglected to say my prayers but ate milk for breakfast. The Doctor and I played at piquet and I lost half a crown. About 10 o'clock we parted and I proceeded to Mr. J-k who entertained me very courteously. I dined here and ate fried chicken. Then went home but was taken in the rain before I got there. I found all well, thank God, and Mr. Dunn was there. My sloop was not discharged from Colonel Hill's sloop till this day, when she was loaded with shingles and sent to Williamsburg and Nurse went in her. Mr. Dunn and I had a great deal of talk till 9 o'clock and then we went to bed. I neglected to say my prayers but had good health, good thoughts, and good humor, thank God Almighty. After we were in bed my wife and I had a terrible quarrel about nothing, so that we both got out of bed and were above an hour before we could persuade one another to go to bed again.

13. . . . About 10 o'clock Mr. Dunn went away and I advised him to reconcile the differences of his parish as much as possible. . . .

14. I rose at 2 o'clock and read two chapters in Hebrew and four leaves in Greek and French Lucian. I went to bed again and lay till 7. I said my prayers and ate boiled milk for breakfast. I danced my dance. Then I wrote a letter to England and put up some seeds for the Bishop of London. About 11 o'clock my cousin Harrison came to see me and desired me to carry some letters for her to Williamsburg. I ate boiled pork for dinner. In the afternoon my cousin Harrison went away and I wrote more letters to England. In the evening I took a walk about the plantation and then wrote some warrants against the general court. . . .

15. I rose at 3 o'clock and read two chapters in Hebrew and five leaves in Lucian (Greek and French). I went to bed again and rose about 7 o'clock. I said my prayers and ate [b-l] for breakfast. I danced my dance. I received a letter from Joe Wilkinson who told me all was well above. To this I wrote an answer. . . . In the evening Captain Randolph's boat came to fetch Mr. C-s and his things. I gave Mr. C-s a letter to the Bishop of London and took my leave of him. Then my wife and I took a walk about the plantation. . . .

16. I rose about 5 o'clock and ate milk for breakfast. I neglected to say my prayers. About 6 o'clock we were set over the creek and proceeded to Williamsburg, after I had recommended my wife and family to God's protection. About 12 we got to Williamsburg. There I ate some cakes and butter and then went to court where we were sworn again. Here we sat till 4 o'clock and then the Governor asked most of the Council to go to dinner and me among the rest. I ate blue wing for dinner. Then we drank a bottle of wine and about 8 o'clock we returned to our lodgings where I read a little in Greek. I said my prayers and had good health, good thoughts, and good humor, thank God Almighty. I sent away my horse by Tom to Colonel Ludwell's in order to return home in the morning.

17. . . . About 8 o'clock Frank Eppes came to my lodgings and I went with him to the Governor to get him a commission to go to the mountains, which he readily gave him. Here I drank some milk tea. About 9 o'clock we went to court where we sat till 12 and then adjourned to see the horse race and I lost 35

shillings. About 4 o'clock we went to dinner at C-t, where I ate boiled beef for dinner. Then we took a little walk and after that had a meeting of the College and then Colonel Digges and I went to the Governor's, where we drank a bottle of claret and were merry till 10 o'clock. . . .

18. . . . About 7 o'clock Robin Beverley came to my lodgings and stayed till 8. Then I went with the governors of the College to wait on the Governor to desire him to accept of our choosing him one of the governors, which he did with an assurance that he would do us all the service he could. Here we drank chocolate. Then I went home and settled some business till 11 o'clock and then went to court, where we stayed till 5 before we went to dinner. I ate boiled chicken and bacon. Then I returned to my lodgings, where I did a great deal of business. . . .

19. . . . About 11 o'clock I went to court, it being the day appointed for trying the criminals. After we had stayed there about two hours we went into Council and then came down to court again, where we stayed till 4 o'clock and then adjourned. . . . In the evening we played at cards and I lost 25 shillings. We played at basset. About 11 o'clock I returned to my lodgings. I recommended to the Governor to get some men from the men-of-war for Colonel Hill's ship. . . .

20. . . . About 10 o'clock I took leave of Captain Isham Randolph, who came to see me. Then I went to court and gave my judgment in several cases. About one o'clock I took some sage and snake-root. Then I returned into court again and there we sat till 3. Then I wrote a letter to my wife and after that went to dinner and ate roast beef for dinner. Then I went to the coffeehouse, where I played at hazard and lost £7 and returned home very peaceful. . . .

21. . . . About 10 I was sent for to Council and went accordingly. Here we were about an hour and then went to court, where we sat till 3. Then I went with the Governor to dinner and ate roast beef for dinner which had been basted with vinegar to make it tender and good. After dinner I went to make a visit to Mrs. Russell in her chamber and drank some tea with her. Then we went down and played at piquet and I lost 10 shillings. The Governor had a letter that the Commodore was come from New York. . . .

22. . . . About 11 o'clock I went to church and heard Mr. Whately preach a sermon. It was very cold this morning and rained much last night. . . .

23. . . . About 9 o'clock I went to wait on the Governor, where I found Colonel Custis. I read my proposal about naval stores to the Governor and he approved of it. Then we went to court. I sat a little while and then returned to my lodgings and prepared my public accounts and continued at them till 3 o'clock. . . . I said my prayers but I committed uncleanness, for which God forgive me. However I had good health and good humor, thank God Almighty.

24. . . . The Commodore came to town last night. About 9 o'clock I went to Council where the Governor read his speech to us and about 11 we went to court and [sat] till one. Then I went home to write and settle accounts with Colonel Digges. About 3 o'clock we went to dinner and I ate boiled beef. Then I went to the coffeehouse where I saw Captain Robinson and a [lieutenant] of the [marines]. I went with them to the Governor's where we supped and played at cards till 10 o'clock. . . .

25. . . . About 9 o'clock we went to Council to consult about the writ of alias capias, and at last we carried 7 to 5. Then we went to court where we sat till 3. Then I went to dine at the Governor's where was the Commodore and Mr. Hamilton the postmaster general, and Captain Garlington. I ate wild duck for dinner. Soon after dinner I waited on the Governor to the capitol where the House of Burgesses were met and chose Major Beverley for speaker, 21 against 16 who were for Mr. Holloway. . . .

26. . . . About 8 o'clock I went to the Governor's where I found the Commodore ready to depart to Kiquotan. I let the Doctor have a bill of exchange for £10 for money. About 9 o'clock we went to court and from thence to Council where the Governor approved of the choice the House of Burgesses made of their speaker. Then he made a speech and delivered it with the best grace I ever saw anybody speak in my life. They passed my accounts of 2 shillings a hogshead. Then we went to court, where we sat till 4 and then went to dinner. . . .

27. . . . About 10 o'clock I went to court, where we sat till 4 o'clock; then we went to Council for half an hour. I went to dine at the Governor's where I ate roast mutton for dinner. After dinner

we drank a bottle of wine and then took our leave. I went to the coffeehouse where I found several of the Council playing at dice and I played with them and won 40 shillings. . . .

28. . . . About 10 o'clock I went to court, where we sat about an hour and then adjourned because several of us were to go to the christening of my sister Custis' child. The Governor and I were godfathers, and Mrs. Ludwell was godmother. I went there in the President's coach and the Governor soon after. About 2 o'clock the ceremony was performed and about 3 we went to dinner and I ate roast beef. I gave the midwife 10 shillings. About 6 o'clock I returned on my brother Custis' horse and when I came home I found Tom who told me all was well at home, thank God, and brought me a letter from my wife and some fish for Mrs. Russell. I wrote a letter to my wife. . . .

29. I rose at 6 o'clock and sent away my man Tom home with a letter to my wife. I read two chapters in Hebrew and some Greek in Homer. I said my prayers and ate boiled milk for breakfast. I went to church about 11 o'clock and heard a sermon of Mr. Taylor. Then Colonel Duke and I went to Mr. Commissary's to dinner and Mr. Hamilton the general postmaster with us. I ate roast mutton. I had a great deal of wit this day, more than ordinary. My cousin Harrison and her daughter were here. About 5 o'clock we took our leave and walked to the coffeehouse where I drank two dishes of tea. Here I sat till 8 o'clock and then returned to my chambers where I read some verses of the Commissary's making. I said my prayers and had good health, good thoughts, and good humor, thank God Almighty. I committed uncleanness this night, for which God forgive me.

30. . . . About 10 o'clock Mr. Bland came to see me. Soon after I went to court but when I found nobody there I went to my chamber in the capitol where I read some Latin. About 12 o'clock we went to court and determined two cases and then went to Council, where several petitions were read and some discourse had about the post. About 4 o'clock we went to dinner and I ate roast goose. I returned to my chambers and drew up a bill against the masters that abuse hogsheads of tobacco. I read some French. Then I said my prayers and had good health, good thoughts, and good humor, thank God Almighty. The fleet was not sailed this morning. The weather grew very cold this evening.

31. . . . I drew an attack against the masters that abuse tobacco

hogsheads. About 9 o'clock Mr. Bland came to see me. Then we went to court, where we sat about two hours and then went to Council and then back again to the court, where we sat till 4 o'clock. Then we went to dinner and I ate turkey. Then Colonel Lewis and I walked to see the Governor's house and then went to the President's where we played at cards and I lost 35 shillings. I wrote a letter to Colonel Hunter which Mr. Hamilton undertook to carry to him. Then several of us went to the coffeehouse where we played at hazard and I won 23 shillings. I wrote a letter to my wife. I did not come home till 11 o'clock; however, I said my prayers and had good health, good thoughts, and good humor, thank God Almighty. The fleet is not yet sailed.

November, 1710

1. . . . About 8 o'clock I went to see Mr. Hamilton at Marot's and went with him to the Governor's where we ate bread and butter and drank tea. About 9 o'clock I came to court where we sat till 4 and Mr. W-r-t-n was reproved for speaking disrespectfully to Mr. Commissary and telling him that he expressed himself as well as another did in the pulpit. We went to Council for half an hour and then Colonel Carter and I dined at the Governor's. I ate mutton for dinner. Then we drank three bottles of French wine. It rained very hard so that we went home about 8 o'clock in the Governor's coach and Colonel Carter set Colonel Corbin and me down at the coffeehouse where we made Colonel Digges treat us. . . .

2. . . . Will Randolph and Mr. Bland came to see me and the first told me of several proceedings of the House of Burgesses. About 10 o'clock I went to court where we sat till about 12 o'clock and then adjourned because Mr. Holloway's trial came on before the committee, who were of opinion that it was a void election. About 4 o'clock we went to dinner, and I ate roast beef. Then I took a little walk with Colonel Duke and then came to the coffeehouse, where I sat till 8 o'clock and then returned to my lodgings. Soon after I went from the coffeehouse there happened a quarrel between Colonel Smith and Mr. Holloway, but Mr. Holloway seemed to be in the wrong. I wrote my judgment concerning the minister and parishioners of Charles Parish which had been referred to me. Colonel Hill came from Kiquotan and told us the fleet sailed this day and his ship among the rest. . . .

3. I rose at 6 o'clock and read a chapter in Hebrew and then company came to me. Indian Peter brought me a letter from home [which] told me that my wife was not like to come down because my daughter was sick. About 9 o'clock I went to court and we sat till one o'clock and then adjourned because Mr. Holloway was called away to the House of Burgesses for his trial and the House judged it a void election. I dined with the Governor and ate fish for dinner. The Governor learned that I intended home tomorrow and so sent a fine [case] to my daughter which I was unwilling to accept but he would have me take it. . . .

4. I rose at 7 o'clock but read nothing because I prepared to go home this day. I said my prayers and ate boiled milk for breakfast. About 8 o'clock I went to court where I sat till 11 o'clock and took horses, which I borrowed of Mr. Clayton and Mr. Jackson, and rode home, where I came about 5 o'clock. I found all my the child. I ate some wild duck for supper and then examined family well except my daughter, who had a little fever but was much better than she had been. I found Mrs. Hamlin there to see how everything stood. I was very weary and so went to bed about 8 o'clock. I neglected to say my prayers in form but had good health, good thoughts, and good humor, thank God Almighty. I gave my wife a flourish in which she had a great deal of pleasure.

5. . . . I settled some things with Mr. Grills, who told me all was well at Falling Creek. About 11 o'clock he and I took a walk to see a fine enclosure which Mrs. Harrison put about her husband's grave which cost abundance of money but will not last. Mrs. Hamlin stayed and dined with us and I ate boiled pork. In the afternoon Mrs. Hamlin went away and I took a long walk about the plantation and found all things in good order. In the evening my daughter was better, thank God. . . .

6. . . . I sent for the tailor to cut my coat shorter. At night my wife and I played at piquet and had a small quarrel about our count. We ate some pears and milk for supper. I wrote a letter to Mr. Will Eppes and sent him some [sage] to cure his looseness. I prepared for my journey to Wiliamsburg. . . .

. . .

8. I rose at 6 o'clock and prepared for my journey to Wiliamsburg. About 7 o'clock I recommended my family to the divine protection and took leave of my wife and took horse about half an hour after. I ate some boiled milk. I met with nothing remarkable on the way

but got to Williamsburg about 12. I sent some fish to the Governor and Mrs. Russell invited me to dinner. About 3 o'clock I went to the Governor's where I dined and ate fish. Here I stayed till about 8 and then went to the coffeehouse where I played at cards till about 9, when the Doctor and the President came. We drank out Colonel Digges' brandy and were merry till 12 o'clock. Then I went home to bed. . . .

9. . . . Colonel Smith and I walked to see the Governor's house and visited Mr. Cary. In an hour we returned to the coffeehouse where we played at cards and I won [18] shillings. I ate some bread and butter for supper. The bill for settling the money passed the House of Burgesses this day. . . .

10. . . . About 12 o'clock we came to the capitol and went into the Council, where two bills were read of no consequence. Colonel Lewis was very drunk with drinking canary. About 4 o'clock we went to dinner and I ate boiled beef. Then we went to the coffee-house where I lost 40 shillings at cards and dice. Mrs. Russell was indisposed again. . . .

11. . . . About 12 o'clock I went to the coffeehouse and found several gentlemen there that got me to cards till about 2 o'clock and then I went with Colonel Digges in his chaise with the Doctor and several others to Colonel Digges his house where we went to supper about 6 o'clock. I ate boiled beef. Then we played at cards and dice till 10 o'clock, and then drank a merry bottle of wine till about 11. When we went to bed it smelled so bad I could hardly endure it. . . .

12. I rose at 8 o'clock and read nothing nor [did] I say my prayers but very shortly. I ate oysters for breakfast. About 10 o'clock we went in the chariot to church, but the Doctor was sent for to Captain Berkeley. It rained a little till the evening. Mr. Taylor preached a short sermon but it was very good. We returned to Colonel Digges' to dinner. I ate boiled mutton for dinner. In the evening the Doctor came to us and told us Mr. Berkeley was better and that Mrs. Burwell was likewise very bad and also Colonel Churchill. At night we played at cards in the belief that there was no hurt in it. . . .

13. . . . Colonel Digges sent for a white negro for us to see who except the color was featured like other negroes. She told us that in her country, which is called Aboh near Calabar, there were

many whites as well as blacks. We played at dice till about 12 o'clock and then we [went] to Williamsburg, but I was so dusted with dirt that I was forced to change my clothes. Yesterday Mr. Ingles had a child burnt to death by fire taking hold of its clothes. We went to the capitol and stayed there about two hours and then I went and dined with the Governor where I ate roast mutton. I had a letter from home which told me all was well except a negro woman who ran away and was found dead. . . .

14. . . . Mr. Salle and several others were to see me this morning. We had news that Mr. Parker was dead and that Colonel Churchill was speechless. About 11 o'clock I went to the capitol and Mr. Jacquelin sent me 24 oranges. We had several disputes in Council concerning the coin. The Governor on several occasions discovered a great inclination to hold the royal P[rerogative?]. About 4 o'clock we went to dinner and I ate boiled pork for dinner. In the evening I took a walk about the town and then went to the coffeehouse and played at cards and lost 30 shillings. About 11 o'clock I returned to my lodgings where I said my prayers and had good health, good thoughts, and good humor, thank God Almighty. I wrote two letters to my wife.

15. . . . I went to court about 11 o'clock where we had several bills read to us and particularly the bill for settling the rate of money and we were all of opinion to settle at 16 pennyweights to the crown. About 4 o'clock we went to dinner and I ate salt fish for dinner. Then we went to the coffeehouse where I wrote a sham letter to Dr. Cocke under the name of Mary F-x. Soon after he came and the letter was delivered to him. Then we played at cards and I lost 10 shillings. . . .

16. . . . Several people came to see me and Mr. Salle among the rest, who desired me to look over the petition of the French to have their 5000 acres of land laid out, in which I assisted them. Major Harrison came to town and told us that Mr. Parker died on Tuesday morning. About 9 o'clock I went to prepare the bill about the money according to the amendment of the Council. About 12 o'clock we went to Council. Colonel Carter came to us and told us that Colonel Churchill was a little better. About 4 o'clock we went to dinner, and I ate boiled beef. Then I took a long walk without the town and returned to the coffeehouse where I played at cards and lost £3 to Colonel Smith. . . .

17. . . . About 10 o'clock I went to wait on the Governor and

found several of the House of Burgesses there with a message to know what he would have done to the house for the Governor. I went with them to the Governor's house where he showed them all the conveniences he proposed. It rained this morning as it had done also in the night. About 1 o'clock I went to the capitol where we amended the bill concerning the tobacco hogsheads. We sat till about 4 and then I waited on the Governor to dinner. I ate fish for dinner. About 8 o'clock we went to the coffeehouse where I played at cards and lost 40 shillings. Captain Smith and Captain Garlington came this night from Kiquotan. . . .

18. . . . Several people came to visit me this morning and Colonel Bassett among the rest. About 10 o'clock I went with him to the Governors and on the way met the two captains of the men-of-war, Captain Smith and Captain Garlington. They told us there was a change in the ministry in England, that a fleet of three men-of-war and 50 merchant ships were expected about Christmas. [W—] we went to the Governor's, where we drank chocolate. About 12 o'clock we came to the capitol and sent the money bill and the hogshead bill to the House of Burgesses with amendments. About 4 o'clock we went to dinner and I ate goose. In the evening I went to see Colonel Duke, who was sick of a fever. Then we went to the coffeehouse where we stayed about two hours and then went home. . . .

19. . . . Daniel came to shave me. About 11 o'clock I walked to church but came there to soon. Colonel Carter and I went to see Colonel Duke and found him still with a fever with the addition of a looseness. Mr. Wallace preached this day but flattered the Governor and recommended the College which did not please at all. After church Colonel Harrison took Colonel Carter and me to dine at Mr. Blair's where I ate boiled beef for dinner. In the afternoon we walked to church again to hear Mr. Blair preach Mr. Whately's funeral sermon, which he performed very well. After the ceremony was over we walked to the coffeehouse, where we stayed the rest of the evening. About 11 o'clock I went home where I said my prayers and had good health, good thoughts, and good humor, thank God Almighty.

20. . . . Mr. Mumford sent to me for the sheriff's place of Prince George for Peter Jones in the room of Will Eppes who died on the 16 of this month, but it was disposed of. About 11 o'clock I went to the Governor's but found nobody. I wrote a letter to Barbados

which I gave to Captain Smith when he gets leave of the Governor to go there. I ate some toast and cider with Colonel Carter at Marot's. About 1 o'clock we went to the capitol where we did very little. About 4 o'clock we went to dinner and I ate boiled beef for dinner. In the evening I went to see Colonel Duke who was much better and there I found my brother Duke. . . .

21. . . . About 8 o'clock I had some visitors and Mr. Blair brought his accounts for me to examine. About 10 o'clock I went to court where most of our time was taken up in these accounts so that we did little business in the upper house. In the House of Burgesses they threw out our hogshead bill and also the bill for dividing our county. Colonel Duke was better and rode out of town. About 4 o'clock we went to dinner and I ate roast goose. In the evening I took a walk and returned in an hour to the coffeehouse where I played at cards and lost my money and went home about 9 o'clock and wrote some verses on the House of Burgesses. . . .

22. I rose at 7 o'clock and read nothing because I wrote some verses and then was interrupted by Mr. Blair who plagued me again with his accounts. I neglected to say my prayers and ate boiled milk for breakfast. I went to court about 10 when we had more dispute about Mr. Harrison's accounts and Mr. Blair was in the right. We did very little business and about 4 went to dinner and ate roast beef. In the evening I walked for half an hour and then came to the coffeehouse and lost 40 shillings. About 9 I went home where I found my man from Westover with letters which told me my daughter and all the family was well, thank God, but only Harry the Indian boy died four days ago. . . .

23. . . . When we had our instructions from the Council we went on the conference with the Burgesses concerning the money bill and used abundance of arguments with them but to no purpose, so that at last we parted and reported what we had done to the Council. About 4 o'clock Colonel Carter and I went to dine with the Governor and I ate wild fowl. One of the burgesses told us that the House had agreed to our amendment of the money bill. We drank two bottles of claret and then went to the coffeehouse. . . .

24. . . . Several persons came to see me, among whom was Mr. Cary to satisfy me about his accounts. Then I went to court where we did some business. I directed a letter to Nat Burwell with a lampoon in it and threw it into the capitol and Mr. Simons found it and gave it him, which put the House of Burgesses into a fer-

ment, but I discovered to nobody that I had a hand in it. I went to my chamber in the capitol and danced by dance. About 4 o'clock we went to dinner and I ate boiled pork. Then we went to the coffeehouse where I played at cards and I lost my money but was diverted to see some of the burgesses so concerned at the lampoon. . . .

25. . . . About 11 o'clock I went to the capitol where we met and read a bill for the impositions which the Governor thought fit to find fault with. It rained still and hindered us from going on our frolic. About 3 o'clock we went and dined with the Governor where I ate some beefsteak. In the evening we went to cards and were merry but I lost about a crown. . . .

26. . . . It rained all night and this morning so as to hinder my going to church. I wrote several things till about two o'clock and then went to Marot's to dinner with the burgesses. I ate roast goose for dinner. In the afternoon we sat and drank a bottle of cider till about 5 o'clock and then adjourned to the coffeehouse. Before we had been there long, in came George Mason very drunk and told me before all the company that it was I that wrote the lampoon and that Will Robinson dropped it. I put it off as well as I could but it was all in vain for he swore it. . . .

27. . . . I neglected to say my prayers but ate boiled milk for breakfast. I wrote more verses against the burgesses. About 9 o'clock Colonel Randolph and Mr. Bland came to see me. About 10 o'clock I went to the coffeehouse where I found several of the Council and from thence went to the capitol where we read several taxes and the Governor sent them several messages which they did not like. It rained again all day. Colonel Carter received the news of his family's sickness which obliged him to ask leave of the Governor to go home. About 4 o'clock five of the Council went to dine at the Governor's where I ate boiled beef. In th evening we went to cards and I won 10 shillings. We stayed till 10 o'clock and then the President's coach carried us to the coffeehouse where I stayed about half an hour and then returned home. . . .

28. I rose at 7 o'clock and read nothing but some English because the head speaker and Colonel Randolph came to see me to discourse about the Governor's message. I said my prayers and ate boiled milk for breakfast. About 11 o'clock I went to the capitol where we dispatched some business. About 2 o'clock the Governor came to us and I endeavored to soften him concerning the passing

of the land bill, but in vain, for notwithstanding he be a gentleman that means well, yet he is too obstinate and [w-l f-t] his own sentiments. . . . Colonel Churchill died this morning.

29. . . . About 9 o'clock John Grills came over and told me my wife was at Queen's Creek where she came last night. He told me all was well at home. I sent to borrow the Governor's coach to fetch her to Williamsburg and went in it myself about 1 o'clock. When I came there I had a sham reprimand for not meeting my wife last night. I caused her to make haste to the Governor's to dinner. We took our leave in half an hour and carried Mrs. Dunn with us to the Governor's who entertained us very handsomely. I ate roast venison for dinner. In the evening we played at cards and the Governor would lend us his coach next day to go to Major Burwell's. About 10 o'clock we took leave and I carried my wife to my lodgings and Mr. Dunn and his wife to Mr. Bland's. I neglected to say my prayers but had good health, good humor, and good thoughts, thank God Almighty. I gave my wife a flourish.

30. We rose at 7 o'clock and I read nothing and neglected to say my prayers. About 8 o'clock Mrs. Dunn came to us. I drank some mulled wine for breakfast. About 9 o'clock the Governor's coach and six horses came to my lodgings to carry us to Major Burwell's and we went soon after and got there about 11. We found the Major very sick and despaired of by Dr. Cocke. I ate some oysters there. There was a consultation between Dr. Blair and Dr. Cocke about him and they agreed on the method to treat him. We stayed here till 2 o'clock and before we came away Nat Burwell told us his wife was sick of the gripes. About 4 o'clock we got to the Governor's where we dined and I ate boiled goose and onions. In the evening we played at cards and my wife received very great charity from the Governor and Mrs. Russell. We stayed till 10 o'clock and were set home in the coach to our lodgings. . . .

December, 1710

. . .

4. . . . I desired Mr. Bland to give his vote for the Commissary to be minister of Bruton Parish and he promised he would and accordingly his vote carried it at night against the inclination of Mr. President. About 11 o'clock I went to the capitol and I learned by

Colonel Ludwell that my wife stayed at Green Spring this day but I could not go there to her because I was ordered to draw an address to the Governor. About 4 o'clock we all went to dine at the Governor's, where Mrs. Russell was indisposed. I ate giblet pie. We stayed till about 8 o'clock and went to the coffeehouse where we played at cards and I won about £4. It was one o'clock before I got to bed. I neglected to say my prayers but had good health, good thoughts, and good humor, thank God Almighty.

5. I rose about 7 o'clock and read nothing because I was busy in drawing the address to the Governor. I said my prayers and ate boiled milk for breakfast. Several were to see me this morning and particularly Mr. Commissary to thank me for my good offices in procuring him this parish. Mr. Eppes came to see me and told me he had been at the mountains and found them easy to be passed in several places. About 11 o'clock I went to the capitol where we stayed till 4 o'clock and my address was read and approved by the Council. We read the Book of Claims and then went to dinner at C-t where I ate boiled mutton. Then we went to the coffeehouse where we played at cards and I won 20 shillings. . . .

6. I rose about 7 o'clock and read a chapter in Hebrew but no Greek because I was hindered by Mr. Eppes who came to give me an account of his journey to the mountains. I ate boiled milk for breakfast but neglected to say my prayers. About 9 o'clock I went with Mr. Eppes to the Governor's and drank chocolate. We stayed there till 10 and then I went to the capitol, where we did a great deal of business till about 4 o'clock, and then I and the Commissary went and dined with the Governor where I ate fish for dinner. We drank a bottle after dinner till about 8 o'clock and then went to the coffeehouse where I stayed talking till about 10 with several gentlemen and Mr. Burwell among the rest, who told me that his wife and father were better. . . .

7. . . . About 10 o'clock I went to see Mr. Holloway and to settle accounts with him but was much disturbed to find how much he had charged me for fees. . . .

8. . . . About 10 o'clock I went to the capitol where I wrote a letter to my wife. Then I went up stairs and danced my dance. I caused a lampoon to be directed to Colonel Smith. About 3 o'clock we went home with the Governor but the servants were out of the way, but when they came the Governor chastised them. I ate boiled pork

for dinner. In the evening we drank a bottle till about 9 o'clock and the Governor gave us some oranges which he had sent him from Barbados. . . .

9. . . . About 9 o'clock Mrs. Russell sent lemons and citrons to my wife. About 10 o'clock I went to the capitol where I met Mr. Holloway and reasoned with him about his accounts but he was on the high rope and gave me back my papers and would have nothing to do with my business which he had but half done. I took him at his word and sent my papers to Robin Beverley. The Governor prorogued the Assembly till April. Then a particular company of us went to dine at the French ordinary where I ate some fish for dinner. We were exceedingly merry and stayed there till about 7 o'clock and then rode to Williamsburg. . . .

10. . . . I read some French. About 11 o'clock I went to visit the President at his lodgings and went with him and Mr. Clayton to church where parson Taylor preached a short sermon. From church I went with the Governor and Mrs. Russell in the coach to dinner. I ate chine and turkey for dinner. In the afternoon we drank a bottle of wine till about 4 o'clock and then I took my leave. The Doctor returned from Major Burwell's who was very sick again and Frederick Jones was also sick of a palsy. . . .

11. . . . It rained much last night. There was a great noise of people drunk in the street good part of the night. About 10 o'clock I borrowed Mr. Clayton's horse to ride to Major Burwell's and got there before 12. I found him with a fever on him but not violent, but he was apprehensive of dying and desired extremely to live a little longer. He begged of me to pray for him and if after his death there should happen a disagreement among his children he conjured me [to] make it up, which I promised him I would. I found there several of his daughters. About 3 o'clock it began to rain and a little after we went to dinner and I ate some roast pig. Then about 4 o'clock I recommended Major Burwell to the protection of the Almighty and took my leave. It rained again before I got to the end of my journey. When I returned I found several letters from England by which I learned that my sister Brayne was dead. I said my prayers, in which I prayed for Major Burwell, and had good health, good thoughts, and good humor, thank God Almighty.

12. . . . About 11 o'clock I went to the coffeehouse where I found several gentlemen of the Council. From thence we went to the Court of Oyer and Terminer and adjourned as soon as we had

117

sworn the jury and went to dine at the Governor's, where I ate some boiled goose and onion sauce. About 4 o'clock we returned to court and one criminal was arraigned for killing a woman after a new fashion. Then we went to the Governor's again, it being the Governor's birth night, and stayed till 10 o'clock and drank a bowl of punch. I desired the Doctor to give six of the Governor's servants £3 and returned to my lodgings. . . .

13. . . . I settled some accounts with Mr. Bland. About 10 o'clock I went to the capitol to the Court of Oyer and Terminer where we proceeded to try the person accused of killing the woman and the jury found him guilty of manslaughter. Then we went to Council where some little matters were dispatched. Then I went to dine with the Governor where I ate boiled beef. After dinner about 4 o'clock my man came from home with the horses and told me my wife was indisposed with a cold and fever. Several of the Council went home and some of us stayed with the Governor till about 9 o'clock. Then I took my leave of the Governor and Mrs. Russell and returned to my lodgings. . . .

14. I rose at 7 o'clock and read nothing because I was preparing to return home to Westover. I said my prayers and ate boiled milk for breakfast. It was very cold weather. However I was resolved to go home because my wife was indisposed. Accordingly I went and took leave of Mrs. Bland and thanked her for all her kindness to me and my servants. About 10 o'clock I took horse and rode away, without calling anywhere till I got home, where I arrived about 4 o'clock and found my wife better and the rest of the family pretty well only two people were sick without danger. I came just as my wife was at dinner with Mr. Dunn and his wife and ate some wild duck. In the evening I looked about me a little and found things in pretty good order. In the rest of the evening I read nothing because of the company that was here. I neglected to say my prayers but had good health, good thoughts, and good humor, thank God Almighty. I gave my wife a flourish, notwithstanding she was indisposed.

15. . . . My wife was better, thank God, but the child was out of order with a cold. I put the pictures in the library and walked about till dinner. Colonel Hill and Colonel Eppes came just time enough to dine with us. I ate roast beef for dinner. In the afternoon I went with the two colonels to the church to hear the people sing Psalms and there the singing master gave me two books, one for me and

118

one for my wife. Mr. Dunn went away and left his wife at our house. In the evening I walked about the plantation to see what work the people had done and found things pretty well. Then I returned home and wrote some verses in the rest of the evening till 9 o'clock. The child was very dull all day and her eyes ran. . . .

16. I rose at 8 o'clock, having first rogered my wife. I read a chapter in Hebrew and some Greek in Lucian. I said my prayers and ate boiled milk for breakfast. I danced my dance and I set things in order in my library. Mrs. Dunn took physic and so did several of my people. The child continued out of order and Nurse was troubled with sore eyes. I ate boiled beef for dinner. In the afternoon my wife and I had a quarrel about learning to sing Psalms, in which she was wholly in the wrong, even in the opinion of Mrs. Dunn who was witness of it. . . .

17. . . . Mrs. Dunn read a sermon in Bishop Latimer which was written in a very comic style. Then we sat and talked till 8 o'clock when we went to bed because I intended to rise in the morning before day. My daughter lay with me. . . .

18. I rose about 3 o'clock and read a chapter in Hebrew and six pages in Lucian. About 6 I went to bed again and lay till 8. I said my prayers and ate boiled milk for breakfast. I danced my dance. The weather was warm again. About 10 o'clock Mr. Bland came from Williamsburg and brought me two letters from England which came from New York but no news. About 12 o'clock came Dick Ward from above to settle accounts with me. He did not tell me that some part of the dam was gone, but Ralph G-p-l-n did tell me there was three feet of it gone. About 1 o'clock I went to the vestry, who gave me the best pew in the church. . . . In the evening I wrote some verses and was very much out of humor. I neglected to say my prayers but had good health, good thoughts, but indifferent humor, without much provocation.

19. I rose about 7 o'clock and read nothing because I prepared to go to Falling Creek. I continued exceedingly out of humor, which was increased by the news of my dam being broken. About 10 o'clock I had a quarrel with my wife about lending my gun to John and about telling me I lied. However I was reconciled before I went away. About 11 o'clock I got on horseback and rode to Colonel Hill's where I only found Mr. Anderson at home with Mr. Finney the minister. About 1 o'clock we went to dinner and I ate

some salt beef. About 2 o'clock I went over the river and rode in two hours and a half to Falling Creek where I found a break in the dam but everything else was well besides. Mr. Grills was in much concern about the dam. I ate boiled milk for supper and then talked with Mr. Grills till 9 o'clock. . . .

20. . . . About 8 o'clock I rode to the Falls where I found things in good order. About 11 o'clock we went over the river and learned that Joe Wilkinson was not on the plantation but was gone with Mr. Laforce to look after his hogs. He had spoiled all the tobacco by house burn and carried several things that belong to me home to his house, for all which reasons I wrote to him to forbear coming any more to my service and appointed Tom Turpin to take care of everything till I sent an overseer. I walked to all the plantation on that side the river and the tobacco was most of it spoiled. . . .

21. . . . About 8 o'clock Tom Osborne came and I agreed to let him be overseer in the room of Joe Wilkinson for £25 a year. Then I took my leave and rode away to Appomattox where I got about 11 o'clock but did not find Mr. Mumford at home. . . . Soon after dinner I went away towards home, where I arrived about 4 o'clock but made some verses on the road. I found several of my family sick and little M-n-g-y dead. I ate milk for supper and wrote verses in the evening. I neglected to say my prayers and had good health, good thoughts, but indifferent humor. However I rogered my wife when we got to bed.

22. I rose about 8 o'clock but read nothing because the sloop came and I was busy in loading her and in punishing Johnny and scolding at S-k-f-r for bringing goods for Mr. Tullitt contrary to my orders. About 10 o'clock I sent her away. . . . In the afternoon my wife and I played at billiards and I laid her down and rogered her on the [trestle]. About 4 o'clock Mr. Bland came on his way to Williamsburg but I persuaded him to stay all night. We sat and talked all the evening. . . .

23. . . . Our daughter began to take drops of ginseng. It was still fair warm weather. We were invited this day to the funeral of Major Burwell, but could not go. I wrote some verses before dinner. I ate some fish for dinner. In the afternoon my wife and I played at billiards and then I went and took a walk about the plantation to see how everything stood. In the evening a negro came from above with venison and wild turkey and told me all

was well there. At night I wrote a letter to the Governor to send with a present of venison and turkey. George the coaler came likewise from the coal-pit and told me all was well there. My wife and I had a little quarrel about nothing. . . .

24. . . . Billy Brayne was taken sick in the night and another negro boy. The woman that was sick was mad this morning. I danced my dance. About 11 o'clock we went to church and took possession of the pew which the vestry gave us. We began to give in to the new way of singing Psalms. I had nobody home with me to dinner. I ate venison. The weather continued warm. In the afternoon my wife and I took a walk about the plantation. In the evening I read a sermon and wrote a letter to Williamsburg. My daughter was a little better, thank God. She drank cider in which rhubarb was infused. . . .

25. . . . About 7 o'clock the negro woman died that was mad yesterday. I said my prayers and ate boiled milk for breakfast. The wind blew very strong and it rained exceedingly. I danced my dance. About 11 o'clock we went to church where we had prayers and the Holy Sacrament which I took devoutly. We brought nobody home to dinner. I ate boiled venison. The child was a little better. In the afternoon I took a long walk and I saw several parts of the fence blown down with the wind, which blew very hard last night. In the evening I read a sermon in Mr. Norris but a quarrel which I had with my wife hindered my taking much notice of it. However we were reconciled before we went to bed, but I made the first advance. . . .

26. . . . I wrote a key of the *Atlantis*. . . .

27. . . . At night I wrote the key of the *Atlantis* and then read some of it. . . .

28. I rose at 4 o'clock and read two chapters in Hebrew and eight pages in Lucian. I went to bed again and lay till 7 and rogered my wife. I said my prayers and ate boiled milk for breakfast. I danced my dance. Then I read some French and settled some accounts till about 12 o'clock when Mr. Mumford came and let me know all was well at Appomattox. . . .

29. . . . Mr. Mumford ate some fried oysters for breakfast and then we went to play at billiards for the rest of the morning. I had two more sick people come down. These poor people suffer for my

sins; God forgive me all my offenses and restore them to their health if it be consistent with His holy will. I ate wild turkey for dinner. In the afternoon Mr. Mumford went away. My poor child continued to have a fever, from which God of his excessive goodness deliver her. In the evening I took a walk about the plantation and was very melancholy on account of the unkindness of my wife. I read several leaves in the *Atlantis* and was much affected with it. . . .

30. . . . Dick came from Falling Creek and told me an old negro of mine was dead and the boy that goes in the sloop very sick. I sent him back with orders to let all my people blood by way of prevention. I read some French till dinner. In the afternoon I read some English and then my wife and I made some punch of [lemons], white sack, and Madeira brandy, and I put it into bottles. In the evening I took a walk with my wife about the plantation. The weather was exceedingly warm. My people seemed to be all better, thank God. At night I read some English in the *Atlantis* till 8 o'clock. I said my prayers and had good health, good thoughts, and good humor, thank God Almighty.

31. . . . My daughter was very sick all night and vomited a great deal but was a little better this morning. All my sick people were better, thank God, and I had another girl come down sick from the quarters. I danced my dance. Then I read a sermon in Dr. Tillotson and after that walked in the garden till dinner. I ate roast venison. In the afternoon I looked over my sick people and then took a walk about the plantation. The weather was very warm still. My wife walked with me and when she came back she was very much indisposed and went to bed. In the evening I read another sermon in Dr. Tillotson. . . . Some night this month I dreamed that I saw a flaming sword in the sky and called some company to see it but before they could come it was disappeared, and about a week after my wife and I were walking and we discovered in the clouds a shining cloud exactly in the shape of a dart and seemed to be over my plantation but it soon disappeared likewise. Both these appearances seemed to foretell some misfortune to me which afterwards came to pass in the death of several of my negroes after a very unusual manner. My wife about two months since dreamed she saw an angel in the shape of a big woman who told her the time was altered and the seasons were changed and that several calamities would follow that confusion. God avert his judgment from this poor country.

January, 1711

1. . . . In the evening came old Harry Cary and Mr. Jackson from Wiliamsburg and brought me a letter from the Governor, very complaisant. I sat and talked with them till 9 o'clock and then went to bed without saying my prayers. . . .

2. . . . My wife was a little better and so was my child, thank God, but C-l-y was extremely ill and so was A-g-y. I tended them as much as I could but God is pleased to afflict me with his judgment for my sins. His holy will be done. . . . I took a melancholy walk. In the evening about 6 o'clock C-l-y died and all the people was [sic] grieved at it. I read a little English and gave the necessary orders about the sick people who were 12 in number. . . .

· · ·

4. . . . Several of the sick people complained of pain in the side and breast and poor A-g-y was very ill. About 11 o'clock Mr. Dunn and his wife came. I spent most of my time in looking after the sick; God grant them a recovery. About 12 o'clock I received a letter from my brother Duke that told me they were all well. I ate roast beef for dinner. In the afternoon Mr. Dunn and I played at billiards a little and then I returned to look after the sick again. . . .

5. . . . My sick people seemed to be all mending except Jenny and A-g-y, God grant them their recovery, if it be his holy will. The child seemed a little [. . .] and so was my wife, who would not dine with us. I ate fish for dinner. I played at billiards in the afternoon with my cousin [Guy] who belongs to the man-of-war and came to see me this morning by the leave of his captain. Then I returned to look after my people. Then my cousin and I took a walk about the plantation but it rained before we came back. The wind was at northeast and threatened bad weather. A-g-y voided three worms, which gave her some ease but did not remove the pain in her side. Upon this, I gave to all the sick people the wormseed because I believe their sickness proceeded from worms in some measure. . . .

6. . . . I removed several things out of the Doctor's closet into mine and was very little with my cousin. I was out of humor with my wife. I ate boiled pork for dinner. In the afternoon Mrs. Dunn went away in the rain. I spent most of my time in looking after my sick. . . .

7. . . . The weather held up so that I and my cousin [Guy] went to church, but my wife was afflicted with the headache and stayed at home. People condoled the sickness of my family. Mr. Anderson gave us a sermon. After church I carried him home with me to dinner and to see my sick people. I ate fish for dinner. Mr. Anderson advised me to give my people cordials since other physic failed, which I did. In the afternoon I did nothing but mind them. . . .

.   .   .

9. . . . In the evening Joe Wilkinson's [wife] came to beg for her husband but I would not speak to her for fear of being persuaded by her tears which women have always ready at command. At night I read some news and drank a bottle of cider. I said my prayers and had good health, good thoughts, and good humor, thank God Almighty.

.   .   .

11. . . . I quarreled with my wife for being cruel to Suky Brayne, though she deserved it. I wrote several letters to Williamsburg to go by Mr. Clayton. The weather was very warm and I had another boy taken sick. I ate roast mutton for dinner. In the afternoon after giving the necessary orders about my people [I] walked to Mrs. Harrison's where was a great deal of company. They were going to dinner but I could eat nothing with them but a little pudding. I stayed till it was almost dark and then returned home where I found my family in the same condition. . . .

12. . . . I stayed there till about 11 o'clock and then returned home, where I found Tom L-d who gave my wife bad language and I gave him chase with my cane but could not overtake him. . . .

13. . . . I went with my people to replant trees. Then I wrote articles between Tom Turpin and me and after read some news till dinner. I ate roast beef for dinner. In the afternoon we planted more trees till the evening and then Dick came from the Falls and told me all the people were well there, thank God Almighty. At night I wrote a letter to Tom Turpin to tell him the terms that I would give him. . . .

14. . . . In the afternoon we took a walk with the child who was a little better but very fretful. I read a sermon of Dr. Tillotson, and in the evening took a walk. At night we had another negro girl dead; God's will be done. We drank a bottle of punch. I said my prayers and had good health, good thoughts, and good humor, thank God Almighty.

124

15. . . . I danced with my wife, who was very merry today and in the evening took a walk with her. Then I took care of all the sick. . . .

· · ·

17. . . . My cousin [Guy] went away this morning and seemed to be much concerned for parting with Nurse. I wrote several letters and read some French and settled some accounts. I ate mutton pie for dinner. In the afternoon I took a walk to visit Mrs. Harrison but she was gone to the Colonel's in Surry. I found Mistress Betty at home but did not stay long with her but returned home and by the way looked for some cedar trees to plant in my pasture. My sick people grew still better. . . .

18. . . . About 10 o'clock I went out to get some cedar trees to plant in my pasture and while I was about it came Colonel Hill and Mr. Anderson, who made me leave the work and go to them. My sick people were much as they were. I ate fish for dinner. In the afternoon I gave them some of my punch which they liked very well. In the evening they went away and I and my wife took a walk about the plantation. . . .

· · ·

20. . . . In the afternoon I went with my people to plant some cedar trees. About 3 o'clock Dick Randolph came with a letter from Mr. Bland to tell me that my friend Colonel Digges was dead yesterday of the fever; upon this I wrote to the Governor to engage him to assist me in getting the two places joined again, and sent Tom with the letter because the express was not to return till tomorrow. . . .

21. . . . At night I read some English about the soul being a spirit. . . .

22. . . . Redskin Peter pretended to be sick and I put a [branding-iron] on the place he complained of and put the [bit] upon him. The boy called the Doc was sent from Falling Creek with a swollen thigh. My sick people were better, thank God Almighty. I received a courteous letter from the Governor by Tom, who brought no news. . . .

23. . . . My sick people were better, thank God, and Redskin Peter was particularly well and worked as well as anybody. We dispatched the sloop away to Williamsburg. Then I reckoned with Mr. Grills and surprised him when he found himself so much in debt.

. . . In the evening I took a walk about the plantation. My wife was extremely out of humor, for I know not what. . . .

24. . . . My wife came into good humor again of herself. The wind was northeast and was very cold. I settled several other accounts and did several little things about the house till dinner. My sick people were all mending, thank God. I ate roast [. . .] and mutton for dinner. In the afternoon I went about the planting of trees and in the evening took a walk about the plantation. It was very cold. At night I ate some oysters and then played at piquet with my wife to oblige her, notwithstanding it was against my inclination. . . .

25. . . . About 11 o'clock Colonel Hill came and told me the rest of his family were singing at church. He told me the ship that is arrived in York River brings an account that our fleet was in the Downs ready to sail in October last. Colonel Hill since the news of his wife's death, which was in July last, has eaten no flesh, which agrees well with him. I ate hog's haslet for dinner. In the afternoon the Colonel went away and I went to plant trees. My two boys, Bannister and Grills, began to learn to sing Psalms. . . .

26. . . . The rain confined me in the house all day. I ate roast shoat for dinner. In the afternoon I looked over my letters from England in order to answer them. My wife and I danced together. It rained all day without holding up one minute. My people kept holiday because of the weather, having nothing within doors to do. At night I read some English and read my old letters. . . .

27. . . . In the afternoon my wife and I took a little walk and then danced together. Then I read some more English. At night I read some Italian and then played at piquet with my wife. Peter came from the Falls and brought me some venison. My overseer wrote me word one of my new negroes was in danger. . . .

28. . . . I exercised my memory with getting things by heart. I thought a great deal about religion. I ate nothing but sallet for dinner. In the afternoon I rogered my wife on the couch. Then I took a little nap. After that I read some more English about the soul and then took a walk, but the rain made me return soon. At night I read more English. Jenny's child was taken sick of a looseness and vomiting. . . .

29. . . . Our cook Moll was taken sick. I caused her to be bled and vomited. Then I went to plant trees and worked very hard about it,

notwithstanding the rain, but I had the precaution to change my stockings. Then I read some English till dinner. I ate cold roast beef. In the afternoon I went to plant more trees. We heard several guns fired at a great distance. In the evening the boatwright and I came to a bargain by which he was to teach John to build a flat for £10. . . .

. . .

February, 1711

. . .

4. . . . About 11 we walked to church and heard a good sermon of Mr. Anderson. After church we ate some toast and drank some mead and went over the creek with our horses where the water was very high and I was very wet and got a violent cold. Mrs. Dunn returned home and we rode to my brother Duke's where we found all well. My sister did not ask us to eat till my brother came home and then I got some milk and potatoes. My cold grew worse. . . .

5. . . . My wife and I quarreled about her pulling her brows. She threatened she would not go to Williamsburg if she might not pull them; I refused, however, and got the better of her, and maintained my authority. About 10 o'clock we went over the river and got to Colonel Duke's about 11. There I ate some toast and canary. Then we proceeded to Queen's Creek, where we found all well, thank God. We ate roast goose for supper. The women prepared to go to the Governor's the next day and my brother and I talked of old stories. My cold grew exceedingly bad so that I thought I should be sick. My sister gave me some sage tea and leaves of [s-m-n-k] which made me mad all night so that I could not sleep but was much disordered by it. . . .

6. I rose about 9 o'clock but was so bad I thought I should not have been in condition to go to Williamsburg, and my wife was so kind to [say] she would stay with me, but rather than keep her from going I resolved to go if possible. I was shaved with a very dull razor, and ate some boiled milk for breakfast but neglected to say my prayers. About 10 o'clock I went to Williamsburg without the ladies. As soon as I got there it began to rain, which hindered about [sic] the company from coming. I went to the President's where I drank tea and went with him to the Governor's and found him at home. Several gentlemen were there and about 12 o'clock

several ladies came. My wife and her sister came about 2. We had a short Council but more for form than for business. There was no other appointed in the room of Colonel Digges. My cold was a little better so that I ventured among the ladies, and Colonel Carter's wife and daughter were among them. It was night before we went to supper, which was very fine and in good order. It rained so that several did not come that were expected. About 7 o'clock the company went in coaches from the Governor's house to the capitol where the Governor opened the ball with a French dance with my wife. Then I danced with Mrs. Russell and then several others and among the rest Colonel Smith's son, who made a sad freak. Then we danced country dances for an hour and the company was carried into another room where was a very fine collation of sweetmeats. The Governor was very gallant to the ladies and very courteous to the gentlemen. About 2 o'clock the company returned in the coaches and because the drive was dirty the Governor carried the ladies into their coaches. My wife and I lay at my lodgings. Colonel Carter's family and Mr. Blair were stopped by the unruliness of the horses and Daniel Wilkinson was so gallant as to lead the horses himself through all the dirt and rain to Mr. Blair's house. My cold continued bad. I neglected to say my prayers and had good thoughts, good humor, but indifferent health, thank God Almighty. It rained all day and all night. The President had the worst clothes of anybody there.

7. . . . I went to see Mr. Clayton who lay sick of the gout. About 11 o'clock my wife and I went to wait on the Governor in the President's coach. We went there to take our leave but were forced to stay all day. The Governor had made a bargain with his servants that if they would forbear to drink upon the Queen's birthday, they might be drunk this day. They observed their contract and did their business very well and got very drunk today, in such a manner that Mrs. Russell's maid was forced to lay the cloth, but the cook in that condition made a shift to send in a pretty little dinner. I ate some mutton cutlets. In the afternoon I persuaded my wife to stay all night in town and so it was resolved to spend the evening in cards. My cold was very bad and I lost my money. About 10 o'clock the Governor's coach carried us home to our lodgings where my wife was out of humor and I out of order. . . .

8. I rose at 7 o'clock and we both got ready to go. I said my prayers and ate boiled milk for breakfast. We expected the Governor at my lodgings and he came about 9 o'clock. We stayed

there a little while and then I walked with him to the house that is building for the Governor where he showed me abundance of faults and found great exception to the proceedings of the workmen. The Governor was pleased to tell me his thoughts about the auditor's place and told me several had made application for it and that one gentleman (that I took to be Holloway) had offered £500 for it. The Governor assisted my wife to get on her horse and then we took leave and rode to Mr. Blair's where we had some milk tea. Then we proceeded to Colonel Duke's where I got 50 black cherry trees for the Governor. We ate some boiled beef for dinner and then sat and talked all the evening. . . .

9. . . . I wrote a letter to the Governor and to my brother Custis about the auditor's place, and then another to Mr. Bland. Then I ate some roast turkey for dinner. My cold was better, thank God. About one o'clock we rode to my brother Duke's and just called to know how they did and then because it was late proceeded on our journey home. The roads were exceedingly bad because of the abundance of rain that had fallen. At Mr. B-s we saw a pretty girl called Mistress King who had £400 to her fortune. About 6 o'clock we got home, where we found all well, thank God Almighty, and my little girl was much recovered in her color. I ate some boiled milk when I came home and was pretty well of my cold but my wife had got a cold in her turn. . . .

10. . . . About 10 o'clock Mr. G-r-t-l came to see me and I sent my boat to Mrs. Hamlin's for his wife. Soon after came Colonel Hill and Mr. Anderson. The Colonel came to purchase some iron but I had none to spare. They all stayed to dinner and I ate pork. In the afternoon it rained but that did not hinder the company from going away, all except Colonel Hill who was so kind as to stay with us. We drank some mead which was very good and talked of several things and among others I encouraged him to endeavor for the auditor's place. The Colonel is a man of no great ambition but a man of honor and good nature. He complained that his head began to ache. . . .

.   . . .

13. . . . I ate some battered eggs and prepared to go to Prince George court. About 12 o'clock I got there and met several people there to do business with and gave my letters to Peter Hamlin. I sold above 100 rights there and saved the people the trouble of coming over the river. Here I saw Mr. Randolph and told him the

Governor was displeased with him for not making more haste with the laws. There was also Mr. Bland, who brought no news from Williamsburg. Mr. Mumford and Mr. Kennon helped me write the certificates of rights. About 3 o'clock I returned home and carried over Colonel Hill, Colonel Eppes, and Mrs. Harrison in my boat to Mrs. Harrison's house where we supped and I ate roast turkey. . . .

. . .

15. . . . I was out of humor and denied some men to catch their hogs on my land because they had bred them there. I read some English and took a walk in the garden. I ate roast mutton for dinner. In the afternoon I walked about the plantation till the evening and then my cousin Harrison came and when she had stayed here about an hour my wife and I walked home with her and did not return home till 8 o'clock. . . .

16. . . . In the afternoon I took a walk with my wife who was melancholy for her misfortunes and wished herself a freak for which I rebuked her. I read some English. In the evening there came a man for rights. I granted him eight. He told me Hal Harrison was extremely sick. I desired him to stay all night but he excused himself. . . .

17. . . . In the afternoon I rode my new horse to see Colonel Eppes and found him extremely bad. From thence I went to see Colonel Hill's ship which he is building and then called at his house to see him and stayed about half an hour. Then I returned home and found all well, thank God. . . .

. . .

19. . . . I had abundance of people with me for rights and I granted more than a hundred and among others Mr. John Simons came for some. I spent all the morning in this business, only I read a little English. I heard that Mr. Hal Harrison was better by a man that came from Surry. I ate roast beef for dinner. In the afternoon I granted more rights. I was very courteous to everybody that came and trusted one poor man because he came a great way. John Grills came from Appomattox and told me Mr. Mumford and all beside were well there. In the evening I took a walk about the plantation and at night John Bannister and I fell out and I gave him a severe reprimand for speaking surlily to me. . . .

20. . . . John Bannister and I were good friends again this morning.

130

[Si] the negro boy was sick this morning and I gave him a vomit which worked well and recovered him a little. I sold 23 rights this morning. Then I wrote a letter to England. Then I read a little English likewise. My daughter was indisposed of a terrible cold. . . .

21. . . . My daughter was taken with a pain in her side and a violent fever. I sent for Drury Stith to let her blood and he was so kind as to do it though he tried twice first. When he had done he went away and would not stay to dinner. Mr. Dunn and his wife came about 12 o'clock. I ate some wild turkey for dinner, but ate too much. In the afternoon Mr. Dunn and I played at billiards. He told me that he heard Hal Harrison was dead. My poor daughter continued sick. I caused her to be put into a sweat which gave her some ease. In the evening I took a walk about the plantation and at night drank some cider with my friend. Mr. Dunn received a letter that made him resolve to go home that night. . . .

22. . . . My daughter continued very sick and complained of her side for which Mrs. Dunn let her blood but she bled but a little, but about 10 o'clock she grew better, thank God Almighty; and I sold 13 rights this morning. Then I read some English. Mr. Doyley came a little before dinner and dined with us. I ate roast beef. In the afternoon Mr. Doyley went away and I read more English and then wrote a letter to England. It rained almost all day so that I could not walk about. At night we ate some bread and cheese and drank some punch and were merry. . . .

. . .

25. . . . I sent my lame boy with Mr. Grills to Mrs. [Hancock] to be cured. We took a walk to see the place I propose to keep my boats in, and the place where I intend to set the gates. About 11 o'clock my sloop came with planks and soon after Mr. Grills went away in my boat. The sloop brought me a letter from Appomattox where all things were well, and a load of tobacco ready. I ate roast beef for dinner. In the afternoon I took a walk about the plantation and met negro P-t-s-n who had been off the plantation and brought some bacon with him, for which I threatened to whip him. Then I found also that John was riding out with the stallion without leave, for which I threatened him likewise. Then I returned home and read some English and then walked out with my wife. . . .

. . .

131

27. . . . I danced my dance and then went to the brick house to see my people pile the planks and found them all idle for which I threatened them soundly but did not whip them. . . . I read some English till 12 o'clock when Mr. Dunn and his wife came. I ate boiled beef for dinner. In the afternoon Mr. Dunn and I played at billiards. Then we took a long walk about the plantation and looked over all my business. In the evening my wife and little Jenny had a great quarrel in which my wife got the worst but at last by the help of the family Jenny was overcome and soundly whipped. . . .

28. . . . I wrote a letter to England and about 11 o'clock rode with Mr. Dunn to visit Colonel Eppes. We found him well recovered. A certain woman that was there had a child that could just go alone who had been with some of the children in the morning but could not be found. All the people on the plantation were looking for it and I went likewise to look [for] it and at last found it, for which the woman gave me abundance of blessings. Then we went to Colonel Hill's where we dined. I ate some fowl and bacon. Several of the Colonel's family were sick and he had lost a young fellow worth £100. . . .

March, 1711

1. . . . The weather would not permit us to go to Mr. Platt's according to invitation. I took a walk about the plantation. Then I wrote another letter to England and after read some English. I ate boiled pork for dinner. In the afternoon I played at billiards with Mr. Dunn and then I wrote another letter to England. Then we took a walk about the plantation. I gave my wife a flourish this afternoon. At night I ate some [broiled] pudding, and had good health, good thoughts, and good humor, thank God Almighty. I sold four rights.

2. . . . A boy from Frank Eppes brought me some venison. The boatwright was affronted that I gave him pone instead of English bread for breakfast and took his horse and rode away without saying anything a word [sic]. . . . In the afternoon I received two letters from Williamsburg by which I learned that Colonel Jenings intends to go to England in the "Lion." . . .

3. . . . The boatwright returned last night again. Mr. Dunn and

Mr. Randolph played 30 games at billiards. I wrote a letter to England and settled some accounts between Captain Webb and me. I read a little English. I ate boiled pork for dinner. My wife endeavored to cut a bone of pork but Mr. Dunn took the dish and cut it for himself, which put my wife into great disorder and made her void blood so that [she] seemed to be going to miscarry and Mr. Dunn had not the manners to ask pardon. He went away in the rain this afternoon and so did Mr. Randolph. . . .

4. . . . My [wife] continued still disordered in her back and belly. However she went to church with Mrs. Dunn in the coach and I walked there. Mr. Anderson gave us a good sermon. After church nobody came home with us. Little Peter came from above and brought news another negro died, which makes 17 this winter; God's will be done. Several others are sick. The Lord have mercy on them, and spare them if it be His will. I ate boiled beef for dinner. In the afternoon Mrs. Dunn went away and I was at the trouble to send John home with her, who did not come back till 8 o'clock. . . .

5. . . . I wrote several letters to the quarters and sent Suky to Manakin Town to Mr. Salle. The weather was warm. I wrote a letter to England. I sold eight rights. I ate some broiled beef for dinner. In the afternoon I removed several of the pictures. I received a letter from Mr. Bland that gave me an account of ill success of our forces in Spain and that some ships were cleared and gone out without the Governor's knowledge and against the orders of the Council, and it is believed it was contrived by Colonel Corbin to be beforehand in his petition for the auditor's place. I was [not c-r-n-t] all day. In the evening my wife and I took a walk to see the boat, where John complained of a pain at the root of his tongue, for which I caused him to be let blood, which gave him ease. . . .

6. . . . John was better, thank God. I wrote the public accounts for the Governor. I resolved to eat no meat today and so I dined on potatoes and butter. In the afternoon I settled some accounts and then went and took a walk about the plantation. My wife was a little indisposed in her belly and in her teeth. At night I sealed up my letters and prepared everything for my journey tomorrow. . . .

7. I rose at 6 o'clock but read nothing because of my journey to Williamsburg. I said my prayers and ate boiled milk for break-

fast. I danced my dance, and gave the necessary orders to Bannister. The weather was clear and not very cold. About 9 o'clock I got on horseback and rode to Mr. Gee's where I had appointed to meet Colonel Hill, who came according to his time. We ate bacon and eggs and then proceeded to my brother Duke's. He was not at home but my sister was and gave us a cast over the river and from thence we rode to Colonel Duke's where we came about 5 o'clock. He could tell us no news. He received us, according to custom, very courteously. We had milk for supper and sat talking till about 9 o'clock before we went to bed. I said my prayers and had good health, good thoughts, and good humor, thank God Almighty.

8. I rose about 8 o'clock but read nothing because Colonel Hill lay with me. However, I said my prayers and ate milk and potatoes for breakfast. The moon changed this morning with a south wind. About 10 o'clock we took leave and rode to Williamsburg and by the way met Mr. Clayton who told us the fleet was come in but knew no particulars. Then we proceeded to Williamsburg, first to Mr. Bland's, who could tell us no more than Mr. Clayton. After I had set myself in order, and Colonel Hill had likewise, we went to wait on the Governor, who received us very courteously and with a particular distinction. He told us two ships of the fleet were come in and the rest, with the two men-of-war, were at hand. We dined there and I ate some roast beef for dinner. In the afternoon I walked with the Governor to the new house, where he showed the improvements he had made. Then I went home with the Governor and stayed with him till 9 o'clock tête-à-tête. Then I went to my lodgings where I said my prayers and had good health, good thoughts, and good humor, thank God Almighty. The Doctor was gone to the north.

9. I rose about 7 o'clock and read a chapter in Hebrew and some Greek in Homer. I ate some boiled milk for breakfast. Mr. Bland came to me about 9 o'clock. I went to the Governor's about 10 and drank some tea with him and Mrs. Russell. About 11 o'clock I walked with him to the new house where Captain [Berkeley] came to wait on the Governor, just come from England, who told him the fleet he left about 500 leagues off. The whole fleet consisted 20 sails besides the men-of-war. He said that Mr. Page was come with him, that Mr. Lane, partner to Mr. Perry, was dead, that Colonel Parke was not arrived in England. We went to dine with the Governor, where I ate some salt fish, but Mr. Holloway

dined there likewise, which put me out of humor. I sent my letters by Peter to Kiquotan to overtake the ships that were going out. About 5 o'clock I took leave of the Governor and went with Colonel Hill to see my sister Custis who was indisposed with a cold. About 9 o'clock we went to bed. . . .

10. . . . My brother and Colonel Hill went to Yorktown this morning. My sister was under great apprehension lest her husband should return again to the Eastern Shore. I promised her in case of Mr. Burwell's death, who was sick, I would use my interest with the Governor to get him the place of naval officer. About 9 o'clock Mr. Clayton came to give me an account of my business in his hands. Among other things we talked of Colonel Digges' family and I desired him to offer Mr. Digges in my name that my wife would take care of his sister because she had nobody to take care of her, which Mr. Clayton thought very kind. About 11 o'clock I took leave of him and my sister Custis and rode to Colonel Duke's, where I got about 2 o'clock and soon after came Colonel Bassett and his wife who dined there with us. I ate boiled beef for my dinner. Colonel Bassett told me the family of Major Burwell was not like to fall out because they had adjusted their differences. About 4 o'clock he and his wife went home and Colonel Duke and I took a walk. . . .

11. . . . About 10 o'clock Colonel Hill came but brought me no letters but told us very bad news of the fleet which wanted some vessels, that six of them were taken and two burnt but he could not tell which they were, that Mr. Lane was dead, that tobacco was worth nothing, that the King of France had coined money which thus [necessitated] anew a beginning of war. Then we went to church and heard Mr. Goodwin preach a good sermon. After church Mr. Goodwin invited us to dinner and I ate fish. Here we saw a fine widow Mrs. O-s-b-r-n who had been handsome in her time. From hence we went to Mr. B-s where we drank cider and saw Molly King, a pretty black girl. Then we went over the river to my brother Duke's. I was not very well because I had eaten too much. . . .

12. . . . About 8 o'clock we took our leave and called upon Mr. Gee and took him with us to Mr. Drury Stith's. We found his wife and son indisposed. It was very hot weather. About 12 o'clock we ate some [brains] for dinner and about 2 we took our leave and I returned home, where I found all well, thank God, except a negro boy called [Si] who had a fever and violent cold. . . .

13. I rose at 8 o'clock and read nothing because Mr. Peter Hamlin came to see me and told me the "Harrison" was come in and had abundance of goods for me. I lent him a horse to go to Colonel Hill's. Then I said my prayers and ate boiled milk for breakfast. I wrote a letter to Falling Creek. About 10 o'clock came Captain Posford and Captain Wilcox, the last of which gentlemen had lost his ship this voyage. They brought me several letters and an account of a great cargo for Williamsburg. These gentlemen parted with their convoy 500 leagues off which was wrong in them because they had much goods in their ships. . . .

. . .

15. . . . I looked over some of the new books that came lately from England by the "Harrison." We rummaged the cellar to know our stock of wine. I wrote a letter to England and then read a little English. I ate mutton for dinner. In the afternoon I unpacked some things. About 3 o'clock my cousin Harrison came to see us. . . .

16. . . . We unpacked the beer that came from England and a great deal was run out. I wrote a letter to England. Captain Posford sent for some planks of oak of 25 feet long but I had none so long. I ate boiled pork for dinner. Moll spoiled a good plum pudding, for which I chastised her. . . .

. . .

18. . . . I took a walk about the plantation and found Mrs. Harrison's horses had broken my fence four times in two days. My wife took a long walk with me and was much tired. . . .

. . .

20. . . . I wrote another long letter to England, about increasing my salary to 400 a year, in which I hope to succeed because I have some friends in the Treasury. I took a walk to see my people at work. Captain Posford sent some of my things up. I made an indifferent dinner this day because Moll had not boiled the bacon half enough, for which I gave her some stripes under which she [b-s-t] herself. I wrote another letter to England in the afternoon. In the evening I took a walk about the plantation with my wife. At night I read in the *Tatler* and ate some bread and new butter. I said my prayers and had good health, good thoughts, and good humor, thank God Almighty.

21. . . . About 12 o'clock Captain Wilcox came and brought me some letters from England and one from the Governor which told me Colonel Hill's ship was arrived in England. . . .

22. . . . About 10 Colonel Hill and Mr. Anderson [came] to see me. I gave them news to read and entertained them with showing them some new books. We rejoiced together at the news of Colonel Hill's ship's safe arrival in England. I ate some beefsteak for dinner. In the afternoon we talked till about 5 o'clock and then they returned home and I took my gun and endeavored to shoot some partridges but could not. At night I read in the *Tatler*. . . .

23. . . . I read some English in the *Tatler*. I ate some roast beef for dinner. In the afternoon Johnny Randolph came and brought me a letter from Williamsburg without any news. He said the Governor came out of Williamsburg on Wednesday and would be here on Saturday. I examined him in Greek and found he had made a great progress. He told me Captain Stith had the dropsy. About 4 o'clock he went away and I took a walk with my gun to kill some partridge, but could not. At night I read some English. . . .

24. I rose at 7 o'clock and read nothing because I was to go meet the Governor. I said my prayers and ate boiled milk for breakfast. The weather was clear and about 9 o'clock I rode in form to Captain Drury Stith's where I had appointed several gentlemen to go and meet the Governor. Here we ate some bread and butter and about 12 o'clock proceeded to [Chickahominy Bridge] and found him just arrived there, with Colonel Bassett and some few gentlemen. After the Governor and Mrs. Russell had rested a little we returned with the Governor to Captain Stith's where we stopped to drink a peach dram, and then went on to my house at Westover where [. . .] gentlemen went to wait on the Governor. It was evening before we got there and about 7 o'clock before we went to supper. We had eight dishes beside the dessert every day. I ate some beef. I gave them several sorts of wine and made them as welcome as I could. After supper all the gentlemen went home and the Governor and the Doctor and I drank two bottles of French wine and talked of many things. The Governor seemed satisfied with his entertainment. I said a short prayer and had good health, good thoughts, and good humor, thank God Almighty.

25. I rose at 7 o'clock and read nothing because of the company. I said my prayers and ate boiled milk for breakfast. About 8 o'clock the Governor came down stairs and about 9 drank some tea and ate bread and butter. It was 12 o'clock before the Governor and the ladies were dressed and then we went to church and heard Mr. Anderson preach. He and three other gentlemen

came and dined with us. I would have no more company for fear of crowding the Governor. I ate some tongue for dinner. The Governor's cook dressed dinner and so it was in good order. The sloop came last night, loaded with planks. After dinner the company stayed till 5 o'clock and then took leave. The Governor and I took a walk about the plantation. He told me that Colonel Bassett agreed to come into the Council again and that he had written to England about it. At night we drank several things but French wine was the chief. About 9 o'clock we went to bed. . . .

26. I rose at 6 o'clock and read nothing. I neglected to say my prayers and ate boiled milk for breakfast and at 9 o'clock I took some milk tea with the company. Several Indians came here yesterday to complain that the Nottoway Indians and several northern Indians had conferred together to cut them off. I told the Governor of it and he sent an order to the Nottoways to forbid them and ordered Colonel Harrison to cause some of the northern Indians to come to him to declare their business. About 10 o'clock several gentlemen came to wait on the Governor, who stayed to dinner, and among the rest Captain Wilcox, who told me Captain John Stith was very bad. We had a very handsome dinner; I ate a partridge. About 5 the gentlemen went away and the Governor, the Doctor, and I took a walk. At night the Doctor was sent for to Captain Stith's and went about 8 o'clock at night. We drank several things. My sister and Mrs. Dunn came this afternoon. I neglected to say my prayers but had good health, good thoughts, and good humor, thank God Almighty.

27. I rose at 6 o'clock and prepared for to wait on the Governor some part of his journey. We ate some bread and fresh butter for breakfast and then rode to Colonel Hill's where the Governor saw Colonel Hill's ship and we ate some roast beef. Here the Doctor came to us and about 10 o'clock we went over the river where we found several gentlemen ready to go with the Governor, among whom was Colonel Frank Eppes. We rode away to Falling Creek where we got about 12 o'clock. The Governor observed my sawmill and dam very nearly and the Doctor was much pleased with it. I brought some wine with me with which I entertained the company. Then we rode to the falls of the river with which the Governor was well pleased. Here all my people and affairs were well. From hence we returned to Captain Webb's who was sick of the gout. However we were very well entertained by his wife who is an excellent woman. I ate some fowl and bacon for supper. We had several gentlemen come over with us and three parsons.

The Doctor and I lay together. I neglected to say my prayers but had good health, good thoughts, and good humor, thank God Almighty.

28. I rose about 7 o'clock and was shaved. I neglected to say my prayers but ate some hashed turkey for breakfast. Captain Webb did not sleep because of the pain he was in. The weather was very cold and snowed a little. However the Governor was resolved to go on and about 10 o'clock we took leave and rode by [Pamunkey] where we passed Chickahominy Swamp and so went to Major Merriweather's, which is a journey of about 26 miles. The Major was a little surprised and was not prepared much for such guests; however he did as well as he could and for fear of the worst I had brought two bottles of wine with me. The Major told the Governor he had not made above one visit in 16 years and that was to a man that was sick. I ate some boiled beef for dinner. The Major sat at the upper end of the table and helped himself first. His wife did not appear. The Doctor's horse was foundered so that he could not go; however he would not believe it. After supper I took a little walk about the plantation, which is level. Our diversion was chiefly in laughing at the Doctor about his horse and he was at last a little angry. I neglected to say my prayers but had good health, good thoughts, and good humor, thank God Almighty. The Doctor and I lay together.

29. I rose about 7 o'clock and neglected to say my prayers. The Governor made me a compliment and would permit me to go with him no farther but the Doctor endeavored to persuade me to it. About 9 o'clock I ate boiled beef for breakfast. About 10 I took leave of the Governor and when I had seen him [to] Pamunkey River, I and the gentlemen with me returned and had one of the Major's sons for our guide as far as Mr. Fleming's where we drank abundance of cider but we could not see his pretty daughters because they were gone to a meeting. Mr. Fleming himself went with us to show us the way to the bridge where I took leave of the gentlemen that had been with me to wait on the Governor and I rode by myself home, where I arrived about 9 o'clock and found all well, thank God Almighty. I gave Mrs. Russell an account of the Governor's health and of his journey and that the Doctor was to ride on her horse because he had foundered his own which she was very sorry for. In the evening we drank a bottle of mead and I ate some toast. My gray horse carried me this journey very well and so did Ch-s-r which Bannister rode for he had taken good care

of them. I said my prayers and had good health, good thoughts, and good humor, thank God Almighty. I rogered my wife with vigor.

30. I rose about 6 o'clock and read two chapters in Hebrew and some Greek in Lucian. I said my prayers and ate boiled milk for breakfast. My wife and I paid all possible respect to Mrs. Russell and I entertained her as well as I could and her conversation was very agreeable. The women drank tea but I drank none with them. About 11 o'clock came Captain Posford and we settled the freight at £12 per ton and I engaged for 100 hogsheads. He told me that Captain Stith was better. He stayed with us at dinner and I ate fish which made me very dry. In the afternoon the Captain went away and I wrote my journal. About 4 o'clock I drank some coffee with the women and talked with them till the evening. Then I took a walk about the plantation. At night we drank a bottle of cider and talked till about 9 o'clock and then the ladies went to bed. I said my prayers and had good health, good thoughts, and good humor, thank God Almighty. I rogered my wife again.

31. I rose about 6 o'clock and read two chapters in Hebrew and some Greek in Lucian. I said my prayers and ate boiled milk for breakfast. My wife told me of the misfortunes of Mrs. Dunn—that her husband had beat her, and that she had complained to Mr. Gee of it, who made Mr. Dunn swear that he would never beat her again; that he threatened to kill her and abused her extremely and told her he would go from her. I was sorry to hear it and told my wife if he did go from her she might come here. I read some news till dinner. I ate boiled beef for dinner. In the afternoon we made a cold tincture. In the evening I took a long walk about the plantation. At night we drank a bottle of French wine. I said my prayers and had good health, good thoughts, and good humor, thank God Almighty. Mrs. Russell has good sense and very good breeding but can hardly forbear being hysterical, notwithstanding it is with good manners.

April, 1711

· · ·

7. . . . I ordered my lambs to be cut and Gilbert assisted my people. I read some English. Mrs. Russell had her fever. About 11 o'clock we went to Captain Stith's, some in the coach and some

on horseback. We were courteously entertained and found the Captain much better than he had been. The Governor's men came over with the horses to carry Mrs. Russell to Williamsburg and they brought me a letter from Mr. Clayton that told me Captain Smith in the man-of-war was come from the West Indies but no ship with him and that Colonel Harrison's vessel was taken with two others. I ate some cake before dinner and then some fowl and bacon. Mrs. Russell was much out of order and could eat nothing. About 5 o'clock we returned home and Mrs. Russell went immediately to bed. . . .

8. . . . I sent away little Peter who brought me word all was well above. Mrs. Russell continued much indisposed and began again to take the bark again [sic] which she has taken nine months without losing her ague above 14 days together. I read a sermon in Doctor Tillotson and afterwards some news till dinner. Mrs. Russell could not come to dinner. I ate boiled mutton. In the afternoon I read some English. Mrs. Russell came down about 4 o'clock and ate some broth but soon brought it up again. In the evening I took a walk about the plantation and at night we drank some cider and I ate some apple pie. We all endeavored to divert Mrs. Russell. I said a short prayer and had good health, good thoughts, and good humor, thank God Almighty.

9. . . . About 7 o'clock Mrs. Russell, after eating bread and butter and drinking some coffee, went away in the Governor's coach and six horses and my sister Custis with her. She was a little better this morning. I excused myself from waiting on her because the General Court was so near. The weather was very hot for them to travel in. I gave the Governor's servants some strong beer before they went and put some meat and wine in the coach for the ladies and their men and some corn also for the horses. . . . In the afternoon I read the news till the evening and then I took a walk about the plantation with my wife and Mrs. Dunn, and the air was very sweet and the birds very merry. I said my prayers and had good health, good thoughts, and good humor, thank God Almighty.

10. . . . Several people came to me this morning and among the rest John Randolph that told me his father was very sick and desired a bottle of sack, which I sent him. I read some news till dinner. I ate roast mutton and sallet. In the afternoon came Colonel Bassett who flattered everything and soon after him Will Randolph and Major Harrison, the last of which gentlemen told me Mrs.

Parker had desired him to take up my mortgage on her estate but he would do nothing without acquainting me first with it. I took this charity very kindly and answered him I had no view but to be paid and should be glad to have so good a paymaster as himself. They went away in the evening and my wife and I took a walk about the plantation. . . .

11. . . . I wrote a memorandum by which Will Eppes was to be bound to me. Then I settled some accounts till dinner. I ate some roast veal for dinner. In the afternoon Colonel Hardiman came with Will Eppes to bind him but that could not be done because his mother was not here. Then I weighed some money. In the evening I took a walk about the plantation. My wife walked with me, notwithstanding she was a little indisposed. . . .

12. . . . I received a letter this morning from Mr. C-s in Barbados which told me the sad news that my father Parke was shot through the head in the Leeward Islands. He told me no particulars because it was a melancholy subject. I told it my wife as gently as I could and it affected her very much but I comforted her as well as I could by telling her that his enemies killed him because he should not make their villainy appear in England. My wife could eat nothing at dinner, but I ate some boiled veal and bacon. In the afternoon I weighed some money and then came my cousin Betty Harrison and Sarah Taylor and stayed about an hour. In the evening it rained and blew hard, the wind northeast so that I could not walk. . . .

13. . . . About one o'clock Mrs. Bassett, my cousin Harrison, Betty Harrison and Sarah Taylor came to dine with us. My wife could not come out for grief. I ate roast mutton for dinner. In the afternoon came Frank Eppes and Will Kennon to visit me and in the evening Robin Mumford who persuaded the other gentlemen to stay all night. About 5 o'clock the ladies went away and with the men I took a walk about the plantation. At night we went to supper and I ate a little veal. . . .

. . .

15. . . . I had a letter from the Falls which told me another negro was like to die. God preserve her and all the rest. I ate some bacon and eggs for dinner. Presently after dinner I recommended my wife and family to God Almighty and went over the creek to my brother Duke's where I found all well and from thence to Colonel Duke's where I ate some custard for supper. It rained by the way. I said

my prayers and had good health, good thoughts, and good humor, thank God Almighty. My brother Duke came with me to Colonel Duke's.

16. I rose about 6 o'clock and read nothing because I prepared for my journey to Williamsburg. I said my prayers and ate milk and bread for breakfast. We stayed here till about 8 o'clock and then Colonel Duke and I took leave of my brother and then rode to Williamsburg where we arrived about 11 o'clock. I set myself in order and then went to court. I sent my man Tom home with a letter to my wife to comfort her for her father's death. I found the news came not only from Barbados but also from Jamaica and Bermudas by which it appeared that he was murdered after a most barbarous manner. The court rose about 2 o'clock. We stayed at the coffeehouse till 4 o'clock and then went and dined with the Governor. I ate fowl and bacon for dinner. Mrs. Russell was very inquisitive after the health of my family but was not well herself. . . .

17. . . . I had several gentlemen come to see me and among the rest Mr. Le Fevre a Frenchman of great learning. Colonel Ludwell came also to learn to be auditor. About 10 o'clock I went to court. While I was there I received a letter from my brother Custis which told me he was not well. We rose about one o'clock and then walked to the Governor's house where we stayed till 4 and then I went with Colonel Ludwell and dined with the Commissary where I ate roast beef for dinner. Mrs. Ludwell was there and very courteous to me. I stayed there till 6 o'clock and then took my leave, notwithstanding they asked me to stay there, but I went home where I wrote till about 9 o'clock and settled some accounts. . . .

18. . . . About 9 o'clock I went to wait on the Governor and saw Mrs. Russell who had her ague again. About 10 we went to court where we sat till about 3 o'clock and nothing remarkable happened and I went with some of my brothers to dine with the Governor. I ate some fowl and bacon. About 5 o'clock we went away and took a walk to the new house and from thence went to the coffeehouse. There came several of the [courteous] young men and we went to gaming and I won five pounds. We played till about 10 o'clock and then I went to my lodgings where I settled some accounts. . . .

19. . . . I settled some accounts and about 10 o'clock went to court where nothing remarkable happened but that Mr. S-l-n was prose-

cuted for beating of George Walker. We had no criminals this court. The court rose about 4 o'clock and some of us went to dinner at Mrs. G-r-t's where we had good victuals and no drink. After dinner Colonel Smith and I took a walk and overtook the Governor and walked with him to the Governor's new house. We walked with him till it was dark and then took our leave and went to the coffeehouse. I stayed here about half an hour and then went home to my lodgings. . . .

20. . . . I wrote a letter to my wife in the morning and another in the afternoon. About 9 o'clock I went into court where we sat till past 5 dispensing justice. My case against Joe Wilkinson was called but not tried this day. I went to dine with the Governor and ate roast mutton for dinner. While I was there the Doctor returned from his journey and told me all were well at Westover and that Colonel Randolph was extremely sick and in great danger. At night I walked to the coffeehouse and drank two dishes of tea. Then I returned to my lodgings. . . .

21. I rose at 6 o'clock and read nothing because my head was full of my case. I said my prayers and recommended my case to God to direct it according to equity and justice. I ate boiled milk for breakfast. Several gentlemen came to see me and Colonel Beverley among the rest. I received an account from England that two ships were lost in which I lost 60 hogsheads of tobacco. God's will be done. About 9 o'clock I went to court and my case against Joe Wilkinson came on and the jury found for me and 3000 pounds of tobacco damages and John Bolling offered to pay it. About 2 o'clock I went out of court and did some business and then returned again and we sat till about 5 o'clock. Then I went to dine at the Governor's and ate tripe for dinner. Colonel Randolph died this evening about 5 o'clock. I went early to my lodgings and did some business with Colonel Robinson. . . .

22. . . . Robin Beverley came to see me this morning and told me his son Billy was come in and had a quartan ague, that he was pretty well improved in his learning but seemed to have bad health. About 11 o'clock Mr. Clayton and Mr. D-r-k came to see me in order to go with me to church. The first of these gentlemen asked me if it was worth my while to be escheator in the place of Colonel Randolph. I thanked him and considered of it. Then we walked to church and heard Mr. Anderson preach. After church I borrowed a horse of Mr. Clayton and rode to Queen's Creek where I found

144

all pretty well and at dinner. I ate some roast beef for dinner. I stayed there with them till almost sunset and then returned to Willaimsburg where I made a visit to Mrs. Bland to console the death of her father. I stayed there all the evening and then went to my lodgings. . . .

23. . . . About 9 o'clock I went to wait on the Governor and asked him for the escheator's place. He would not promise me but gave me great hope by the compliments he was pleased to make me. I also begged leave of him to go to England to manage Colonel Parke's affairs. He was pleased to tell me he would always be ready to grant me that and likewise to make any man my deputy that I pleased. John Bolling desired my interest with the Governor for the escheator's place but I told him honestly that I had asked for it myself. Then we went to court where we sat till 5 o'clock and then all the council went to dine with the Governor because it was Saint George's day. I ate boiled beef. We were very merry in the evening in drinking the healths and in making the Commissary drink them by the help of Colonel Harrison that sat next him. About 9 o'clock we took leave and some of us went to Colonel Bray's where some company was dancing. I stayed there about an hour and then went home. . . .

24. . . . About 9 o'clock I went to Council where I procured a patent for the gold mines for Colonel Hill. Then I went to my office above stairs and settled some accounts. About one o'clock the court sat and a new trial was ordered in Branch his case concerning his land near Falling Creek. Mr. Holloway was very sullen against me. The court rose about 5 o'clock and I went to dine with the Governor. I ate roast beef for dinner. At night we diverted ourselves with some Indians. . . .

25. . . . About 9 o'clock I went to Council where the Governor heard several disputes about entering for land. About noon we went to court and sat till about 4 o'clock and then the governors of the College met and chose five new members and the Governor was chosen Rector but he was displeased that we did not turn Mr. Blackamore out of the school and Mr. Le Fevre in. He also showed abundance of disorder because we did not choose Dr. Cocke one of the College but we excused ourselves because he was not an inhabitant. We chose Mr. Le Fevre professor of philosophy and mathematics with a salary of £80 a year. Colonel Smith and I dined at Marot's and I ate roast beef. . . .

26. . . . Abundance of company came to see me about business so that I could not go to court till 10 o'clock. I did not stay there long but went off the bench again about my accounts. The court sat till about 5 o'clock and I went to Mrs. G-r-t's to dinner and ate boiled beef. I paid for all the days I had been absent, three bits for every day. Then Colonel Smith and I took a walk to take the air. In the evening I went home to my lodgings and did a great deal of business and settled abundance of accounts but could read nothing. . . .

27. I rose about 6 o'clock and read nothing because I had my public accounts to write. I said a short prayer and ate boiled milk for breakfast. Several people came to me; however I used no ceremony but wrote on till I had finished my business and then I went to court where I just saved my day, because the court was just on rising. Then we went to Council and Colonel Ludwell examined my account and found an error in it which cost me some trouble to rectify. About 6 o'clock the Council rose and I went to dinner with the Governor where I ate boiled beef. It rained a little in the evening. At night I went to the coffeehouse where I stayed about an hour and then went to my lodgings where I settled some accounts. I neglected to say my prayers for which reason I was guilty of uncleanness. I had good health, good thoughts, and good humor, thank God Almighty.

28. I rose about 6 and read nothing because we were to go by 7 o'clock to Council. This made me neglect to say my prayers though not to eat boiled milk for breakfast. They passed my quitrent accounts in Council and got the warrants signed. I settled the Governor's account and adjusted several other matters and took leave of several of the members of the council. Mr. Commissary got £5 as ordinary by his [teaching] us. I dined with the Governor and ate salt fish for dinner. In the afternoon my man came with my horse and brought me word all was well at home, thank God. I took leave of the Governor and Mrs. Russell and then took a walk and afterwards went to the coffeehouse where I took leave of more of my friends and then went to my lodgings where I settled some accounts. I said my prayers and had good health, good thoughts, and good humor, thank God Almighty. I gave the Governor's men 5 shillings apiece.

29. . . . I settled all my affairs and then went to Mr. Bland's to take my leave, which I did about 9 o'clock. Then I rode to my sister Custis' and found them pretty well, only my sister was

melancholy. I comforted her as well as I could and then took a walk with my sister and brother in the orchard. About one o'clock Dr. Cocke came from Williamsburg and soon after we went to dinner and I ate boiled beef. In the afternoon we sat and talked till 3 o'clock and then I took my leave and went to Green Spring, and the Doctor returned home. I found a great deal of company with Colonel Ludwell who went away in the evening and we took a walk and romped with the girls at night. I ate some partridge and about 10 went to bed. I said a short prayer and had good health, good thoughts, and good humor, thank God Almighty. I had wicked inclinations to Mistress Sarah Taylor.

30. . . . I took my leave about 6 o'clock and found it very cold. I met with nothing extraordinary in my journey and got home about 11 o'clock and found all well, only my wife was melancholy. We took a walk in the garden and pasture. We discovered that by the contrivance of Nurse and Anaka Prue got in at the cellar window and stole some strong beer and cider and wine. I turned Nurse away upon it and punished Anaka. I ate some fish for dinner. In the afternoon I caused Jack and John to be whipped for drinking at John [Cross] all last Sunday. In the evening I took a walk about the plantation and found things in good order. . . . The weather was very cold for the season. I gave my wife a powerful flourish and gave her great ecstasy and refreshment.

May, 1711

1. I rose about 8 o'clock because the child had disturbed me in the night and read a chapter in Hebrew and some Greek in Lucian. I said my prayers and ate boiled milk for breakfast. I wrote to Mr. Randolph to have some copies of his county records and sent G-r-l with the letter. I caused Bannister to draw off a hogshead of cider which was very good. . . . I forgave Anaka, on my wife's and sister's persuasion, but I caused Prue to be whipped severely and she told many things of John Grills for which he was to blame, particularly that he lost the key of the wine cellar and got in at the window and opened the door and then because he had not the key the door was left open and anybody went in and stole the beer and wine &c. In the evening I took a walk with my wife and sister. . . . I received a letter with some records from Will Randolph. I gave my wife a short flourish.

. . .

3. . . . I read some law and searched for precedents. In the evening my wife and I took a walk about the plantation and when we returned we found Captain Posford's boat come with my things from Williamsburg. By that came some letters from England which told me the Duke of Argyle was made General in Spain. . . .

4. . . . Nurse sent for her things which were delivered. I settled some accounts. My sick people were better, thank God Almighty. My sister Duke and Colonel Eppes came and stayed to dinner. I ate pork and peas for dinner. In the afternoon my sister went home and the Colonel went away and then I went and read some law till evening. Then I took a walk about the plantation to see how everything was but my wife stayed at home and was melancholy. At night I read more law. I said my prayers and had good health, good thoughts, and good humor, thank God Almighty. I gave my wife a flourish.

5. . . . In the afternoon I took a walk to see what John was doing and then returned home and read more law till the evening, when my wife was well enough to walk with me about the plantation. Just as it was dark came Mr. Clayton from Williamsburg and brought no news only that Mrs. Russell was going to Pennsylvania for her recovery which some think is to lay a great belly there but this is a malicious idea. At night we ate bread and butter and drank some wine till about 10 o'clock. I neglected to say my prayers because of company but I had good health, good thoughts, and good humor, thank God Almighty for it. Captain Posford was here this afternoon and told me our nurse was drunk aboard his ship and the smith lay with her.

6. . . . Mr. Clayton and I went into the library to consult some law books concerning my case with John Giles. We stayed there till dinner. I ate tongue for dinner. In the afternoon Mr. Clayton and I walked to Mrs. Harrison's who looked a little grave but afterwards she cleared up and was in good humor. She gave us some strawberries and milk. In the evening we returned home. My sick people were better. At night we drank a bottle of wine and my wife with us. . . .

7. . . . It rained this morning, which hindered me from going to the court above to hear my case but Mr. Clayton went, however, in the rain. They could not unload the sloop because of the rain. I settled some accounts till dinner. I ate broiled mutton. In the

afternoon I settled more accounts and then took a walk to the brick house to see them [manage] tobacco and I found P-t-s-n smoking there for which I drubbed him very much. In the evening it held up a little and we got 40 hogsheads ashore. My wife and I walked in the garden. At night I read some English and then my wife and I ate some roast mutton with great pleasure. . . .

8. . . . About 9 o'clock came Captain Posford and Mr. Rogers and the last [offered] his service as a lawyer and I promised to employ him in Henrico. He then desired to know whether I would take Spanish money for Mrs. Parker's debt. I told him I would. They went away soon. About 12 came Mr. Clayton and let me know the court above had done me all the injustice they could in my case. I ate pigeon and bacon for dinner. In the afternoon Mr. Clayton went to Mrs. Harrison's and I took a walk about the plantation. In the evening I could not walk for fear of rain and so I read in the *Tatler*. At night came Mr. Mumford and Mr. Clayton returned from Mrs. Harrison's. We drank a bottle of claret. . . .

9. . . . My wife and daughter were both indisposed, the first with breeding, and the last with a fever. . . .

10. . . . My daughter was a little better, thank God, but my wife was indisposed by fits as women are in her condition. I went into the garden and ate some cherries. . . . I read some Greek in the new edition of Homer. In the evening I took a walk and ate some cherries at M-n-s. The season has happened so late this year that cherries are three weeks more backward than they used to be. . . .

11. . . . I sent Tom with some cherries and green peas to the Governor at Williamsburg. I dreamt last night that I received letters from England with a paper of funeral biscuits, by which I expect letters from thence to tell me of the death of Colonel Parke very soon. I settled several accounts and then went and ate some cherries. Dr. Cocke came just before dinner and so did Colonel Hill and Mr. Anderson. They brought no news but that Mrs. Russell was gone to Pennsylvania for her health in order to leave her distemper there and put it out to nurse. I ate fish for dinner. In the afternoon we diverted ourselves till about 6 o'clock and then Colonel Hill and Mr. Anderson went home, notwithstanding I invited them to stay. In the evening we took a walk about the plantation and then at night drank a bottle of wine and were very merry till about 10 o'clock. . . .

. . .

17. . . . About 11 o'clock came Mr. [Gee] to endeavor to get me to be his security for being sheriff but I put him off as courteously as I could. About one o'clock came Mr. Burwell and his wife, Mistress Judy Wormeley, Mrs. Harrison and her daughter to dine. I ate salt fish. In the afternoon it rained very hard so that my people could not proceed to put up the gates. However we were as merry as we could. In the evening Mrs. Harrison and her daughter went away in the coach and the rest of the company stayed. . . .

. . .

20. . . . I ate some green peas for dinner and was out of humor because the butter was melted oil and scolded at Moll for it. After dinner I took a walk about the plantation to see how everything stood. Then I ate some cherries. My wife was much out of order. I read some English in the *Tatler* and then my wife and I took a walk about the plantation. She was much out of humor with her indisposition, as she generally is. . . .

21. . . . I ate some beans and bacon for dinner. In the afternoon Mr. Mumford and I played at billiards and I won a bit. Then we went and got some cherries but we found to our great surprise that the wild pigeons had eaten all the black-hearts. Then we took a walk about the plantation and particularly saw the colt. It was very hot this afternoon. . . .

22. . . . Mr. Mumford cut my young horse and then he and I went and shot wild pigeons with bows and arrows and then wrote some verses to try if I could translate Homer with any success. A little before dinner came Mrs. Dunn and told us her husband wished to go to Stafford to live. I ate green peas for dinner. In the afternoon Tom returned and brought me a kind letter from the Governor but no news. Mr. Mumford and I played at billards and he won a bit and then went away. I read some English in the *Tatler* and then went with my wife and Mrs. Dunn to walk about the plantation. At night we drank some syllabub. . . .

23. . . . The salt came this morning, about 400 barrels which I ordered to be taken ashore. It was very hot. I began this day to make my will, which I never had done before in my life. I ate bacon and pigeon for dinner. We consulted by what means to persuade Mr. Dunn not to go away to Stafford County to live and agreed the best way would be to persuade him to go to England. About 3 o'clock Mrs. Dunn went home. It thundered and threatened rain but it did not rain. In the evening the master of the salt

ship came and he agreed next week to send up 100 barrels of salt to my store at Appomattox. I walked with him in the garden and said my prayers. . . .

24. . . . My sheep began this day to be sheared. It threatened rain this morning and about 11 o'clock rained so that we were forced to leave shearing. I wrote more of my will. My sloop came from Falling Creek with planks and other shipping. I ate some beans and bacon for dinner. In the afternoon Captain Posford called here and told me Mr. Blair was at next house. About 3 o'clock there came a terrible gust of wind and rain that blew up several trees by the roots and tore many more and threw down my fence. However it did no mischief to the house nor to my sloop but it was soon over, thank God. In the evening I took a walk about the plantation to see what damage I had sustained. In the evening I read some English in the *Tatler* till it was time to go to bed. . . .

25. . . . About 10 o'clock Mr. Blair, his wife, and Mrs. Harrison called here and at the same time came Mr. Cairon, the minister sent for Manakin Town. He gave me two letters from the Bishop of London and one from the Leeward Islands containing a copy of my father Parke's will, in which, I thank him, he gave me nothing but gave his estate in this country to my sister Custis and his estate in the Island to the daughter of Mrs. Chester. We gave the company some cherries, coffee, and wine, but [they] did not stay above an hour and then went away to Colonel Hill's but the French minister, who stayed to dinner. . . . About 4 o'clock Mr. Bland came on his way to Jordans but had no news only that a rich ship from Carolina was taken by the Cape. In the evening I caused him to be set over the river and then took a walk about the plantation. . . .

26. . . . My wife continues very sick and peevish in her breeding and uses but little exercise. The wind was east and pretty cold. At night I read in the *Tatler*. . . .

27. . . . About 11 o'clock we went in the coach to church and heard a good sermon of Mr. Anderson. Then we received the Sacrament and there were more communicants than ever I saw here. We invited nobody to dinner. I ate roast pigeon and asparagus. In the afternoon came my cousin Betty Harrison by whom I sent a letter to Colonel Bassett because she was to go there tomorrow. Then I ate some cherries with her but she would drink nothing. . . .

151

28. . . . About 7 o'clock I had got everything ready and rode on M-r-s-l to Colonel Randolph's to visit the poor widow who desired my good offices with Mr. Perry in her behalf, which I promised. Here I met Mr. Anderson, Mr. Finney, and Mr. Brodie who were going to the Manakin Town and they persuaded me to go there with them. Here we ate some roast shoat. Then we took leave and rode to Falling Creek, where I found all well, but heard that S-r-y a negro woman was dead at Burkland. God's will be done. On the way I saw Mr. Laforce and demanded the debt of him but he gave me no satisfaction and I threatened to sue him. The three parsons stayed with me at Falling Creek till 6 o'clock and then they went to Mr. Tullitt's and I stayed here and ate for supper some chicken pie. I talked with Mr. Grills about my business and then said a short prayer and had good health, good thoughts, and indifferent good humor, thank God Almighty.

29. I rose about 6 o'clock and read a little in Homer. I said my prayers and ate boiled milk for breakfast. Then I walked to the mill where I took horse and rode to Mr. Tullitt's to call for my company. Here I saw abundance of work done and many conveniences made. The company went to breakfast but I could eat nothing with them and therefore walked in the garden. About 10 o'clock we mounted and proceeded to the Manakin Town but they rode very slowly. Mr. Finney and I went to Mr. Salle's and ate some eggs, and then went to Mr. Phillipe's and from thence to the coalpit where we found all well and George told me they had pressed through the rock and found very good coal. We stayed here about half an hour and then returned, the parsons to Mr. Phillipe's and I to Mr. Salle's. But they came to me in about an hour. Mr. Anderson and Mr. Finney stayed to supper with us but Mr. Brodie went over the river with Tom Randolph and fell out of the boat and hurt himself. We had some French cookery for supper. Mr. Finney went over the river but Mr. Anderson stayed and lay with me, no very clean bedfellow. . . .

30. I rose at 6 o'clock and Mr. Finney came to us and told us of the misfortune of Mr. Brodie. Mr. Anderson went to him to let him blood and returned in an hour and told me he could not ride with us. There was a very good breakfast but I ate nothing but milk. About 8 o'clock we took our leave and rode very slowly to Falling Creek. Mr. Anderson's horse was very poor. While of the expedition among the French, I recommended peace and union to them and conjured them to be courteous to Mr. Phillipe notwith-

standing he was removed, which Mr. Salle promised me they would. We got to Falling Creek about 12 o'clock, where I made a bargain for some good land. Captain Webb came there and about one we went to dinner and I ate some chicken pie. About 2 o'clock we rode away and came to the Hundred about 5 o'clock. I stayed at Colonel Hill's and ate some milk and raspberries and then took my leave and got home just as it was dark, and found all well only they told me old P-r-s-n was dead. . . .

31. . . . My wife was indisposed and had been ever since I went from home. Tom was sick and I gave him a purge which worked very well. I believe his sickness proceeded from my threatening to whip him for not taking care of the horses. It was exceedingly hot today. I ate salt fish for dinner but had no great stomach because I breakfasted too late. In the afternoon I wrote some of my will till the evening. I sent Captain Posford some cherries and some beans. In the evening I ate some cherries and then took a walk about the plantation, and my wife was with me very sick. At night I read some English in the *Tatler*. . . .

June, 1711

1. . . . My wife was a little better this day. I wrote a letter to the Governor to give him an account of my expedition to Manakin Town. . . . Mrs. Dunn came about 6 o'clock and told us that the Governor would not recommend her husband to the parish in Stafford. We had a syllabub. . . .

. . .

3. . . . I received a complaint that one of my steers had broken in again to Mrs. Harrison's cornfield. I had put a yoke on his neck and put him into the great pasture but he jumped out notwithstanding, on which I resolved to kill him rather than keep anything injurious to my neighbor. I ate a broiled pigeon for dinner. . . .

4. . . . I wrote two letters which I sent by Bannister to [Henrico Court]. I threatened Will Wilkins for stealing the apples and denying it when he had done, but I forgave him. It was extremely hot. I practiced some arithmetic till dinner. I ate some dry beef but had no stomach to eat. In the afternoon I began to write my will fair and about half did it. In the evening I took a walk with my wife who had been pretty well all day. At night I caused the

steer to be killed that had broken into my cousin Harrison's cornfield and sent her part of it to make her amends. . . .

. . .

6. . . . In the evening Will Randolph came and the French parson who told me that Captain Smith on his way from New York had taken a privateer of 90 men. We had a gust in the evening but little rain. Mrs. Harrison and Mrs. Eppes called here. At night the French parson and his three sons went on board their boat to go up the river. . . .

7. . . . It was so hot I could not dance. The French parson and his three sons could not go last night and so came and ate some raspberries and milk here and when they went away I gave them some roast beef and bread. About 11 o'clock came Colonel Eppes. I got him to be a witness to my will. There came a man for my advice about a boy that had received a kick from a horse, which I gave him as well as I could. . . .

8. . . . I received news that one of my mares was killed by a snake or spider for she was swelled much. I had also an account of one of my negro's death above by Will Bass who came over to account with me. . . . I took a walk about the plantation and ordered the colt that had lost his mother to be brought home and fed with milk. I drank some syllabub at night and then said my prayers and had good health, good thoughts, and good humor, thank God Almighty. My sloop came this evening from Appomattox with tobacco.

9. . . . About 10 o'clock came Captain Jones to visit me and I showed him my library with which he was pleased. About 11 o'clock Mrs. [Hancock] came with a negro boy that she had in care [or cure] and I gave her five pounds for his care. . . .

10. . . . It was so hot I could not go to church. Mr. Anderson came and brought me my watch which he had injured by breaking one of the wheels. He drank some cider and went away to church and about 12 Mr. Grills went away also. I ate some boiled pork for dinner and was angry with Moll for neglecting to boil some artichokes for dinner. I wrote a letter in answer to Mr. [Gee's] in which he had asked my advice. . . .

11. . . . I prepared for my journey to Williamsburg. I ate some roast pigeon for dinner. In the afternoon I got everything ready

154

and then took a nap for about an hour and then washed and dressed me and about 5 o'clock was set over the creek and proceeded on my journey. I got to the ferry about 9 o'clock and there drank some milk. I got to Williamsburg about 11 o'clock and after saying my prayers lay on the bed without sheets and slept very well. . . .

12. I rose about 6 o'clock and read 100 verses in Homer and then got ready to shave me. I ate boiled milk for breakfast. Mr. Bland and Mr. Clayton came to see me. About 9 o'clock and past Colonel Duke and I went to wait on the Governor, who received us very kindly. I drank some cider and after staying about an hour we went to court where two men were [tried] for felony and both found guilty. I saw the French prisoners [that] were taken in the privateer by Captain Smith to the number of 88. They made but a poor figure. About 4 o'clock the court rose and I and Mr. Holloway settled our difference. I showed Mr. Clayton my father Parke's will but he could find no error in it. About 5 o'clock I went with four others of the Council to dine with the Governor. I ate boiled mutton for dinner. About 8 o'clock all the company went away except myself and I stayed till 12 with the Governor and we drank about two bottles of French claret but the Doctor was very dull all the time. Then I went to my lodgings. . . .

13. I rose about 6 o'clock and read nothing because of going to court early. However I ate my milk first and then went to the coffeehouse and got my papers together and went to court where one of the prisoners was burnt in the hand and the other ordered to the whip. Then we went to council where several things were debated and particularly the affairs of Carolina which are in great confusion. Kit Robinson was made naval officer in the room of Colonel Corbin. The Court of Admiralty of [c-p] to [try] the privateer and she was made prize. Then we had a meeting of the directors of the town and agreed to build a market place to which we all contributed. About 4 o'clock we went to dine with the Governor and I ate boiled veal for dinner. I stayed about an hour after dinner and then took my leave and went to my lodgings to prepare to go home with Colonel Ludwell. I went and took leave of Mrs. Bland and then we rode to Green Spring where I found all well. We sat and talked till about 10 o'clock and I took leave because I was to go in the morning early. . . .

14. I rose at 4 o'clock and came away without seeing anybody, notwithstanding it rained. I said my prayers on the road. When I

was got about 12 miles it began to rain and I put in at W-l-k [Wilkes' ?] and drank some milk and when I came away I promised him a pair of wool [cards] if he would fetch them. I stayed there about an hour and then took horse and had good riding half a mile before it rained again very hard. However, I rode through it and got home about 10 o'clock, where I found all well, thank God, but I was wet with the rain. I shaved myself and drank a glass of wine. I ate some pigeon for dinner and Mrs. Dunn dined with us, whom I found here. In the afternoon came Captain Posford came [sic] and told me he had done caulking and tarring my sloop, for which I thanked him as I did for some oatmeal he brought. He stayed about an hour. My wife hid this afternoon, and so did Mrs. Dunn. . . .

15. . . . It was very hot today but my wife was well. I wrote some letters to Williamsburg and settled some accounts. We began to weave and blue pieces went into the loom by Mrs. Dunn's direction. I ate some roast mutton for dinner. In the afternoon I settled some other accounts and then ciphered and read some French till the evening. Then I took a walk about the plantation and then swam in the river to wash and refresh myself. At night I drank some syllabub with Mrs. Dunn but my wife was out of humor and would drink none. . . .

16. . . . About 9 o'clock came [Wilkes ?] for his wool [cards] that I promised him and also Mr. Mumford to tell me all was well at Appomattox. He hindered me from reading but I wrote a letter to the Governor. Then Mr. Mumford and I played at billiards till dinner. I ate some boiled fish and roast mutton. In the afternoon we played at billiards again and I lost two bits. We ate some cherries and drank some cider. In the evening both Mr. Mumford and Mrs. Dunn returned home and I went to walk about the plantation. I quarrelled with John for letting some bitches run about. . . .

17. . . . It was exceedingly hot and my wife was indisposed in the morning. I gave John Grills leave to go and see his mother married. I wrote a letter to England about my father Parke's will and desired Mr. Perry to give me [credit] for the £1000 which my father Parke ordered him to pay me. I ate roast mutton for dinner. In the afternoon I gave my wife a flourish and then refreshed myself with a nap. Then I wrote a letter to Mrs. Custis and another to Captain Posford to desire him to deliver my letters at Williams-

burg, and his seaman came for them. I read some French till the evening, and then took a walk about the plantation with my wife. Then we returned and ate some milk. Just as we went to bed it began to rain exceedingly and thundered. . . .

18. . . . John Grills returned about 9 o'clock and told us that Colonel Hardiman's son had the smallpox on board Colonel Harrison's vessel that is come from Barbados and that nobody would go near him. . . .

19. . . . Will Kennon was married this day to Colonel Frank Eppes his daughter.

. . .

23. . . . My wife was indisposed and was threatened with miscarriage. I again persuaded to bleed but she could not be persuaded to it. It rained again and I believe it was the rain that disposed my wife to that infirmity at this time. . . . I repeated my petition to my wife to be bled and at night she did try but could not suffer it. I drank some syllabub and gave my daughter some with me. I said my prayers and had good health, good thoughts, and good humor, thank God Almighty. I had a small quarrel with my wife because she would not be bled but neither good words nor bad could prevail against her fear which is very uncontrollable.

24. . . . My wife was a little better, thank God, and gave me hope she would avoid miscarriage. Mr. Anderson came before church to see if he could do any service to my wife but I thanked him and told him she was better. I went with him to church, where I saw Peter Hamlin, who had no letters from Barbados for me. People were afraid of him because one of his people had the smallpox. Mr. Anderson gave us a good sermon against speaking ill of our neighbors. There was no news. I brought Captain Posford and Captain L-th-m home with me and found Mrs. Dunn there and my wife worse than she was. I ate some pigeon and bacon for dinner. In the afternoon we endeavored to persuade my wife to bleed but she would not . . . .

25. . . . My wife grew worse and after much trial and persuasion was let blood when it was too late. Captain Stith came about some [n-l] he said he lent my father 20 years ago. Mr. Rogers came also about Mrs. Parker's business. My wife grew very ill which made [me] weep for her. I ate roast mutton for dinner. In the afternoon my wife grew worse and voided a prodigious quantity

of blood. I settled some accounts till the evening and then took a walk about the plantation. Before I returned my wife sent for me because she was very weak and soon after I came she was delivered of a false conception and then grew better. I sent for Mrs. Hamlin who came presently. I said my prayers and had good health, good thoughts, and good humor, thank God Almighty.

26. . . . Mrs. Dunn went home and so did Mrs. Hamlin. I received a letter from the attorney general to send his accounts, which I did and wrote a letter to Mr. Bland by him. My wife was extremely mended and very cheerful, thank God. I settled some accounts till dinner. I ate some boiled mutton for dinner. In the afternoon I took a nap by my wife and then went and read some French. I lent my wife some pictures to divert her. Then I went and showed my people how to manage some hay they had mowed out of the swamp. . . .

27. . . . I settled several accounts and wrote three bills of lading. I wrote by my wife that she might not tire herself with reading. . . . When my wife heard that Peter Hamlin had the smallpox she said that she should have them likewise because his mother had been here two nights ago and she had laid on her sheets.

28. . . . My wife had the headache severely this morning and had a small fever. I wrote a letter to Mr. Randolph and sent Bannister with it. It rained a little this morning. My wife grew worse of her fever and her pain in the head. I comforted her as well as I could. . . . I sent for Mrs. Dunn and would fain have sent for the doctor but my wife would not let me because she said she should be better in the evening and I think her fever did abate a little. Then I took a walk about the plantation. I said my prayers and had good thoughts, good health, and good humor, thank God Almighty. Mrs. Dunn could not come today but would tomorrow morning. I gave my wife some Venice treacle.

29. I rose at 4 o'clock and sent away Grills for Dr. Cocke and Tom for Mr. Anderson for my wife was very bad. She could not sleep this night, which made her headache continue and also her fever. She vomited up her Venice treacle. I read a chapter in Hebrew. I said my prayers and ate some milk for breakfast. About 10 o'clock Mr. Anderson came and advised us to put spirits of [salt] into her drink to stop her vomiting, which it did. My wife grew a little better and got a little sleep. Mr. Rogers came and

paid me £166 for Mrs. Parker. I let Mrs. Harrison know my wife was very ill and she came. I ate some dry beef for dinner. In the afternoon my wife grew much better and her fever abated. In the evening the company went away. George Smith came from Manakin Town and told me all was well at the coalpit and Falling Creek. I took a little walk. Just as it grew dark Doctor Cocke came and found my wife pretty well but he brought no news. Mrs. Dunn came a little before him and I ate some dry beef with them for supper. . . .

30. I rose at 5 o'clock and settled accounts with George Smith and wrote a letter to Falling Creek but could read nothing. I neglected to say my prayers but had milk tea and bread and butter for breakfast with the Doctor. I wrote a letter to England. My wife slept very well and was much better this morning. The Doctor ordered her nothing but a bitter drink made of camomile flowers and ginseng root, which she was to drink morning and evening. My sloop came from Falling Creek and I ordered to unload her. John W-l-s came and told me that the negro I had put to apprentice to him was lame and desired I would order him to be cured. I told him it was his business to take care of that, who had the service of his labor. I ate some roast lamb for dinner. In the afternoon we diverted my wife and were very merry till the evening and then Mrs. Dunn returned home and the Doctor and I went into the river and afterwards drank some syllabub. My wife was better and better, thank God. I said a short prayer and had good health, good thoughts, and good humor, thank God Almighty. Mr. Bland came here without any news from Williamsburg.

July, 1711

1. . . . In the afternoon I gave the Doctor four pieces of gold for his trouble in taking care of my wife, but I gave it him and desired him to give my service to Suky and give her the money. About 3 o'clock he went away. . . .

2. . . . About 9 o'clock there came an express with a letter from the Governor with one from Colonel Hunter, governor of New York, by which I learned there was an expedition on hand which I judged to be against Canada and that all the money in my hands was to be sent there. My wife was indisposed a little and very much out of humor. Mr. Anderson and several other gentlemen of

the vestry came down just before dinner. I asked them to dine with me, which they did. I ate veal for dinner, but gave my wife none, which bred a mortal quarrel when the company was gone. I endeavored to reconcile myself to her and to persuade her to eat but she plagued me a great while before she would. . . .

3. I rose about 5 o'clock and wrote a letter to the Governor and to Dr. Cocke and then sent away the express. . . .

4. I rose about 5 o'clock but read nothing because I prepared to go to Williamsburg, notwithstanding I was indisposed. I ate some milk for breakfast and said my prayers. It was a coolish morning so that I thought it would be a cool day. About 11 o'clock I went over the creek and so rode to Williamsburg, having commended my family to God Almighty. It proved a hot day and I was very much affected with my journey. When I came to the ferry I was faint and drank some milk and water, which was wrong. Then I rode to Colonel Ludwell's, where I drank abundance of water. Here I stayed about two hours and then proceeded to Williamsburg where I arrived in the evening. I drank some cider with Mr. Bland and then went to the Governor's where I found him just returned from Kiquotan where he had been concerning matters about the marines that were to go on the expedition to Carolina. The Governor told me he should buy 1000 barrels of pork for Colonel Hunter. Here I drank some syllabub and then went to my lodgings and went to bed and was taken with an ague which was succeeded with a fever which went away in a sweat towards morning. I slept very little. I said a short prayer to God and had very good thoughts, good humor, but bad health, but God's will be done.

5. I rose about 8 o'clock and found myself indisposed. However I did some business. I said a short prayer and ate some water gruel for breakfast. My man Tom had a headache and a little fever. I ordered him to be let blood. About 11 o'clock I went in the President's coach to the Governor's but before I went the Doctor came to see me. I drank some tea at the Governor's and was much out of order. However I went with the rest to Council where I could not hold up my head. It was agreed in Council that the revenue of two shillings per hogshead ought not to be applied to the supply of New York, but only quitrents. It was also agreed that it was necessary to endeavor to stop the seditious proceedings in Carolina and send some forces there and the Governor was pleased to say he would go in person. About 3 o'clock we went to the

Governor's to dinner and I went among the rest but could eat nothing but water gruel. I found myself a little better and then took leave of the Governor and went to my lodgings where I said my prayers and then went to bed. My man was grown very ill. God's will be done. I had a bad night of it and could not sleep well, notwithstanding I had an intermission of the fits. Poor Peter Hamlin died of the smallpox, for want of attention.

6. I rose about 8 o'clock and found myself pretty well but I learned my man continued bad. I said a short prayer and ate water gruel for breakfast. Several persons came to see me and I settled several accounts. The captain of the French privateer came to see me and lamented the necessity of his going to old France. About 11 o'clock my ague came with more violence. The Doctor was gone to York and I resolved to go, sick as I was, to Colonel Ludwell's in order to go home the next day in Captain Posford's boat. I asked the President to lend me his coach, but he made several excuses and therefore I sent to beg that favor of the Governor, who readily granted it, and about 5 o'clock came in his coach and offered me everything he had. I was very ill; however I went away a little after 5 o'clock and before 7 got to Colonel Ludwell's where they took great care of me, but I went to bed as soon as I could and had a fever all night and could not sleep till morning. God's will be done.

7. I rose about 9 o'clock and was pretty well, thank God, and without much ceremony took my leave and went in the Governor's coach to the water-side where I went into Captain Posford's boat. I gave the Governor's man 10 shillings and in about five hours I came very easily home where I found all well, thank God. I was pretty well the rest of the day but ate nothing but water gruel and drank some apple drink and sugar tea. I ordered Captain Posford's men to be well treated for their care of me. Before I came from Williamsburg I had given the best orders I could about my man Tom and desired Mr. Bland to get an old woman to attend him and had sent Bannister home before me with my horse to prevent my wife going to Williamsburg to take care of me, which would not have been fit for her in her weak condition. I had also made the Governor the compliment that if I had been well I would have waited on him to Carolina. I said a short prayer and went to bed where I slept very indifferently, God's will be done. I took some snakeroot stewed in wine and water to make me sweat. However I sweated but little.

8. I rose about 8 o'clock and was pretty well and ate some water gruel. I said a short prayer and sat up till 1 o'clock and then came my ague violently and Colonel Hill and Mr. Anderson came from church and found me very ill. I went to bed and had a very severe fit. I took more snakeroot and sweated very much with it, but it made my hot fit the worse and last the longer. I was not very dry nor did my head ache at all, or my back. I drank sage tea and some apple drink. At night came Dr. Cocke out of pure friendship and not as a doctor. He gave me some comfort but said little to me that night because he would not disturb me. Only he did not approve of the sweats that I took. I sweated all night and could not sleep but in the morning the fever went off and left me very weak.

9. This day I was so weak I could not rise but I was without a fever, but the Doctor would not give me the bark because there would not be time before next fit to take quantity enough to prevent the next fit and if it did not prevent it, it would make it worse. I could eat nothing and took little or nothing but sage tea. The Doctor told me he would stay with me till I was safe, notwithstanding he neglected a great deal of other business. Several came to see me but the Doctor would let nobody to me because when people are weak company do them mischief. The Doctor assured me I should have but one fit more which pleased me much in my weak condition. Everybody was concerned for my sickness and my people attended me very well and particularly Mrs. Dunn. The Doctor comforted my wife so that she was very easy, thank God Almighty. I slept very little all night, nor could I command my thoughts enough to pray but I addressed myself to heaven to be restored.

10. I was a little easy this morning but had nothing but sage tea. The weather was [. . .] but I was very hot notwithstanding. I had a good intermission, thank God, but I lived in fear of the next fit, which came about 11 o'clock with terrible violence. My cold fit lasted four hours and the hot fit [. . .]. It was much the most violent I ever had in my life. The Doctor said he had not seen such a one and if I had another he believed it would turn to the quartan fever. It is not possible to describe the uneasy condition I was in but God enabled me to bear it, thanks to His holy name. The fit did not go away till the evening and then the bark was prepared for me and I took it every three hours.

11. This morning about 6 o'clock I began to be easy and con-

162

tinued to take the bark every three hours, but at first it purged me and gave me four stools. This obliged the Doctor to give me laudanum with the bark and made me drink a drink made of burnt hartshorn. He also gave me barley cinnamon water to stop the purge and it succeeded very well. I swallowed the bark like milk and took two ounces. Mr. Rogers was here yesterday and paid off Mrs. Parker's mortgage and I surrendered it to him. I was very weak-kneed and could eat nothing but bark and drink [whey] drink made of burnt hartshorn. The Doctor was very merry with Mrs. Dunn. In the evening Mr. Clayton came to see me, which was very kind. He brought me no news. My mouth was very clammy and I washed it with water very often to cool it. In the evening I began to look very yellow which the Doctor took for a good sign that the medicine had taken effect. Mr. Clayton lay at Mrs. Harrison's.

12. I was a little better this morning and the bark had thrown the distemper into my skin and I had the yellow jaundice in a great degree for which the Doctor prescribed turmeric. . . . Captain Posford sent often to know how I did. Mr. Clayton came this morning, but the Doctor would not let him or anybody else come up to see me. Colonel Hill and Mr. Anderson came to the house and dined here but I saw them not. Blessed be God, I lost my fit this day. The Doctor ordered the bark to be mixed with the turmeric without my knowledge so that I took three ounces of bark in all. I was very weak and had a clammy mouth and no stomach. Nor could I sleep but distracted sleep but I was easy, thank God Almighty.

13. I found myself better this morning though my jaundice was full on me. The Doctor saw me in a good way and so took his leave but he took nothing for all his trouble, which amazed me. However the Doctor did not go till after dinner. I gave him a million of thanks since he would take nothing else and his man led a horse to Williamsburg for Tom who was perfectly recovered. My jaundice began to clear up and I grew better and ate some rice. I got up just to have my bed made and went to bed again. I was thirsty and drank sage tea. In the evening my wife sang to me but however I could not sleep well. I began to say my prayers in order again and to give God thanks for my recovery. Tony came from Appomattox and told me he had brought in above 400 skins.

14. I found myself a little better and my jaundice vanishing away by degrees. I said my prayers and ate some chicken broth for

breakfast. About 10 o'clock I got up and sat in the great chair all day. About 2 o'clock came Tom from Williamsburg and brought me a letter from Mr. Bland. Tom was very well again, thank God. . . . In the evening I said my prayers and my wife and Mrs. Dunn sang to me and I slept better than I had done.

15. . . . I got up about 11 o'clock and went down stairs, thank God, for the first time. My beard was very long but I would not shave it. . . .

.   .   .

17. I slept pretty well last night and was better this morning. I dressed me early and went into the hall. I said my prayers and ate eggs for breakfast. . . . Colonel Hill told me Mr. Anderson could not leave his wife, who expected to lie in every moment. The Colonel stayed till the evening. I did a pretty deal of business and tired myself. . . .

18. . . . I wrote a letter for England and set my wife to writing one to the Duke of Argyle. I ventured to eat a pear. I settled several accounts. About 12 o'clock I took a little nap and then went into the library. I ate some broth and lamb for dinner and ate a great deal. In the afternoon I ate some Virginia cherries and some watermelon. I took a little walk in the garden. I sent John Grills in the morning to Williamsburg with an account of my health to the Doctor and wrote merrily. . . . I shaved my beard and head.

.   .   .

August, 1711

1. . . . It was court day and I had some business there about the negro woman that was dead. About 11 o'clock came Colonel Hill and Mr. Anderson and Mr. Platt and about 12 I went with them to court and the suit against me was dismissed. I brought the persons mentioned before home to dinner and I ate boiled pork for dinner. In the afternoon I sent a bottle of wine to Mrs. Eppes who could not come from court. I read some French when the company was gone. In the evening it threatened more rain. However I took a walk in the garden. The rain blew over. John Pleasant's mill dam was carried away so that nobody could come from Henrico County to court. . . .

2. . . . In the evening I walked about the plantation. Somebody

shot a poor mare and drove her into my lane to make people believe that my people had done it. I suppose it was Mrs. Harrison. . . .

3. . . . My wife was peevish which made a little quarrel between us. I ate roast lamb for dinner. In the afternoon put several things in order and then I wrote a letter to Falling Creek and sent the sloop away. I also wrote to Mr. Randolph to prepare the release for John Giles who offers to take £20 for his right to Falling Creek. Then I read some Latin and French till the evening and then I took a walk into the orchard where there were few apples. . . .

4. . . . I beat Prue for staying with my milk at the cowpen and telling a lie about it. Mr. Anderson came and desired to be set over the river because the ferry man could not hear him, which was done accordingly. I was indisposed with beating of Prue, and tired. I settled some accounts till dinner. . . . I could not walk in the evening because there was likely to be a terrible gust of thunder and rain which happened accordingly and it rained exceedingly and thundered, and it seems killed a horse at Captain John Stith's. Captain Drury Stith I heard was recovered of his ague and drank nothing but cold water just drawn from the well. . . .

5. . . . I prepared to go to church but as soon as I was dressed I found my ague began to return on me again about 11 o'clock. The ague was not very violent but the fever was and lasted till the evening. Bannister brought me home some English letters from Bradley of an old date with an account from him of 36 shillings a hogshead that went by the "Harrison." This price did not mend my fever. However, about 5 o'clock it began to abate and left me in a sweat. I drank nothing but wine and water and not too much of that because I was not exceedingly dry. I made some short ejaculations but my head was not enough composed for prayers. I went to bed as soon as it was dark but did nothing but sweat and slept very little. God's will be done. I had deserved his judgment.

· · ·

7. . . . I began to have a small looseness which made me a little weak. However, I came down and walked about till about 12 o'clock and then my ague came which, notwithstanding it was short, disordered me extremely and made me vomit up all I had eaten and drunk that day. This alarmed me so much that I sent for Dr. Cocke. But when I had done vomiting I found myself

pretty easy again. In the afternoon my fever came with terrible violence and to cool it I ate some watermelon which Captain John Stith sent me. . . . I had letters from Manakin Town that told me their minister Mr. Cairon was like to die. God's will be done.

8. . . . About 5 o'clock came the Doctor who expected to find me very ill. However he pronounced me worse than I thought myself and began to recommend the bark to me which I refused to take because I thought I should get well without it. In the evening my sister Custis came because she heard I was dangerously ill and when she came the Doctor and the three women made such a hubbub and noise that I retired upstairs and told the Doctor the bark was a fit remedy for him to prescribe because it made people deaf. I slept about half the night, thank God Almighty.

9. I was not so well as yesterday morning but was faint and weak and lay in bed till 10 o'clock. I ate some rice and currants for breakfast, which did not well agree with me. My wife and Mrs. Dunn had a quarrel about several matters, which ended in good humor again presently. About 12 o'clock I found myself very uneasy and went up into my chambers and vomitted a little and then I was better but had a little fever. About 2 o'clock I came down stairs again. The Doctor shook his head and told me I was in a bad condition and believed I could not get well without the bark. However he would not insist on it since I had so much aversion to it but would prescribe me a bitter draught which possibly might cure me but he doubted it. I told him I was better than he thought but that I would take his bitter draught. In the evening I ordered the coach for my sister and the Doctor to go to Mrs. Harrison's but my sister out of her great modesty would not go alone in the coach with the Doctor, and so Mrs. Dunn went with them. My fever was moderate all the evening, thank God Almighty.

10. I was better this morning, thank God; however I lay in bed till 10 o'clock and drank tea there with my sister Custis there [sic]. I had my will signed this morning. . . .

11. I slept very well all night, thank God, and scarcely moved out of one place, and also slept till 10 o'clock in the morning, which I imputed to the drink made of the root of dandelion and whey, of which I drank a bottle full. . . .

12. . . . I ate three roast apples and a little muskmelon and drank some canary after them. I wrote my journal and walked about and

was very well but weak. At night I drank some bitter draught and then laid [*sic*] on the couch and gave audience to my people. . . .

13. . . . Mr. Mumford told me he had been sick but that all was well at Appomattox, and that my trader went out last week. He told me the parson of Manakin Town was better again. We talked of several businesses and particularly a sickness of which he said he had four hogs perish since he saw me, which makes 8 in all. . . .

14. . . . In the afternoon came Bannister's mother to account with me. We found the balance more than £9 which I would not take from her in consideration of her son's good service. She was very thankful and gave me her blessing. It was very hot this afternoon. I ordered Mr. Mumford to let Mrs. Eppes know she need trouble herself to bring her son no more because I would keep nobody that would not follow orders. I ate some watermelon and peaches and drank some canary. I learned that Mr. Rogers was sick and I sent him some Spanish flies. . . .

15. . . . About 12 o'clock came Colonel Eppes who told me Tom Cocke was dead and that Mr. Rogers was very sick. He stayed and dined with us. I ate a snipe for my dinner. In the afternoon I received a letter from the Governor with orders to exercise all the militia under my command because we were threatened with an invasion, there being 14 French men-of-war designed for these parts. I immediately [sent] to Colonel Eppes to get the militia of this county together and sent orders to Colonel Frank Eppes to do the same in Henrico County. In the evening I wrote a letter to the Governor, to make my excuses for not going to council tomorrow. . . .

16. . . . Tom returned last night from the Falls and told me all was well there and at Falling Creek. I sent him with my letters to Williamsburg. This was the first day of my dressing myself again and my head was shaved. . . .

17. In the morning about 6 o'clock I took the bark, taking it in hartshorn water for eight doses running. I lay in bed all day and ate nothing but bark of which I took an ounce. I slept pretty much in the day and sweated. The bark did not purge me as it did last time but it made me deaf and dazed me so much that I lay in the same place and almost in the same position for more than 30 hours together. In the afternoon came Mr. Bland on his way to

Williamsburg. He was not well himself. He stayed with me about two hours and then took his leave. The water I made was not of so red a color as before I took the bark. My wife sat up till 11 o'clock and Mrs. Dunn till 2 to give me my dose of bark and I slept pretty well between whiles, thank God Almighty.

18. I took my last dose of bark about 7 o'clock this morning. I was very deaf and my head was giddy. Mr. Anderson came about 9 o'clock and sat with me an hour and about 10 I rose and had bread and butter and tea for breakfast which I ate with some taste. This made me sweat. My sloop came early this morning with walnut planks and unloaded some of it here and was to carry the rest to Williamsburg. At dinner I ate some apple dumpling. In the afternoon I was a little faint. . . .

19. . . . My wife and Mrs. Dunn went to church where several people had the goodness to ask for me. About 12 I ate some mutton broth and about 2 I ate two small fish and some roast mutton and ate pretty heartily, thank God. I was better in the afternoon and not so giddy in my head. . . . I slept pretty well and had a pollution in my dream.

20. . . . I sent further orders to Colonel Frank Eppes about the militia and gave them to Colonel Littlebury by word of mouth and walked about in the garden pretty much without being tired. I said my prayers and had good health, good thoughts, and good humor, thank God Almighty. I drank some canary and snakeroot when I went to bed but I could not sleep well, I had so many projects come into my head, but I slept the latter end of the night without waking till day, nor had I any polluting dream as I had the night before.

21. . . . There came a man for 12 rights of land. There came also an express from the Governor concerning the militia, a copy of which I sent to Colonel Eppes with my orders to put it in execution. I wrote to the Governor and to Mr. Bland by the express. I ventured to dress myself today and was very easy and well. I ate some mutton for dinner. In the afternoon I prepared some infusions of the bark to take at the end of the week. I read some French and in the evening I wrote to Colonel Frank Eppes to send with a copy of the Governor's letter to me. . . .

22. . . . Bannister went this morning to Henrico to carry my letter to Colonel Frank Eppes. I ate some squirrel and onions for dinner.

I caused Moll to be beaten for not making the shoats [fat]. I cleaned my pistols this afternoon. . . .

23. . . . I rose about 8 o'clock and drank a glass of red wine in which the bark had been steeped, and about 9 had some tea and bread and butter. Then I was shaved. It was cool after the rain. I had a letter from Captain Drury Stith that he had a fever but all the other officers came except John Eppes who was sick likewise. We discoursed of several matters relating to the militia and about the beacons and we agreed on the places where they were to be put. They dined with me and I ate some pigeon. In the afternoon came Colonel Frank Eppes and several gentlemen with him. We settled several matters and named several officers and then they all went away. Soon after they were gone I received a letter from the Governor dated yesterday that two French men-of-war and several privateers were arrived and ordering me to send away to Jamestown 25 gunners out of each county to work on the battery there. I sent away orders after my two colonels this night. My wife was frightened and would hardly go to bed, but was persuaded at last, but I could not sleep for thinking of our condition and what I was to do. I said my prayers devoutly and had good health, good thoughts, and good humor, thank God Almighty. I drank my bark.

24. I rose about 6 o'clock and dispatched several orders. I sent for my guns and ammunition from Appomattox and I sent away the plate and several things of value to Captain Drury Stith's that place being more secure than this. I sent to Major H-n-t to send an express as soon as any privateer appeared at his house. I got my arms in order and made cartouches. I ate a roast pigeon for dinner. In the afternoon Mrs. Harrison and her daughter and Mr. Cocke came to hear what news concerning the enemy and were pleased to hear I had heard no further about them. I told her when I learned the danger was near I would sent her word and defend her. They went away about 4 o'clock and I began to read some French and to write in my journal. Tom returned from Major H-n-t without an answer and John returned with the cart from Captain Drury Stith's and said the things got there well but that the Captain was not at home. . . .

25. I rose about 6 o'clock and found my sloop come. I wrote a letter to the Governor, to Dr. Cocke, and Mr. Bland, and sent some venison to the Governor by Tom. The people of my sloop told me there was news that our fleet was taken. My boat came in

the night from Appomattox and brought what ammunition they had there with an account that Mr. Mumford was very sick and therefore I [*or* they] sent for the Doctor to come to him. About 9 o'clock came Colonel Hill and Colonel Frank Eppes to give me an account what he had done. I gave them some bread and butter and cheese and some strong beer for breakfast. Colonel Eppes went away again about 11 and soon after his brother Littlebury came and he told me the beacons would be all up this day. . . . The Frenchman made me a great number of cartouches and cleaned my arms. At night I received a letter from Mr. Salle about the affairs of the Manakin Town. . . .

26. . . . I drank my bark and found myself very well, thank God. My wife and Mrs. Dunn rode out this morning with the child. About 12 o'clock Tom returned from Williamsburg with letters from the Doctor and Mr. Bland for the Governor was not at home. They told me that Colonel Milner of Nansemond had sent an express yesterday about noon which said that 15 French men-of-war were come within the Cape and with several other ships and had landed several thousand men on the Eastern Shore. I believe this not all true. I ate a partridge for my dinner. In the afternoon came Billy from the Falls with an account that all was well there, but they were in fear of the Indians and therefore he wanted powder. I sent him a pound and wrote a letter to him and to Tom Osborne. . . .

27. I rose about 6 o'clock and I found myself pretty well but I read nothing because I prepared to go to meet my captains in Henrico. I said my prayers and ate roast partridge for breakfast. About 11 o'clock I went to Colonel Hill's where I stayed about an hour and then in his boat I crossed the river and he and Mr. Anderson went with me. When we came to Isham Eppes' I found all my officers there and settled several matters and gave away several troops and particularly one to Frank Eppes. They all seemed to be very vigorous and [polished]. When I came away I recommended to them to inspire the men with vigor and then we passed the river again and I dined at Colonel Hill's and ate some boiled beef. About 4 o'clock Bannister came with a letter from Major H-n-t which told me that the Governor had sent an express to Colonel Ludwell that 7 ships were come up James River and so the militia of James City were ordered to Williamsburg. Upon this I sent orders to Colonel Eppes to march all the militia to the lower part of the county which was done accordingly and an

alarm given. I went home, where I found Mrs. Harrison, but heard no more news this night. . . .

28. . . . Dick Cocke came to hear what news and told me the alarm took through the county and all the people would be together about 2 o'clock. He would not stay to drink. Presently after came Colonel Littlebury Eppes, come for news likewise, and as soon as he was gone came Major Wynne and told me that Prince George County were all in arms because of the alarm of Henrico. I told him the reason of it. He said John Bolling set such a heap of straw on fire in the night that it caused two beacons of Prince George to be set on fire. The Major had his holsters at his girdle and an armor bearer that carried his pistols, which made a good figure. He would not stay to dinner. I ate a roast chicken for dinner. In the afternoon I read some French and Latin. In the evening came Mr. Bland's boy with letters from him and Dr. Cocke that told me the seven ships supposed to be French that entered into James River were English. As soon as I received this account I sent away expresses to the militia of Henrico to let them know it, that they might go home if they pleased. I also sent an account of it to Prince George for the same reason. This was just as I suspected, and everything seemed quiet again, thank God. . . .

29. . . . I sent Tom to Colonel Bassett's for my accoutrements and John with the cart for our things at Drury Stith's. I also sent away the sloop to Appomattox for tobacco. I received a letter from Colonel Ludwell with an order to send other men to Jamestown because those I sent before complained of their crops and the danger of their families for which reason he was resolved to discharge them except the Governor ordered him otherwise. I took this letter ill and sent an answer to it that the Colonel won't like. I ate some crab for dinner, which Will Parish brought over. In the afternoon I read some French and set my closet in order. I unpacked my things that came from Drury Stith's. In the evening I took a walk in the garden. Mr. Chamberlayne brought me a letter from Robin Mumford that told me he was better. After it was dark came Dr. Cocke but he brought no news. . . .

30. . . . About 11 o'clock came Drury Stith and soon after him Mr. Anderson, Colonel Hill, and several other gentlemen of the vestry which was to meet this day and I went with them to church. We appointed people to positions of [l-n] of the parish. I brought Colonel Hill and Mr. Anderson home with me to dine with the

Doctor. I ate roast duck for dinner. In the afternoon they went away to Mrs. Harrison's and the Doctor and I played at piquet with my wife, and the Doctor won the pool. In the evening we took a walk and then drank a bottle of wine. . . .

. . .

September, 1711

1. . . . John [Cross'] wife came to try to beg for her husband but she did not succeed. A man brought some peaches for which I likewise ordered him a pair of wool cards. I spent most of the morning in setting right my books in the library. I ate some crab for dinner. . . .

2. . . . I went on horseback to church, where I found two troops and a company of foot drawn up. I viewed them and found several without arms, four of whom I ordered to Jamestown to relieve as many others. Then we went into church and heard a good sermon from Mr. Anderson fit for the occasion. After church the militia were drawn up again and I viewed them and then returned home and Colonel Eppes went home with me. . . .

3. . . . In the afternoon came Captain H-n-t and told me the Governor told him his letter of marque was good and he might go when he pleased. I offered him £10 a ton but he said he would ride to York and try his fortune there before he would take that and so he went away. . . .

4. . . . I was not well, nor I was not sick, but out of order a little, I believe for want of sleep. I settled several matters in the library. The weather was grown warmer, the wind at southwest. About 12 o'clock came Colonel Frank Eppes and his son Frank and Tom Randolph to discourse about the militia of Henrico. I ordered that every week two troops should range at the head of the river and if they found any Indians on patented land to take away their guns. . . . I was a little displeased with my wife for talking impertinently. . . .

5. . . . I danced my dance, though with little vigor. Then I read some French. About 12 o'clock Mr. Clayton came from Mrs. Harrison's where he lay last night. He told me the men-of-war and land forces designed against Canada sailed from Boston the first

of last month. . . . I desired Mr. Clayton to tell the Governor I would send 2000 palisades to Jamestown and Williamsburg. . . .

6. . . . About 10 Mr. Clayton went away and then I went to bed again because my head ached. I took the bark every three hours and lay and dozed very much and sweated a little. I slept enough to cure my headache. I ate nothing all the rest of the day but bark. My wife gave it me and looked after me with a great deal of tenderness. I was in a perfect state of villainous health and had no [current] thanks. I said a short prayer and had good humor, but very indifferent thoughts and health. I slept pretty well but not much at a time, thank God Almighty.

7. . . . I got ready to go to church, this being fast day. The captain of the ship called here and told me he had not been at York as he intended. He seemed resolved not to take less than £18 a ton. About 11 o'clock I rode to church where I found two troops and a company drawn up in pretty good order. Mr. Anderson gave us a good sermon for the occasion. After church I reprimanded Will Irby for not being at his post and reviewed the men and then came home very faint so that I could not keep the fast but ate some cold chicken for dinner. . . .

8. I wrote two letters to the Falls and sent others to get the palisades. I read nothing this morning but I said my prayers and had tea and bread and butter for breakfast. I found myself pretty well and had a good stomach. We prepared to ride to Mrs. Randolph's and then ate again about 12 o'clock and I ate a partridge. . . . Tom Randolph had been sick and was a little better. At night I ate some cold roast mutton for supper and drank beer, which I have not done since I came to Virginia. Captain Bolling came over with Will Randolph and we sat up till 10 o'clock. . . .

9. I rose about 8 o'clock, having first rogered my wife. I read a little in my commonplace book. I said my prayers and drank chocolate for breakfast. Notwithstanding the bad weather we prepared to go to church but it did not rain, however. Will Randolph's troop waited on me to church and within a quarter of a mile of the church three more troops met me in good order and I took their courtesy very kindly. I viewed all the troops and found them in as good condition as might be expected and we went into church and Mr. Finney gave us a good sermon. After church I reviewed the troops again and spoke several things kindly to them. . . . I

took leave of Colonel Eppes and all the officers and men and after drinking two drams of peach brandy we returned to Mrs. Randolph's but I would not let any of the troops wait on me but returned home. My wife in returning had a gentle fall from her horse. . . .

· · ·

20. . . . About 11 o'clock I went to the coffeehouse but before I went I gave [Harry] four great pomegranates for the Governor which grew at Westover. Mr. Holloway was better this day. About 1 o'clock we went to dinner at the coffeehouse and I ate a fricassee of chicken for dinner. In the afternoon we played at piquet till the evening and then Mr. Robinson and I took a walk to the new house and after viewing that we went to the Governor's and found him at supper. I sat down with him and ate some roast beef. He was extremely tanned. He received me kindly. I delivered him my list and the report of the militia of my counties with which he was well pleased. . . .

21. I rose about 6 o'clock and read nothing. I said my prayers and ate milk and pears for breakfast. I settled some affairs with Mr. Bland concerning the pork account and about 9 o'clock went to the Governor's where I drank tea and ate bread and butter. One of the Governor's servants gave me abundance of letters which came from Kiquotan, in one of which was an extraordinary [?] of the Duke of Argyle and the Earl of Orrery. I was a long time in discoursing with the Governor concerning what should be done with obstinate Quakers, and about 11 o'clock took my leave and then rode away to Colonel Duke's. The weather was hot but I got there in 2½ hours. Here I found my brother James Duke who was not very well. About 2 o'clock I ate some stuffed chicken and about 4 we took the Colonel with us and went to my brother's and called at Mr. B-s where we saw the brunette that married Dr. Burbage. We found my sister well and all the family. We drank some thick cider and I ate some milk. Then I retired to my chamber and said my prayers and had good health, good thoughts, and good humor, thank God Almighty.

22. . . . About 7 o'clock I took my leave of the Colonel and all the family and rode home in 2½ hours and found my family well, thank God, only Sue had lost her child and 10 of the Falls cattle were missing. I stayed at home but two hours and then changed horses and rode to Colonel Hill's in order to go over the river to meet my militia. I told the Colonel all the news I knew and then

passed the river and found Captain Isham Eppes' troop of horse and Captain Bolling's troop of dragoons. I reviewed them and then we marched away to Captain Bolling's house where we lighted and drank persico. Here we met Captain Kennon's troop of dragoons and in about half an hour proceeded to Mrs. Kennon's where we dismissed the troops. I was received with great courtesy and ate boiled beef for supper. I ate very heartily, having had no dinner. . . .

23. I rose about 7 o'clock and found the weather grown very cold, the wind at northeast. I said my prayers and ate boiled milk for breakfast. All the rest of the company drank drams plentifully. Everybody showed me abundance of respect. About 10 o'clock the whole company went to breakfast and I among them and I ate some stewed fowl. About 11 we went to church with Will Kennon's troop to wait on me and there we found Captain Jefferson's, Captain Bolling's, Captain Eppes', and Captain Worsham's troops and companies which made a good appearance. Everybody respected me like a king. Mr. Robinson gave us a sermon and when church was done I reviewed the troops again and then with all the officers we went to Colonel Eppes' to dinner and I ate boiled beef. All the drink I used was cider. We were very merry all the evening only the Colonel had his ague moderately. . . .

24. I rose about 7 o'clock and said my prayers and then went down to the company. The Colonel was better this morning. About 9 o'clock everybody else went to breakfast on meat but I drank only some chocolate, and about 10 o'clock took our leave and I went attended with about 10 persons, all officers except the Parson Robinson, to Captain Bolling's, who gave us some persico, of which I drank plentifully and about 2 o'clock we went to dinner and I ate some blue-wing pie. In the afternoon we stayed about an hour and then took our leave but I could not persuade the officers to return but all went with me to the Hundred and saw me safe in the ferryboat. I thanked them all for the honor they had done me. When I got over the river I just called on Colonel Hill and he gave me a piece of a pint bottle of wine. Then I rode home, where I found all well, thank God. I said my prayers and had good health, good thoughts, and good humor, thank God Almighty. I rogered my wife.

25. . . . I was displeased with John for giving away the sweetbread of the hog he killed and threatened to whip him. I ate fried pork

for dinner. In the afternoon I weighed some money and put several things to rights and settled several accounts, and in the evening took a walk with my wife about the plantation and were very kind to one another. At night I wrote my journal and then read some French. . . .

26. . . . I settled several accounts and wrote some of my journal in arrears. It was fine warm weather but there was great want of rain for the grass. I ate roast pork for dinner. In the afternoon I rogered my wife in the billiard room. Captain H-n-t came and told me he had but 70 hogsheads on board and the reason was because people gave notes for tobacco which was not ready. About 4 o'clock I took a walk with him to Mrs. Harrison's to inquire when she would send her tobacco. She gave us apples and wine and told me that Colonel Harrison was very much indisposed and drooped without being sick and believed he should never see Williamsburg again. In the evening we returned home where all was well, thank God. At night I had several people whipped for being lazy in the morning. . . .

27. . . .I understood that Drury Stith had beaten Dr. Irby's son for being refractory which was well done. I read some Latin in Terence till dinner and then I ate some boiled pork. In the afternoon I went with Bannister to the store to examine my stock of nails. When I returned I read more Latin. About 3 o'clock came my cousin Harrison and her daughter, Betty Bassett and her sister. I gave them wine and cider and was very courteous to them. About an hour after came Mrs. Cargill who told us there was a man-of-war come in. They stayed here till 8 o'clock and then there came so few horses that Betty Bassett and Betty Harrison stayed all night. I ate some bread and butter with them and we were very merry. . . .

. . .

29. I rose about 7 o'clock, having rogered my wife this morning. I read a chapter in Hebrew and some Greek in Lucian. I said my prayers and ate boiled milk and rhubarb for breakfast. I danced my dance. The weather grew cold with a northwest wind. I sent Tom to Appomattox for the pistols and bullets for the prizes at the general muster. I made an abridgment of the laws concerning the militia till dinner and then I ate some bacon fraise. In the afternoon I wrote again and then looked over my arms that I design for prizes. . . .

. . .

October, 1711

1. . . . I prepared my business to go into the upper county and about 11 o'clock my wife and I ate each of us a blue wing and then committed our family to God's protection and then set out for Colonel Hill's where we got by one o'clock and at 2 we went to dinner and I ate some boiled beef for dinner. I persuaded Mr. Anderson and Nanny B-k-r to go with us over the river and see Captain John Bolling, where we came about 5 o'clock in the evening. He was just come from Henrico court. We had abundance of victuals for supper and I ate boiled beef. Everything was very clean and well dressed beyond any other house in that county. We spent the evening in conversation till about 10 o'clock and then we took leave of the company and retired. I said a short prayer and had good health, good thoughts, and good humor, thank God Almighty.

2. I rose about 7 o'clock and found the weather cold, which was the more troublesome because the chimney smoked. I said my prayers shortly and read nothing because the company was all up. I drank some persico and about 10 o'clock had a family breakfast and I ate some blue-wing pie. After breakfast came Robin Mumford who told us that his wife was very sick, and soon after came Captain Kennon. About 11 we took horse and rode to Captain Jefferson's where the militia of that side of the river was drawn up. I viewed them a little and because they were not all come I went to Captain Jefferson's house where we drank some persico and then returned into the field where I caused the troops to be exercised by each captain and they performed but indifferently for which I reproved them. [Massot] one of the French was drunk and rude to his captain, for which I broke his head in two places. When all was over we went to dine with Captain Jefferson and I ate some roast beef. My horses got out of the house where they were put and ran away, for which I was angry with Tom. Most of the company went home with John Bolling and got drunk, but I said a short prayer and had good health, good thoughts, and good humor, thank God Almighty.

3. I rose about 7 o'clock and found it had rained a little but it soon cleared up again. I said a short prayer and catched [sic] a little cold because the room had no glass window. We sent several ways for my horses and they were brought about 10 o'clock. Mr.

Anderson was called out of his bed to go to a woman that wanted to receive the Sacrament. About 11 o'clock I ate some mutton for breakfast, and several of my captains came to go over the river with me, where we got about 2 o'clock but in the meantime the Major had exercised his men on the north side. Then I ordered the men to be drawn in single [file] along the path where the men were to run for the prize, and John Hatcher, one of Captain Randolph's men, won the pistol. Then I caused the men to be drawn into a square to see the men play at cudgels and Dick O-l-n won the sword, and of the wrestling Will Kennon won the gun. Just as the sun went down our games ended and then I took leave and we went to Frank Eppes' where I ate boiled beef for supper. Mr. Anderson and Mr. Finney came over with us and had both lost and Mr. Finney said several inscrutable things. My cold a long dispute about several mysterious things in which they were was increased. . . .

4. I rose at 7 o'clock and my wife shaved me with a dull razor. I persuaded Mr. Anderson to go and visit Tom Osborne who was very sick, while I went to the militia court, but we ate our breakfast first and I ate some boiled beef. About 11 o'clock we went to the militia court, where Captain Bolling and I had a dispute about fining Mr. M-r-s-l, one of my overseers, because he affirmed [they ought to buy such negroes as make a corps]. We fined all the Quakers and several others and the Captains agreed to send for trophies. Captain Royall neither came nor returned a list though he had two Quakers in his company. I spoke gently to the Quakers which gave them a good opinion of me and several of them seemed doubtful whether they would be arrested or not for the future. I told them they would certainly be fined five times in a year if they did not do as their fellow subjects did. The sun set before we had finished and then we rode to Frank Eppes' with design to proceed to Captain Webb's, but it was so late I could not persuade my wife to go so we stayed there and I ate beef again for supper. I said my prayers and had good health, good thoughts, and good humor, thank God Almighty.

5. . . . About 10 we took leave of the family and rode to Falling Creek where we got about 12 o'clock and found all well, thank God, and the dam almost finished. Mr. Anderson came to us a little after we got there and told me Tom Osborne was in no danger of his life but was extremely fretful. We went to the tannery and saw everything that was to be seen, which pleased my wife

very much. Then we went to the house to dinner and I ate some roast beef. About 3 o'clock we went away to the Hundred where we arrived about 6 o'clock and just called to ask how Mr. Anderson and the rest of the family did and then proceeded home, where we found all well, thank God. We ate some milk and potatoes and then I read some Latin. I said my prayers and had good health, good thoughts, and good humor, thank God Almighty.

6. I rose about 7 o'clock and read some Hebrew but no Greek. I said my prayers and then prepared to go to the general muster of this county. My wife and daughter went in the coach and I rode on horseback and got into the field about 11 o'clock and was there before several of my Captains. However, I found Captain Drury Stith and Captain Eppes there and I caused them to exercise their men till the others came. The first had his troop in good order but the last had his very indifferent and did not exercise them himself. When the rest came I reprimanded them for staying so long, nor was any of their men in order. About 2 o'clcok our prizes began and Will M-r-l got the prize of running and John S-c-l-s the prize of cudgels and Robin Easely the prize [of] wrestling. All was finished about 4 o'clock and then we went to Captain Stith's to dinner and I ate some boiled beef. Then we took leave and got home about 7 o'clock and found all well, thank God Almighty. . . .

7. . . . I received a letter from the Governor by express by which I learned that 60 people had been killed by the Indians at Neuse and about as many at Pamlico in North Carolina and that he would meet me at Major Harrison's. However, I could not go till tomorrow because I had invited company to dine with me and accordingly Mr. Cole, Mr. Roscow, Mr. [Tayloe], and Captain H-n-t came and dined with me. I ate blue wing for dinner. These young men behaved themselves very well and seem to have good understanding. They stayed till about 5 o'clock and then went away in Captain H-n-t's boat. My wife and I took a walk in the evening and at night we had a game at [p-l-y]. . . .

8. I rose about 7 o'clock and read nothing because I prepared myself to ride to Major Harrison's. I said a short prayer and ate boiled milk for breakfast. About 10 o'clock I got over the river and proceeded on my journey but went a little out of my way. However I got there about one o'clock and found the Governor, Colonel Harrison, and Colonel Ludwell, which last had been sick. They reproached me for staying so long, but I excused myself be-

179

cause the express had not brought me the letter till yesterday. About 2 o'clock we went to dinner and I ate boiled beef for my part. After dinner we sat in council concerning the Indians and some of the Tributaries came before us who promised to be very faithful to us. It was agreed to send Peter Poythress to the Tuscaroras to treat them and to demand the Baron Graffenriedt who was prisoner among the Indians. It was also resolved that the militia of Prince George, Surry, and Isle of Wight should rendezvous at Nottoway town on Wednesday next and the Governor be there with them to show some part of our strength to the Indians. In the evening came several gentlemen and Mr. Bland among them with letters for the Governor from Carolina which told him how backward the people of that country were to [advantage] themselves. About 10 o'clock we went to bed. Colonel Ludwell and I lay together. . . .

9. I rose about 7 o'clock and got myself ready because I heard the Governor up. We had chocolate for breakfast, of which I drank four cups. About 10 o'clock the Governor went over the river; I begged of him to go to Westover but he told me very kindly that when he went there it was for pleasure but this was not the time to take pleasure in. I told him I would meet him at Colonel Harrison's this day sennight and so took my leave. However I stayed with the Major till dinner and ate boiled beef for my part. The Major would fain insinuate some unkind things against Mr. Mumford which I told him I would inquire into. About 2 o'clock I took my leave with Mr. Bland and got home about 5 o'clock and everybody was well and my wife at Mrs. Harrison's. . . .

10. . . . John [Cross] came to me but would not agree by fair means to go to work at Jamestown but chose rather to go to prison out of pure conscience. I ate boiled beef for dinner. Just after dinner came John Giles to receive the £20 I was to give him for his right to Falling Creek. I wrote three letters and sent by him to desire some of my captains to meet me at Nottoway Town. . . .

11. . . . About 10 o'clock came Captain H-n-t to buy planks and soon after him came Captain Drury Stith and after him Captain John Eppes, Captain Sam Harwood and Captain Hamlin. I persuaded them to stay and dine before we went to the martial court and fined as many people as came to 4500 pounds of tobacco. We made an order that the fines returned by each captain should go towards his trophies. Mr. Bland called on his way to Williamsburg.

In the evening I took a walk and beat Jenny for being unmannerly. At night I read some Latin in Terence. . . .

12. . . . It rained in the morning but that did not hinder Mr. Mumford from coming to know if I had any service before the General Court. I told him what I had heard at Major Harrison's concerning him but seeming however not to believe it. He protested solemnly he was innocent and I believe he is. About 11 o'clock came Colonel Hill, Mr. Finney, and Mr. Anderson. We diverted ourselves in the library till dinner and then I ate pigeon and bacon. Mr. Finney had appetite of his usual vigor. It threatened rain which hastened away my company, all except Robin Mumford, who had the discretion to stay all night and it was well he did, for it rained extremely. . . .

.   .   .

16. I rose about 6 o'clock and prepared everything for my journey, notwithstanding it threatened rain. I put up my baggage and then ate some boiled milk for breakfast. I recommended my family to the divine protection and went over the river in order to proceed to Colonel Harrison's with my man Bannister with me, and my people that went with the baggage were gone before we got over the river. It was 2 o'clock before I got to Colonel Harrison's. However I was there two hours before the Governor. The Colonel treated me with strong water. About 3 o'clock came Colonel Hill and Mr. Platt and John Hardiman and after 4 came the Governor and several gentlemen volunteers with him and particularly Dr. Cocke and Mr. Graeme the Governor's cousin. About 5 o'clock we went to supper and I ate some boiled beef. At night some of the volunteers drank hard but I went to bed and said a short prayer and the Doctor lay with me. I had good health, good thoughts, and good humor, thank God Almighty. Will Robinson lay in the room and disturbed us with his groaning.

17. I rose about 7 o'clock and found the Governor up. I drank some strong water. I said a short prayer and about 8 o'clock we sat to a family breakfast and I ate some roast mutton. About 9 we took leave of Colonel Harrison and got on our horses with Captain Hal Harrison's troop to wait on us. Captain John Allen's troop met us on the road and about 3 o'clock we met Colonel Ludwell and soon after got to Nottoway town where we met abundance of the militia. We had just time before night to settle our quarters and to look about us. Several of us lay in the King's cabin with the Governor, where we lay on new mats and our

cabin was covered with other mats. I found my baggage well received but one of the horses was sick. No less than eight of my Henrico captains came over to meet the Governor, which compliment he took very kindly. Both they and all the volunteers supped with the Governor under his marquee and I ate venison pasty. The Governor appointed a guard for the fort of about 100 men. Several of the Tributary Indians came here to meet the Governor. The Doctor lay with me but our lodging seemed very hard at first and we were incommoded with the smoke at first. I said a short prayer and had good health, good thoughts, and good humor, thank God Almighty. We talked almost all night. We lay in our morning gowns and breeches.

18. About break of day we were waked with the reveille and rose about 6 o'clock and then took a walk about the town to see some Indian girls, with which we played the wag. I ate some gingerbread and drank tea with the Governor for breakfast. Then we got on our horses to take a review of the militia and assigned to each county its post and gave the militia of the Isle of Wight the head because we were in their county. While we were in the field the Governor modelled the horse and put commanders at the head of them. There were about 700 horse besides volunteers and about 900 foot, and there were about 30 volunteers among whom were three parsons. About noon the Governor sent about 30 horses to meet the Tuscarora Indians at the Saponie town. After the Governor had reviewed the horse on both wings he dismissed them about 4 o'clock and sent all except those appointed for the guard that they might provide themselves with lodgings in the neighborhood. About 5 we went to dinner with the Governor and I ate some venison. All the volunteers dined with the Governor. At night we drank a bottle till about 10 o'clock, and then went to bed. I said a short prayer and had good health, good thoughts, and good humor, thank God Almighty.

19. I rose about 6 o'clock and found it cold. We drank chocolate with the Governor and about 9 o'clock got on our horses and waited on the Governor to see him put the foot in order. [He] divided the companies and made them about 50 men each, and made captains over them, though when he came to Surry he found it difficult to get captains because everybody refused the Governor and made him so angry that he swore at several which was a thing he seldom did. The Doctor went away about 10 o'clock privately with pretence of some business but it was to go to Mrs. Russell. We

182

ate gingerbread all day long and saw the Governor exercise the foot. I drew up the volunteers into a company or troop and commanded them under the name of the Governor's Guard and we placed ourselves on the right. About 3 o'clock the Tuscarora Indians came with their guard and Mr. Poythress with them. He told the Governor that the Baron was alive and would be released but that Mr. Lawson was killed because he had been so foolish as to threaten the Indian that had taken him. About 6 o'clock we went to dinner and I ate some roast mutton. At night some of my troop went with me into the town to see the girls and kissed them without proceeding any further, and we had like to have been kept out by the captain of the guard. However at last they let us in and we went to bed about 2 o'clock in the morning. I neglected to say my prayers but had good health, good thoughts, and good humor, thank God Almighty.

20. I rose about 6 o'clock and drank tea with the Governor, who made use of this opportunity to make the Indians send some of their great men to the College, and the Nansemonds sent two, the Nottoways two, and the Meherrins two. He also demanded one from every town belonging to the Tuscaroras. About 9 the Governor mounted and we waited on him to see him exercise the horse and when all the militia was drawn up he caused the Indians to walk from one end to the other and they seemed very much afraid lest they should be killed. The Governor did nothing but wheel the foot, and Colonel Ludwell and I assisted him as well as we could. About noon the Governor ordered lists to be taken of the troops and companies that the people might make their claim to be paid, because they had been on the service five days. When this was done he gave liberty to the people to go home, except a troop and company for the guard that night. Then we went and saw the Indian boys shoot and the Indian girls run for a prize. We had likewise a war dance by the men and a love dance by the women, which sports lasted till it grew dark. Then we went to supper and I ate chicken with a good stomach. We sat with the Governor till he went to bed about 11 o'clock and then we went to Major Harrison's to supper again but the Governor ordered the sentry to keep us out and in revenge about 2 o'clock in the morning we danced a [g-n-t-r] dance just at his bed's head. However we called for the captain of the guard and gave him a word and then we all got in except Colonel Ludwell and we kept him out about quarter of an hour. Jenny, an Indian girl, had got drunk and made us good sport. . . .

21. I rose about 6 o'clock and we began to pack up our baggage in order to return. We drank chocolate with the Governor and about 10 o'clock we took leave of the Nottoway town and the Indian boys went away with us that were designed for the College. The Governor made three proposals to the Tuscaroras: that they would join with the English to cut off those Indians that had killed the people of Carolina, that they should have 40 shillings for every head they brought in of those guilty Indians and be paid the price of a slave for all they brought in alive, and that they should send one of the chief men's sons out of every town to the College. I waited on the Governor about ten miles and then took leave of him and he went to Mr. Cargill's and I with Colonel Hill, Mr. Platt, and John Hardiman went to Colonel Harrison's were we got about 3 o'clock in the afternoon. About 4 we dined and I ate some boiled beef. My man's horse was lame for which he was let blood. At night I asked a negro girl to kiss me, and when I went to bed I was very cold because I pulled off my clothes after lying in them so long. . . .

22. I rose about 7 o'clock and understood by Colonel Hill that he [f-s-t] away last night. I said a short prayer and then drank some chocolate for breakfast. About 9 o'clock we took leave of the Colonel and the rest of the family and rode home with Colonel Hill and Mr. Platt and Mr. Hardiman, who went with me part of the way. I got home about 11 o'clock and found Mrs. Hamlin there who wanted some physic for her son Dick who had the gripes and I gave her a purge. Captain Eppes and Colonel Eppes came just before dinner and sat down with us and I ate venison for dinner. All my family was well, thank God, and so were all my people above, thank God. In the afternoon I settled my affairs to go to Williamsburg tomorrow. In the evening my wife and I took a walk about the plantation. . . .

23. . . . About 9 o'clock I took leave of my wife and daughter and was set over the creek and was angry with Tom for forgetting the strap of my portmantle and I was displeased with Eugene for forgetting his cape. It rained all the way I rode to Williamsburg, where I got about 3 o'clock pretty wet. Then I got ready to go to court that I might not lose my day and accordingly did save it. I made my honors to the Governor and to the gentlemen of the council and took my place. We sat in court till about 5 o'clock and then the Governor took me home to dinner and there I found Mrs. Russell returned from her travels. I ate boiled beef for dinner. The

Governor told me that our design upon Canada had miscarried by the fault of the Admiral. About 8 o'clock we went to the coffeehouse were I played and won 50 shillings. About 10 I went to my lodgings and wrote a letter to my wife. I said my prayers and had good health, good thoughts, and good humor, thank God Almighty.

24. . . . . About 9 o'clock I went to court where I sat diligently till noon and then I ate some gingerbread. Nothing very remarkable happened but in all cases they dispensed judgment very equally. We sat till the evening and I went again with the Governor to dine, as he said, to eat some of my own venison. We had a rumor that the Duke of Marlborough had gained another victory in Flanders and that the French had failed in their enterprise upon Brussels. About 8 o'clock I went to the coffeehouse where I fell to playing with some of the young men and won £9. . . .

25. . . . . Colonel Hill called to see me and let me understand all was well above. About 9 o'clock I went to court and heard several cases but none remarkable. About noon I returned to my chambers and wrote in my journal and then went into court again and we sat till it was dark and then I went home again with the Governor because the rest of the Council sneaked away in the dark. I ate some boiled beef for supper. About 8 we went to the coffeehouse and got Mr. Graeme with us. We played at whist and I lost 5 shillings. . . . Billy Beverley came to see me with his father.

26. I rose about 7 o'clock and read nothing but wrote a letter to my wife to send by Colonel Hill to invite her over to see Mrs. Russell. I said a short prayer and ate boiled milk for breakfast. Then I went to the capitol to read some law books and about 9 o'clock went into court, where I sat till noon and then I went up stairs and wrote in my journal. I ate some gingerbread. Nothing came before us very remarkable; however we sat till about 5 o'clock and then I slipped away lest the Governor should ask me again to dine with him. Several of us went to dine at Marot's where I ate a good fricassee of chicken, and drank Virginia wine that was [tolerable]. When dinner was over we went to the coffeehouse and played at cards and I lost 5 shillings.

27. . . . . I wrote another short letter to my wife by Mr. Platt. I had several people come to see me at my chamber. About 10 o'clock I went to court where I sat diligently all day because two of the

judges went home. However I got time to settle accounts with Colonel Waters. We sat till it grew dark and dispatched a great deal of business. Then I went home again with the Governor to dinner and ate some salt fish. We drank some French wine till almost 10 o'clock and then we took leave and I went home to my lodgings. Two or three days ago the Governor put Gilbert his coachman into prison for his insolence. . . .

28. . . . I got Daniel to shave my head. I continued to rain. However I went to church purely because I thought it my duty but I went in the President's coach. There were few people at church and no ladies but Mrs. Russell. Mr. Robinson gave us a good sermon but very sadly delivered. After church the Governor asked me to dine with him but I was engaged to the Commissary. Colonel Carter and I went in the President's coach to the Commissary's and I ate roast goose for dinner. Mrs. Blair was in good health and very good humor. It continued to rain; however we took our cloaks and walked home. I went to my lodgings and wrote a great deal in my journal. . . .

29. . . . About 9 o'clock I went to wait on the Governor but he was not at home and I walked after him to the new house and found him there and saw several of the Governor's contrivances, and particularly that for hanging the arms. About 11 o'clock I came with the Governor to court where we sat till about 3 and then I went up stairs and danced my dance and wrote a letter to England. Then I returned to court where we stayed till about 5 and then I went home with the Governor and ate venison for dinner and then drank a bottle till 8 o'clock. Then we went to the cofleehouse, where we played at cards till 10 and I won 25 shillings. Then I returned home and I committed manual uncleanness, for which God forgive me. I neglected to say my prayers but had good health, good humor, but indifferent thoughts.

30. . . . About 10 o'clock I went to court where I sat till about 2 and then went up stairs and danced my dance and wrote a letter to England. Then I returned into court where we sat till about 5. Then I went with the Governor to dinner and found the weather very cold. I ate venison pasty for dinner and then we drank a bottle till 8 o'clock. Afterwards we went to the coffeehouse where I played at piquet and won 5 shillings. In the evening Colonel Smith and Colonel Carter were at Marot's and somebody cast a brick from the street into the room which narrowly missed Colonel Carter. . . .

31. . . . About 10 o'clock I went to court where I sat till about 3 and then I went up stairs and danced my dance and wrote a letter to England. About 4 I returned to court and we sat till past 5. Then we went to dine at Marot's and I ate roast veal for dinner. About 8 o'clock we went to the coffeehouse and I had not been there half an hour before Eugene came and told me that my wife was at my lodgings. I instantly went home and found her there. She told me all was well at home, thank God, this morning. I neglected to say my prayers but had good health, good thoughts, and good humor, thank God Almighty. I rogered my wife. The weather was very cold.

November, 1711

1. I rose about 8 o'clock and read nothing because I had a great deal to say to my wife. We sent some ducks and pigeons to the Governor and my wife sent to Mrs. Dunn to come to her. I drank chocolate for breakfast and about 10 o'clock went to court but the Governor was not there. I sat till about 3 o'clock and then went to my lodgings where I wrote in my journal till 4 o'clock, and then went to the Governor's to dinner and found my wife there. I ate venison pasty for dinner. In the evening we played at cards and I won. We put a trick [on] the Doctor who left 10 shillings on the table and we took it when he turned his back and left it for the cards when we had done. About 10 o'clock we went home in the Governor's coach. . . .

2. I rose about 7 o'clock and read nothing because my wife was there, nor did I say my prayers, but ate boiled milk for breakfast. About 10 o'clock I went to the capitol and sat all day in court without once going away and by night we made an end. Then I waited on the Governor home to dinner where we found Mrs. Churchill and several other ladies and my wife among them. The table was so full that the Doctor and Mrs. Graeme and I had a little table to ourselves and were more merry than the rest of the company. I ate roast beef for supper. In the meantime the Doctor secured two fiddlers and candles were sent to the capitol and then the company followed and we had a ball and danced till about 12 o'clock at night and then everybody went to their lodgings, but I neglected to say my prayers but had good health, good thoughts,

and good humor, thank God Almighty. Mrs. Russell was my partner.

3. I rogered my wife this morning and rose about 7 o'clock. I neglected to say my prayers but had boiled milk for breakfast. Mr. Beverley came to see my wife and breakfasted with us. About 10 o'clock I went to the capitol to write letters because I would not be disturbed, and my wife went to see her sister. The weather was grown warmer. I wrote three letters to England. About 1 o'clock I ate some gingerbread and drank sage and snakeroot, and then wrote more letters. About 5 o'clock I returned to my lodgings and put up my letters and because Mrs. Churchill and Mrs. Beverley were at Colonel Carter's lodgings I went there and found the Colonel with the President and Mr. Clayton almost drunk. They would fain persuade me to drink with them but I refused and persuaded the Colonel not to suffer the ladies to wait on him so long. Then I went to the coffeehouse and had the misfortune to affront the President without saying anything to provoke a reasonable man. After that we went to [p-l-y] and I won £18 and got home before 11 o'clock. I neglected to say my prayers but had good health, good thoughts, and good humor, thank God Almighty. I let Mrs. Churchill know that I owed her £40 of which her husband had kept no account.

4. . . . About 10 o'clock came my sister Custis to dress here who told me the Major was better. About 11 the coach was sent by the Governor to carry the women to church and I walked. Mr. Commissary gave us an indifferent sermon. When church was done we went to the Governor's to dinner and I ate some boiled venison, though my stomach was not so good as usual. About 4 o'clock we went to see the new house and there we found Mrs. Blair and Mrs. Harrison. When we had tired ourselves there the coach set the women home and the Governor and I went to the coffeehouse where we stayed about half an hour and then I went home to my lodgings and read some of the public news till about 9 o'clock. . . .

5. . . . About 9 o'clock came Mrs. Bland and invited my wife and Mrs. Dunn to dinner and the Governor sent and invited me by Mr. Robinson, together with all the governors of the College that were in town. The College presented their verses to the Governor by the hands of the Commissary and the master. About 11 o'clock I went to the capitol and wrote a letter to England and set Grills to

copying letters for me. About 2 o'clock I went to the Governor's to dinner and found there Mr. Commissary and the master of the College and Johnny Randolph as being the first scholar, who at dinner sat on the Governor's right hand. I ate roast mutton for dinner. The Governor was taken sick before we rose from table but it soon went over. In the evening Mr. Bland took a walk to the College, and the Governor, Mrs. Russell, and several ladies came to see the bonfire made by the boys. At night we went to the Governor's to spend the rest of the evening till 10 o'clock and then we went home. . . .

6. . . . My wife and her sister and Mrs. Dunn waited on Mrs. Russell to Nat Burwell's, but I could not possibly go with them and therefore committed them to the care of the Doctor, who gallanted them. About 11 o'clock I went to the capitol, where I danced my dance and wrote several letters to England. The old Frenchman came to desire me to get him a passage to England, which I promised to do when Captain H-n-t comes down. I stayed and wrote at the capitol till about 5 o'clock because it rained so hard that I could not get away. However at last I ran through it to the coffeehouse, where I sat an hour before anybody came. At last came Mr. Clayton from York but had no news. Soon after came Mr. Robinson and he played at piquet with me and we neither won nor lost. . . .

7. . . . I paid £500 to Mr. Tullitt for the College. About 10 I caused my secretary to be brought to my lodgings from the capitol. The wind blew very hard at northwest so that my wife and her company could not come from Gloucester. Some of the burgesses began to come and the House met and adjourned. I dined upon gingerbread because I could find no company to dine with. About 3 o'clock I went to the capitol and wrote letters to England and danced my dance. About 5 o'clock Mr. Clayton came to me and told me my wife and the other gentlewomen were returned from Gloucester and were at my lodgings. I went to them and gave them some victuals and a bottle of wine from Marot's. My sister Custis and Mrs. Dunn went to Queen's Creek and my wife went to bed and I went to the coffeehouse where I won 5 shillings and stayed till 9 o'clock. I neglected to say my prayers and had good health, good thoughts, and good humor, thank God Almighty.

8. I rose about 7 o'clock and read nothing because my wife was preparing to go away home. I neglected to say my prayers and ate

boiled milk for breakfast. About 9 we went to the Governor's who showed me his speech. I entreated for Gilbert but could not prevail. I drank some tea till about 11 and then went in the Governor's coach to the capitol where he made his speech to the Council and Burgesses. Then I started a project of paying the ministers in money and laying 3 shillings more on tobacco and everybody was pleased with the reason of it. About 2 o'clock I dined with the Council at Marot's and ate mutton for dinner. Harry W-l-s walked from hence to Jimmy Burwell's and back again in less than three hours for a wager of two guineas, but was almost spent. I took a walk to see the College and Governor's house and in the evening returned to the coffeehouse where we played at cards and I won 20 shillings. . . .

9. . . . Mr. Bland came to see me and so did Frank [Ballard] and told me Mr. D-k was resolved to marry Mrs. Young in spite of all his friends. I went to prayers with the Burgesses and then we met as upper House but did nothing more than adjourn. Then I danced my dance and wrote my proposal but learned that the Governor was against it because it was no provision for more powers than are at present. About 2 o'clock we dined at Marot's and I ate roast veal for dinner. In the afternoon we went to the [?] coffeehouse where we fell into gaming and I won about £8 in all at piquet and dice. . . .

. . .

13. . . . Mr. Graeme and I went out with bows and arrows and shot at partridge and squirrel which gave us abundance of diversion but we lost some of our arrows. We returned about one o'clock but found that Frank Lightfoot had broken his word by not coming to us. About 2 o'clock we went to dinner and I ate some venison pasty and were very merry. In the afternoon we played at billiards and I by accident had almost lost some of my fore teeth by putting the stick in my mouth. Then we went and took a walk with the women and Mr. Graeme diverted himself with Mrs. Dunn. In the evening came Mr. Mumford who told me all was well again at Appomattox. We played at cards and drank some pressed wine and were merry till 10 o'clock. I neglected to say my prayers but rogered my wife, and had good health, good thoughts, and good humor, thank God Almighty.

14. I rose about 7 o'clock and gave all the necessary orders to my people. I recommended myself and family to God and then ate

some cold venison pasty for breakfast. I settled my business with Captain H-n-t and delivered my letters to him. Then we took our leave and were set over the creek and then proceeded on our journey and about 3 o'clock we got to Green Spring but neither the Colonel nor his lady were at home and therefore we stayed but half an hour and then went on to Williamsburg where we got about 5. I dressed myself and went to Colonel Bray's where the wedding had been kept and found abundance of company there. I dined and ate some chicken pie and then we went to dancing and the bride was my partner but because Colonel Bray was sick we went away before 10 o'clock to the coffeehouse where I won 5 shillings of the President. . . .

15. . . . About 10 o'clock Colonel Ludwell [came] to my lodgings. He stayed about half an hour and then we went to the capitol where I danced my dance and wrote in my journal. Then I went into council where our address to the Governor was read and Colonel Lewis and myself were ordered to wait on the Governor to know where and when the council should wait on him with it, and I walked him so fast that when he came there he could hardly speak. The Governor gave us some strong water to warm us and then we returned. . . .

16. . . . About 9 o'clock I went to the Governor's where I stayed about an hour and then went to the capitol where we read a bill concerning rolling houses the first time. About 11 the Governor came and the President read our address to him with an indifferent grace. About 2 o'clock we dined at Marot's and I ate some fish for dinner. My mouth was sore with the blow I had with the billiard stick. About 4 o'clock Jimmy Burwell and I resolved to go to the wedding at Mr. Ingles' and went away in his coach and found all the company ready to go to supper but we ate nothing with them but some custard. After supper we began to dance, first French dances and after country dances till about 11 o'clock and then most of the company went to Williamsburg but I stayed with Jimmy Burwell and Jimmy Roscow and James Bray, got drunk and went home by myself about 12 o'clock. . . .

17. . . . Mr. Ingles entertained us very generously and is a very good and courteous man. We took our leave about 8 o'clock and returned in Jimmy Burwell's coach to Williamsburg and went away to the capitol where we read a bill concerning horses the first time. Then we adjourned and I went to Colonel Duke's who

entertained me with good cider and toast. The weather threatened rain or snow. About 1 o'clock I went again to the capitol and danced my dance and wrote in my journal. Then I read Italian for an hour. After which I took a walk round the town till about 5 o'clock, and then went to the coffeehouse and won 5 shillings of the President. . . .

18. . . . About 11 o'clock the President called upon me with his coach to go to church where Mr. Paxton gave us a sermon that was very good. After church Colonel Duke and I dined with the Commissary and I ate roast turkey for dinner. Mrs. Blair was not very well. In the evening Colonel Duke and I took leave and walked to Colonel Bray's and found him much better but the design was to visit Mrs. B-r-d [bride?] before she went up to Captain Llewellyn [Eppes?]. We diverted ourselves with the girls till about 9 o'clock and then took our leave and wished them a good journey the next day. . . .

19. . . . I went to the Governor's but he was gone to the new house and I went there to him and found him putting up the arms. Captain H-n-t came over and could hardly prevail with the Governor to let him go; however I interceded for him and got leave. About 2 o'clock my sister Custis sent horses for me and about 3 I rode to make her a visit and found them pretty well and their whole family. About 6 o'clock we went to supper and I ate some roast beef. Then we talked about dividing the land of old Colonel Parke between them and me. Some words were spoken concerning selling some of Colonel Parke's land to pay his debts but my sister would not hear of it. I said my prayers and had good health, good thoughts, and good humor, thank God Almighty.

20. I rose about 7 o'clock and my brother and I appointed Mr. Bland and Mr. [Keeling] to divide the land of old Colonel Parke and agreed my sister should have the choice. I said my prayers and ate boiled milk for breakfast. About 9 o'clock I took leave and rode to Williamsburg where I found my man Tom with a letter from home, that told me all were well except my daughter, who had fallen down and cut her forehead. I wrote a letter to my wife and sent Tom home. Then I went to the capitol and read some bills. The Governor was there. We sat till two o'clock and I went to dinner at the Governor's and ate roast beef. About 4 we went away and I went and wrote in my journal and afterwards went and recommended the business of the College to some of the burgesses

192

and then went to the coffeehouse where I won of Dr. Cocke 45 shillings at piquet. . . .

21. I rose about 7 o'clock and read nothing because I went to the committee for making the port bill and stayed there about an hour. Then I returned and said my prayers and had boiled milk for breakfast. Then I went to the capitol and danced my dance and did some business with Mr. Holloway. Then I went down to the Council and read some law and the Governor came among us and stayed about an hour. About 2 o'clock we rose and went to dinner and I ate fish. Then Colonel Smith and I played at billiards and I won half a crown. Then we took a walk and afterwards went to the coffeehouse and played at whisk but lost 15 shillings. Then we played at dice and after losing £10 I recovered my money and won £8. . . .

22. . . . Mr. Bland came to see me and told me he would go about the dividing of old Colonel Parke's land as we desired. About 11 I went to the capitol where I found the Governor, who had letters from the Governor of North Carolina which gave a terrible account of the state of Carolina. He had also a letter from the Baron by which he had a relation of his being taken with Mr. Lawson by the Indians and of Mr. Lawson's murder. The House of Burgesses brought their address of thanks to which the Governor answered them that he would thank them when he saw them act with as little self interest as he had done. About 3 o'clock we went to dinner and I ate some roast goose. Then I took a walk to the Governor's new house with Frank W-l-s and then returned to the coffeehouse where I lost 12 pounds 10 shillings and about 10 o'clock returned home very much out of humor to think myself such a fool. . . .

23. . . . About 10 o'clock I went to the capitol where I danced my dance and then wrote in my journal. It was very cold this morning. About 11 o'clock I went to the coffeehouse where the Governor also came and from thence we went to the capitol and read the bill concerning ports the first time. We stayed till 3 o'clock and then went to dinner.to Marot's but could get none there and therefore Colonel Lewis and I dined with Colonel Duke and I ate broiled chicken for dinner. After dinner we went to Colonel Carter's room where we had a bowl of punch of French brandy and oranges. We talked very lewdly and were almost drunk and in that condition we went to the coffeehouse and played at dice and I lost

£12. We stayed at the coffeehouse till almost 4 o'clock in the morning talking with Major Harrison. Then I went to my lodging, where I committed uncleanness, for which I humbly beg God Almighty's pardon.

24. I rose about 8 o'clock and read a chapter in Hebrew and some Greek in Homer. I said my prayers and ate boiled milk for breakfast. Colonel Carter and several others came to my lodgings to laugh at me for my disorder last night. About 10 I went to the coffeehouse and drank some tea and then we went to the President's and read the law about probate and administration. Then I went to the capitol and danced my dance and wrote in my journal and read Italian. This day I make a solemn resolution never at once to lose more than 50 shillings and to spend less time in gaming, and I beg the God Almighty to give me grace to keep so good a resolution if it be His holy will. . . .

25. . . . About 11 o'clock Mr. Clayton came to see me and I desired him to lend me his horse to ride to Queen's Creek. About one my brother Custis called on me and I went with him home and found all the family well. Just before we sat to dinner Dr. Cocke came to us. I ate some roast beef for dinner notwithstanding my cold, which continued violently. We were merry till the evening and then we drank a bowl of punch made of French brandy and oranges which I drank for my cold and ate roast apples with it. . . .

26. . . . My sister agreed to divide her grandfather's land without any intervention of [f-r-n] and she also agreed to the sale of some of the land and negroes of her father to pay his debts. About 10 o'clock we took leave and went to Williamsburg but there we did not meet to do business till almost 2 o'clock because we had not enough in town. We read two bills and then went to dinner and I ate chicken pie but was not well after it. In the evening we went to the coffeehouse where I received a letter from Mr. Perry and an account of £5 a hogshead for tobacco. . . .

27. . . . James Bray invited me to the wedding of his daughter this day but the weather was so bad I made my excuses by the Commissary. We sat at the President's house where we had a good fire. I received a letter from home by my sloop that brought some coal on her way to Kiquotan with palisades. We read several bills and the Governor came to us and made his exceptions to some clauses in the bill concerning probate and administration, which we

194

resolved to amend. We sat till about 4 o'clock and then went to dinner and I ate some roast mutton. In the evening we went to the coffeehouse where I played at cards and won 25 shillings. . . .

28. . . . I had a gentleman that came to buy the quitrents of Nansemond County but we could not agree. About 10 o'clock I went to the capitol where I wrote in my journal and danced my dance, and then went to the coffeehouse where I found several of the council but not ready to go to council, and so some of us took a walk to the Governor's house where we found the Governor looking over the workmen. It was exceedingly cold. Then we returned to the President's lodgings where we read some bills and afterwards adjourned to the capitol where the House of Burgesses brought an address to the Governor in which they desired him to make war on the Indians and the council afterwards advised him if no other method would procure satisfaction from the Indians then to make war on them. About 4 o'clock we went to dinner and I ate some roast beef. In the evening we played at cards till 7 o'clock and then I went home and read some Greek and looked over several papers relating to the estate of old Colonel Parke. I said my prayers and had good health, good thoughts, and good humor, thank God Almighty.

. . .

December, 1711

1. . . . In the afternoon I had my head shaved but Bannister had set the razor so bad it was practically murder to me. In the evening I took a walk about the plantation and overlooked everything and found several things out of order, for which I scolded at John. At night Peter came from above and brought a wild goose that was very fat. L-s-n seemed to be a little better. My wife and I had a small quarrel about nothing. . . .

2. . . . I ate some wild duck for dinner and in the afternoon took a walk about the plantation and saw everything and considered what was to be done and did not return till the evening and then I found Mr. Mumford come over the river and he told me that Captain Evans and another Indian trader were come from Carolina and had brought abundance of skins. He told me also that the

Tuscarora Indians were come in to tell us what their nation would do. . . .

. . .

4. . . . I took my leave and was set over the creek and so proceeded through the snow to Williamsburg. It was very cold so that I was forced to alight off my horse to walk two several times. I got to Williamsburg about 3 and dined with the council and I ate mutton for dinner. Then I went to the Governor's to consult the doctor about L-s-n and he gave me his directions in writing. Then we played at piquet and I won 20 shillings. I went home about 9 o'clock and wrote a letter to my wife and another to Mr. Ludwell to beg some linseed. I said my prayers and had good health, good thoughts, and good humor, thank God Almighty. It was terribly cold this night that I could not be warm in bed.

5. . . . Abundance of company came to my lodgings and some burgesses among them, with whom I discoursed about the unreasonable taxes on several things. I settled some accounts and then I went to the capitol in my boots because of the snow. The wind came to south and it grew a little warmer, thank God. My man Tom returned home. We rejected the bill concerning the gold coin and began to make a bill about negroes. We sat till about 3 o'clock and then went to dinner. I ate some roast chicken. We sat and discoursed till the evening and then went to the coffeehouse where I lost 10 shillings at whisk. . . .

6. . . . About 11 o'clock we went to the capitol and read the horse bill and sent in down with a message that we adhered to our amendment. We made some steps to making another negro bill but made nothing of it. About 3 we adjourned and I went to dine at the Governor's and I ate some venison for dinner. Then I went to the coffeehouse where I lost £4 at piquet. . . .

7. . . . Several people came to my lodgings and Mr. Custis among the rest who came about selling some of Colonel Parke's land and negroes to pay his debts. About 11 I went to the capitol, where we sat in council about Mr. Cary's accounts and the Governor insisted that he was incapable of the business and should be turned out and the council were of his opinion. We went to dinner about 3 and I ate some wild duck for dinner. Then Colonel Smith and I took a walk and in the evening went to the coffeehouse, where I played again at piquet and won of the Doctor about

£4 and about 11 o'clock went home, where I said my prayers and had good health, good thoughts, and good humor, thank God Almighty. Gilbert, the Governor's man, was sent this day on board the man-of-war.

8. I rose about 8 o'clock and read a chapter in Hebrew but no Greek because Mr. Custis came to me again and several other people. I said my prayers and ate boiled milk for breakfast. Colonel Ludwell invited me to go to Green Spring but I excused myself, notwithstanding several pretty women were there. About 10 o'clock I went to the capitol where the Governor gave audience to the Tuscarora Indians and engaged them to promise to cut off those Indians that committed the murder in Carolina. The weather was warm. . . . We had some French wine sent by Captain Garlington to the Governor. About 7 o'clock I went home to my lodgings and wrote a letter to my wife with directions concerning L-s-n. . . .

9. . . . About 10 o'clock came my brother Custis and stayed till 11 o'clock and we went to church, where I saw Billy Cole's wife, who was very pretty. Mr. Finney gave us a sermon and a very indifferent one. After I went with my brother and sister Custis to Mrs. [Whaley's] to dinner where we had a turkey and bacon, very well dressed. In the afternoon we sat and talked till about 4 o'clock and then I took leave and walked some part of the way with Mr. Custis, and he told me of some slander he had heard of me, which came from Mrs. Russell. I had my usual way of contempt for it. In the evening I went to visit Colonel Bray where I stayed till about 8 o'clock and then went to my lodgings where I washed my feet. . . .

10. . . . I had several gentlemen come to my lodgings and among them Mr. Custis who desired me to go to the committee to attest my wife's consent to selling some of Colonel Parke's estate to pay his debts, which I did accordingly. Then I went to the capitol where we read the money bill the first time and heard the treaty they passed with the Tuscarora Indians. . . .

11. . . . Frank Eppes came to see me but I was in great haste to go to Council, where the Tuscarora Indians were to sign the treaty with the Governor, which they performed accordingly. Then we [went] into court where we were sworn as judges of the Court of Oyer and Terminer and then we went to church to hear the

Commissary preach the [assize] sermon, which was very indifferent. Then we returned to court where Betty J-r-d-n was convicted of burglary for breaking the Governor's house. . . .

12. . . . I went to the capitol and we went into court to pronounce sentence of death upon Betty J-r-d-n and she plead her belly. Then we went into Council and excepted against several things in the money bill. We had a hot dispute and Colonel Ludwell and Colonel Carter quarreled before the Governor, who laughed at them to himself. We sat till about 4 o'clock and then went to dinner. The House of Burgesses sent us up several bills and that for selling some of the land and negroes belonging to my sister Custis among them, which we read the first time. . . .

13. . . . I neglected to say my prayers because there came company that hindered me, but I ate three custards for breakfast. Colonel Bassett came among the rest. I received letters from my overseers above by which I learned that all were well there. About 10 o'clock I went to the capitol where a jury of matrons were impanelled to inquire if Betty J-r-d-n was quick with child and their verdict was that she was quick. Then we went to Council and read several bills and sent a message concerning amendments to be made to their money bill. We rose about 4 o'clock and then went to dinner and I ate roast duck. My man Tom came from home and told me poor L-s-n died on Sunday morning last but that all else were well, thank God. . . .

14. . . . It threatened rain; however I wrote a letter and sent Eugene home with it to let my wife know why I could not come. Several gentlemen came to my lodgings but about 10 o'clock I went to see Colonel Carter and found him better. Then I walked to the capital where I danced my dance; then we went to Council and read some bills the third time and particularly Mr. Custis his bill. Then we examined Mr. Cary's accounts and found several articles wrongly charged. . . .

15. . . . About 10 o'clock I went to the capitol where we received an answer from the House of Burgesses to our proposals to amend their money bill, who refused to allow of those amendments. Mr. Robinson told some of the Council that the Governor was for having the bill passed notwithstanding the Burgesses had refused our amendments. However I was against it though I was very ready to oblige the Governor in anything in which my honor was not

concerned. We made some amendments to the bill for raising the land forces and sent it away down and then rose and I walked home with the Governor to dinner and ate some boiled mutton for dinner, and then drank a bottle of French wine till about 8 o'clock and then walked home to my lodgings. . . .

16. . . . A man came to me for rights and because it was matter of necessity I let him have some rights. I did not go to church but rode to Jimmy Burwell's where I got about one o'clock before the people came from church, but they came about half an hour after. Here I found Colonel Eppes, John Bolling, and Robin [Bolling], which last was ill of the colic. I never had seen Mrs. Burwell, who is a pretty woman, nor did I ever see Suky the Doctor's maid, who was not ugly but much gone to the flesh. About 3 o'clock we went to dinner and I ate some boiled beef. In the afternoon we took a walk, notwithstanding it was very cold, till the evening and then we sat by a good fire and were merry till about 10 o'clock, and then I took my leave and went to bed next door to the nursery. I said my prayers and had good health, good thoughts, and good humor, thank God Almighty. One of Major Burwell's children disturbed me in the night so that I could not sleep.

17. I rose about 7 o'clock and read nothing but a little Dutch. However I said a short prayer and ate boiled milk for breakfast. The weather continued very cold. Robin Bolling was better and he and I went to shoot with bows and arrows. When that was over we returned and I drank some chocolate. About 10 o'clock we took leave and returned to Williamsburg, where we heard that a ship was come into Rappahannock from London which brought word that our fleet got well to England. The Doctor and my brother Custis came to my chambers and from thence we went to the capitol where we heard that the Indians were forming a conspiracy against the English and that a Nottoway Indian told a negro of it. We had a conference about the bill that lay the taxes but the Burgesses had orders to discourse about the title of the bill and not the substance of it. . . .

18. . . . I settled the pork account and then went to the capitol where I danced my dance. Then we went into Council and read some of the claims. The Governor let some of us know he would not pass the bill for the impositions. About 12 o'clock I danced my

dance again and read some Italian. We settled the rangers and then went to dinner and I went with the Governor home and ate boiled beef for dinner. Then we drank a bottle of claret and then went to the coffeehouse where I lost 30 shillings. . . .

19. . . . Captain Holt came to me to favor him in a protested bill by forbearing him, which I did. About 10 I went to the capitol where we sent a message to the Burgesses to confer with them about their imposition bill but they denied us it on account of its being the province of the Burgesses to raise money after which method they pleased. We resented this usage, but the Governor came and gave audience to the Saponie Indians and then made the Burgesses a speech which was a severe reflection upon their proceedings and in which he told them he could not pass their imposition bill because it was insufficient and [unusual]. . . .

20. . . . Several gentlemen came to my lodgings and I settled several accounts with them and particularly with Dr. Cocke I settled his [p-l-y] account and he owed me £24. About 11 I went to the capitol where I danced my dance and read some Italian. Nothing was done in Council but signing a warrant and petition though the House of Burgesses [laid] some faults on us. I danced my dance again because I was cold. Mr. Custis came to town and would have me go home with him but I could not because the young men came to town. About 4 o'clock we went to dinner and I ate some roast chicken and after dinner we drank a bowl of punch and were merry with Colonel Carter, who went away about 7 o'clock in the evening. Then we went to the coffeehouse where we played at dice and I won £4. . . .

21. I rose about 7 o'clock and read nothing because I was to write out the Governor's account, which I did. I said my prayers and ate custard for breakfast. The weather was very cold. About 9 o'clock I went to the Governor's to settle accounts with him but he was not at leisure. When I returned I went to the coffeehouse where I played a game at piquet and won 15 shillings. Then I went to Mr. Clayton's and settled Colonel Churchill's account and desired him to write a deed of partition between my brother Custis and me of old Colonel Parke's land. Then I returned to the capitol where I danced my dance. We prepared a protest against the proposal of the House of Burgesses not to grant us a conference on the money bill. . . .

22. . . . About 10 o'clock Mr. Bland came and he went with me to the Governor's where we balanced accounts with him and he made me allow him 6 percent for the difference of money. I inquired of him whether I might not pay the contingent charges in money and charges sterling and he agreed that I might. I desired leave to go home, but the Governor told me he should speak to the House of Burgesses on Monday and would have the Council there. About 12 I went to the coffeehouse where the gentlemen of the Council were and I told them the Governor's mind and they agreed to be there. About 2 o'clock I went again to the Governor's in the President's coach to dinner and ate beefsteak. . . . I endeavored to reconcile the Governor to the Burgesses but in vain.

23. . . . I wrote out a chronology of the Bible which the Governor lent me and did not go to church, God forgive me. About 12 o'clock Dr. Cocke came to me in order to go to Queen's Creek and we got on horseback about one and rode there and [found] them pretty well. The weather was cold and had hindered them from going to church likewise. We waited till 3 o'clock for dinner and then I ate some turkey and chine and after dinner we sat by a fire and chatted and were merry, without much scandal to our [talk]. The Doctor was very pleasant company, as he commonly is. We had some roast apples and wine, with which we diverted ourselves till about 10 o'clock. . . .

24. . . . It was very cold and had frozen very hard. However, about 10 we took leave and rode to Williamsburg. Mr. Bland came to my lodging and told me he had bought Mr. Brodnax's land for me that lay near the Falls and was to give him £165 for it. Then I went to the coffeehouse, where I met all my brothers of the Council that were in town. About 12 o'clock Colonel Ludwell and I went to the Governor's to learn from himself how long he intended to keep us and to persuade him to give leave to the House of Burgesses to adjourn for a month without their asking, which he at last consented to. He asked us to dine but we [. . .] to the rest of the Council and dined with them at the coffeehouse and I ate some beef for dinner. I paid all my debts and about 3 o'clock we went to the capitol to expect· the coming of the Governor, who adjourned the assembly till the 24th of January and then we all took leave and went away and I went to Queen's Creek and surprised a good company there. I ate some toast and cider and roast apples and sat and chatted till 10 o'clock and then I recommended the com-

201

pany to the divine protection and said a short prayer and had good thoughts and good health and good humor, thank God Almighty.

25. I rose about 7 o'clock and read nothing because I prepared for my journey to Colonel Duke's. However I said my prayers and ate boiled milk for breakfast. The weather threatened snow but it did not frighten me from taking my leave about 11 o'clock, but before that I wrote a letter to Mr. C-s and enclosed to Mr. Graeme who was to go soon in the man-of-war. About 2 o'clock I got to Colonel Duke's and found both him and his old woman in good health, only the last was grown very deaf. We sat and talked till about 4 and then we went to dinner and I ate some wild duck. In the meantime the Colonel sent a negro man to see whether the river was open at my brother Duke's and he brought word it was, and therefore I took leave of the Colonel and his old countess and rode away to the river and with some difficulty got over as soon as it was dark. I found all well there and we drank a bottle of wine. About 9 o'clock I went to bed. I said my prayers and had good health, good thoughts, and good humor, thank God Almighty.

26. I rose about 7 o'clock and read nothing because I prepared for my journey. However I said my prayers and ate boiled milk for breakfast. It was cold and threatened rain or snow. About 9 I took leave and rode towards home and between Captain Stith's and home I met my wife and Mrs. Dunn going to Williamsburg to see what was become of me, but they turned back with me home where I found all well, thank God Almighty, except old Jane who was very ill of a fever. About 3 o'clock we went to dinner and I ate some wild goose. In the afternoon I looked about and found all things in good order. Mr. Anderson dined with me and after dinner gave old Jane the Sacrament. He stayed with me till the evening and then returned home. I inquired of my people how everything was and they told me well. Then I gave them some rum and cider to be merry with and afterwards read some Italian and wrote two letters to my overseers. I said my prayers and had good health, and good thoughts, and good humor, thank God Almighty. I rogered my wife [lustily].

27. . . . I danced my dance and said my prayers devoutly and then walked in my library because the ground was wet. In the evening I wrote in my journal and caused several of my people to be let blood by way of prevention. . . .

. . .

29. . . . Poor old Jane died this morning about 9 o'clock and I caused her to be buried as soon as possible because she stank very much. It was not very cold today. I danced my dance. . . . I ate some broiled goose for dinner. In the afternoon I set my razor, and then went out to shoot with bow and arrow till the evening and then I ran to breathe myself and looked over everything. At night I read some Latin in Terence till about 10 o'clock. . . .

30. . . . The weather was very clear and warm so that my wife walked out with Mrs. Dunn and forgot dinner, for which I had a little quarrel with her and another afterwards because I was not willing to let her have a book out of the library. About 12 o'clock came Mr. Bland from Williamsburg but brought no news. He stayed to dinner and I ate some roast beef. In the afternoon we sat and talked till about 4 o'clock and then I caused my people to set him over the river and then I walked with the women about the plantation till they were very weary. At night we ate some eggs and drank some Virginia beer and talked very gravely without reading anything. . . .

31. . . . In the afternoon I weighed some money and then read some Latin in Terence and then Mr. Mumford came and told me my man Tony had been very sick but he was recovered again, thank God. He told me Robin Bolling had been like to die and that he denied that he was the first to mention the imposition on skins which he certainly did. Then he and I took a walk about the plantation. When I returned I was out of humor to find the negroes all at work in our chambers. . . . My wife and I had a terrible quarrel about whipping Eugene while Mr. Mumford was there but she had a mind to show her authority before company but I would not suffer it, which she took very ill; however for peace sake I made the first advance towards a reconciliation which I obtained with some difficulty and after abundance of crying. However it spoiled the mirth of the evening, but I was not conscious that I was to blame in that quarrel.

January, 1712

1. I lay abed till 9 o'clock this morning to bring my wife into temper again and rogered her by way of reconciliation. I read nothing because Mr. Mumford was here, nor did I say my prayers,

for the same reason. However I ate boiled milk for breakfast, and after my wife tempted me to eat some pancakes with her. Mr. Mumford and I went to shoot with our bows and arrows but shot nothing, and afterwards we played at billiards till dinner, and when we came we found Ben Harrison there, who dined with us. . . . I took a walk about the plantation and at night we drank some mead of my wife's making which was very good. I gave the people some cider and a dram to the negroes. . . .

2. . . . A little before dinner came Ben Harrison in his best clothes, because he happened to come yesterday in his worst. He dined with us and I ate roast beef and before we had done Colonel Hill and Mrs. Harrison came and the Colonel ate some pudding with us, but Mrs. Harrison ate nothing. They went away about 4 o'clock and then my wife and I went to walk about the plantation and saw some young trees that Tom had planted this day. . . .

3. . . . I gave Anaka a good scolding for letting Billy Brayne have a hole in his stocking. In the afternoon I set my razor and then went to prune the trees in the young orchard and then I took a walk about the plantation and my wife and Mrs. Dunn came to walk with me. . . .

. . .

5. . . . About 9 o'clock came Major Harrison and the captain of the "Pelican." I gave them a bottle of sack. Then we played at billiards and I won 7 shillings, and sixpence. About one o'clock we went to dinner and I ate some boiled beef. In the afternoon we were merry and made the Quaker captain drink the Queen's health on his knees. About 2 o'clock came my brother and sister Custis and sat down to dinner. They brought no news. My sister was much tired. In the evening the captain and Major Harrison went away to Mrs. Harrison's where I understood that Mr. Clayton was come. We drank a bottle of wine at night. This day a negro of mine at Falling Creek had a tree fall on his head and had his brains beat out. . . .

. . .

9. . . . About 10 o'clock Major Harrison and his brother Harry went away but the rest of the company was persuaded to stay a day longer, only Parson Finney, who went away likewise. Mr. Clayton and I took a walk till dinner and then I ate some roast mutton which was very good. My sloop went away this morning

to Falling Creek. In the afternoon we were merry without drinking. . . . We drank some of my best wine and were merry but would not let the women part from us. About 10 we ate some bread and cheese and drank a bottle on it, and about 11 we went to bed. My wife had got some cold and was disordered in her hip. I neglected to say my prayers but had good health, good thoughts, and good humor, thank God Almighty, only I was a little displeased at a story somebody had told the Governor that I had said that no Governor ought to be trusted with £20,000. Little Peter brought a wild goose with him and two ducks.

10. . . . About 11 o'clock my company took leave and went away and then I could do everything which too much company had hindered me from. . . . Redskin Peter pretended he fell and hurt himself but it was dissimulation. I had a cow die this day. . . .

11. . . . In the afternoon I set my razor and then went into the new orchard and trimmed the trees till the evening and then I took a walk about the plantation. Redskin Peter was very well again after he had worn the bit 24 hours and went to work very actively. Before I came in I took a run for my health. . . .

12. . . . In the afternoon I went into the orchard and trimmed the young trees till I was called away by one of the girls who told me that Mr. Peter Butts would speak with me. His business was to desire me to get a sheriff's place for his brother and in order to persuade me to it told me several things of Ned [Goodrich] and how he had once hindered my man Tony from paying £30 for lying with an Indian wife. . . .

13. . . . About 12 o'clock Mr. Bland came on his way to Williamsburg. He stayed and dined with us and I ate some boiled beef. In the afternoon we sat and talked about the news that came in my last letters till about 4 o'clock and then Mr. Bland went away to Captain Stith's and I went to walk about the plantation and went into the swamp, which was frozen very hard . . . .

.   .   .

20. It rained very hard in the beginning of the night and towards morning it snowed exceedingly and continued till about 9 o'clock. I rose about 7 and caused a path to be made to the kitchen, to the library, and to the house office. . . . In the afternoon because I could not walk I danced my dance and then walked in the library

till night and considered what [obligation] to make to the Governor for saying no Governor ought to be trusted with £20,000. . . .

21. . . . I was out of humor because I missed a book out of the library which I thought my wife had taken for Mrs. Dunn without my knowledge, but she denied it. Mr. Peter Poythress came to our house and brought me a letter from my brother Custis who told me the Governor was angry about what I had said concerning the £20,000. . . .

22. I rose about 7 o'clock and read nothing because I prepared to go to Williamsburg. The weather was cloudy and it rained about 10 o'clock. I said my prayers and ate boiled milk for breakfast. About 11 o'clock came Colonel Eppes and Colonel Hill, the first came to inquire what he should do further about the rangers because people refused. They stayed [till] 12 o'clock and then went away. I ate some tripe and then notwithstanding it rained resolved to ride as far as my brother Duke's and accordingly I recommended my family to heaven and got on my horse about 2 o'clock and got to Mr. Duke's about 5 and there I found the Colonel and all in good health. In the evening I ate some roast beef and Mr. Duke gave us a bottle of wine. . . .

23. I rose about 7 o'clock and found it had snowed very much and continued so to do and the wind blew hard at northeast. I said my prayers and because I could get no milk I ate some hashed beef for breakfast. About 10 o'clock the wind began to abate and then we made a shift to go over the river with our horses and then rode to Colonel Duke's and there I ate some toast and cider. All this time it continued to snow but held up about 2 o'clock and then I took leave of the Colonel, who promised me to follow me next day, and rode in about three hours to my brother Custis' and found them all well there. Here I ate nothing but some boiled milk for supper. We talked about Mrs. Russell and the Governor, not much to the advantage of the first. My sister loves to talk a little scandal of her neighbors. . . .

24. . . . I was a little perplexed what to say to the Governor to extenuate what I had said but I was resolved to say the truth, let the consequence be what it would. About 12 o'clock I and my brother went to town and lighted at my lodgings. Then I went to the coffeehouse where I found Mr. Clayton and he and I went to the Governor. He made us wait half an hour before he was pleased

206

to come out to us and when he came he looked very stiff and cold on me but did not explain himself. At last several of the council came in and paid their compliments to the Governor, who invited us to dinner and six of the council dined there and I ate some boiled pork for dinner. We stayed till it was dark and then went to the coffeehouse. . . . There were 25 of the Burgesses met today which was more than could be expected, considering the weather.

25. . . . We had nothing to do but meet in order to adjourn and the Burgesses did little else unless it was to adhere to their Book of Claims, which put the Governor out of humor with them. The weather was very cold and much snow on the ground, so that I went with boots. About 2 o'clock Colonel Smith and I went to the Governor's to dinner and I ate some cod sounds. I perceived Mrs. Russell to be very cold and stiff in her behavior to me. However we were pretty easy. . . .

26. . . . I wrote a letter to my wife. The weather was clear and good; however I wore my boots. The Governor continued stiff to me but I took no notice of it but behaved myself very courteously to him, when he came in my way. About 3 o'clock we dined at Mrs. [Serjanton's] and I ate roast chicken for dinner but we were forced to dine in the kitchen but however it was very good and we made a shift to be very merry and contented. Nothing of moment was done this day either by the Burgesses or us. In the evening we went to the coffeehouse where I lost £6 at piquet. . . .

27. . . . I had my head shaved by my old man Daniel, who told me he was to live with Mr. Page. About 11 o'clock came Colonel Smith. We stayed in town and Colonel Duke and we walked to church where we expected Parson Anderson to preach but he disappointed us so that Mr. Commissary was forced to give us a sermon. After, we went home with the Commissary to dinner and I ate some roast goose and we were very merry with a dream Colonel Duke had concerning Mrs. Harrison. . . .

28. . . . We dined at 2 o'clock this day because the Governor was to come at 3 o'clock to make a speech to the Burgesses. I ate some boiled pork for dinner. The Governor made a very long speech and much softer than the last. When that was done we went to the coffeehouse where the governors of the College were to meet about several matters and particularly about Tanaquil Faber and they turned him out of his place but gave him, however, his salary

207

for the whole year. They agreed to give Mr. Tullitt £400 to build up the College hall. Then we played at piquet and I lost £7. . . .

29. . . . Several gentlemen came to see me and particularly Major Harrison, who told me that my wife came on Friday last to Colonel Harrison's and the next day to his house with Mrs. Ludwell, where she stayed till Monday morning. He paid me £3 he owed me. About 12 o'clock I went to the capitol where I danced my dance. Major Custis came to town and told me all was well at his house. The Doctor came to me at the capitol and we talked about the Governor being out of humor with what I had said concerning the £20,000. We met just to adjourn and then went to dinner and I ate some wild duck. In the afternoon I took a walk to the Governor's new house and so returned to the coffee-house where we played at dice and I played with good luck and won 50 shillings clear and the Doctor was among us. About 10 I went home and said a short prayer and had good health, good thoughts, and good humor, thank God Almighty, but in bed I committed uncleanness for which God forgive me. My man Tom brought me a letter from home by which I learned that all were well, thank God, but my little panther which he brought for the Governor died by the way.

30. . . . I wrote a letter to my wife which I sent home by Tom again with my horse. Several people came to see me and I received 3 pounds, 15 shillings for my first escheat from Major B-s. The weather was warm but cloudy, the wind southeast. The Governor went to church but I did not because I heard of it too late but went to the coffeehouse where I played at piquet and won 50 shillings. Then I went to the capitol where I danced my dance and then read some Italian till 3 o'clock and then went to dinner and ate some roast turkey. After dinner I took a walk to the College and the Governor's great house. . . .

31. . . . About 10 o'clock our doorkeeper came to me and told me that the Governor was going to the capitol with the Council. This made me get ready and then I went to the capitol where I found the Governor complaining that the House of Burgesses had passed several resolutions which made it plain they intended to spend their time only in dispute and then he commanded Mr. Robinson [*i. e.*, Robertson] to order the speaker and the house to attend him and when they came he dissolved them after a short speech and then proposed how he should perform the treaty made with

the Indians. Everybody was silent for some time and then I said notwithstanding there was no money in my hands belonging to the Queen; however rather than either Her Majesty's interest or the country's should suffer I would advance £500 to pay the Indians with in case they performed their treaty. The Governor took [it?] and the rather because nobody seconded me. Then we rose and I went home with the Governor in his coach to dine with him. I ate some boiled goose for dinner. Several of the Burgesses came after dinner to take leave of the Governor and about 5 o'clock I took my leave and went to the coffeehouse where I played till about 2 o'clock in the morning and neither won nor lost. I said a short prayer and had good health, good thoughts, and good humor, thank God Almighty. I desired the Doctor to give the servants 5 shillings each for me. I advised the Governor to finish the fort at Point Comfort and pay it out of the contingency charges, which he seemed to agree to.

February, 1712

1. . . . I ate boiled milk for breakfast and recommended myself to heaven in a short prayer. I took leave of Mrs. Bland and thanked her for all her kindness and ordered Grills to give her servants money. Then I went to the coffeehouse to pay my debts and went from thence to the Commissary's where I stayed to dine and I ate goose giblets for dinner. In the evening I went to Major Custis and found him a little out of humor that I had not come there to dinner. However that was soon over. He gave me some very good cider. We talked about all our affairs till about 10 o'clock. . . .

2. I rose about 7 o'clock and prepared for my journey. My brother and sister agreed to go with me to Mount Folly. I said my prayers and ate boiled milk for breakfast. About 10 o'clock we were ready and got on horseback and by the way saw Skimino mill and then called on George Keeling and I threatened to arrest him about a bill of exchange. Then we went to Mount Folly and rode about the Neck and found it fit to raise [the stock]. About one o'clock we ate some cold roast beef which we had brought with us and then away we went to Colonel Duke's and by the way my brother Custis and I made a bargain that I should have the land and negroes that were to be sold by act of Assembly, and pay all Colonel Parke's debts. About 4 o'clock we reached Colonel Duke's just as it began

to rain. The Colonel was very kind but had no more than one bottle of wine. I ate some cold chicken for supper and then we sat and talked till 9 o'clock. . . .

3. I rose about 9 o'clock and the reason I lay so long in bed was to consider about our bargain whether I had best agree to it or no. I said a short prayer and ate boiled milk for breakfast. It rained all day so that we could not start from hence. I was computing the profit of my bargain almost all day. We sat by a good fire and discoursed our affairs till 2 o'clock and then we went to dinner and I ate some roast turkey but we had no wine and only bad cider so that we were dull through the bad weather and had nothing to arm our spirits. However we made a shift to wear out the day in chatting and the Colonel is always good company and is kind as far as he is able. I wrote several heads of agreement between my brother Custis and myself. Colonel Duke and his maid were ready to quarrel several times by which I told him it was plain he was too familiar at other times, but the Colonel denied it stiffly. . . .

4. I rose about 7 o'clock and wrote out the articles of agreement between Mr. Custis and his wife and myself. I said my prayers to bring a blessing on our business and ate boiled milk for breakfast. At last we signed and sealed our bargain and God Almighty give it a blessing. The weather was grown clear and warm. I desired the Colonel to take care of my rent tobacco. About 11 o'clock we took our leave of the Colonel and of one another and about two miles from thence I met my brother Duke who turned back with me again and we went over the river to his house, where I found my sister well and her child. My brother's boat was not good but because I came often that way I promised to present him with a boat if he would send for it. I went with him to his mill and then took my leave of them and rode home, where I got about 4 o'clock and found all well, thank God. I ate some partridge for supper. We talked away the evening and I told my wife of the bargain and she was not pleased with it. . . .

5. I rose about 8 o'clock, my wife kept me so long in bed where I rogered her. I read nothing because I put my matters in order. I neglected to say my prayers but ate boiled milk for breakfast. My wife caused several of the people to be whipped for their laziness. I settled accounts and put several matters in order till dinner. I ate some boiled beef. In the afternoon I ordered my sloop to go to Colonel Eppes' for some poplar trees for the Governor and

then I went to visit Mrs. Harrison that I found in a small way. She entertained me with apples and bad wine and I stayed with her till evening and then I took a walk about my plantation. . . .

.   .   .

7. . . . Tom returned about 11 o'clock and brought me several letters by which I learned that the Indians continued still their hostilities in Carolina. . . .

.   .   .

9. . . . In the afternoon I read some more Latin in Terence and played with my girl and then took a walk about the plantation. My wife was a little indisposed with the coming of her moon. . . .

10. . . . About 12 o'clock came Mrs. Stith to visit my wife. . . . Mrs. Stith stayed with us all the afternoon till the evening and then went away, after which we took a walk and my wife burst herself with laughing. In the evening Tom returned from my brother Duke's and brought me some letters. At night I read nothing but we drank a bottle of wine to the health of all our friends. . . .

11. . . . About 2 o'clock I proceeded to Mr. Fleming's where I got about 5 o'clock. Here I met Mr. Custis, who told me his family was well. We were courteously used here, and I saw two pretty daughters of Mr. Fleming. . . .

12. . . . Mr. Custis and I talked about all our affairs. I sent one of my servants with a negro shoemaker, which I had bought of Mr. Custis, to Falling Creek. About 9 o'clock I ate some chicken for breakfast and about 10 took our leave and rode up to the quarters at Parke [Level]. We saw everything there and then went to Parke Hall. . . . In the afternoon we went over the river to Parke Meadow and from thence to Parke Manor, which two plantations are in King William County. We found the land extraordinarily good and very level. Then we returned over the river to Parke [Level] where we ate some boiled shoat; then we discoursed of all our affairs. . . .

13. I rose about 7 o'clock and said a short prayer and ate milk for breakfast. Mr. Custis removed several of his negroes and those which I had bought were still on the plantation. About 10 o'clock we rode to the plantation called Mount Pleasant and examined

everything and I found all the plantation in good order. Then we returned to Parke Hall and went over the river and walked about the low ground at Parke Meadow which had the best timber I ever saw. It rained a little in the afternoon. I was much pleased with this land. Captain Anderson came to account with Mr. Custis and they had a dispute which Mr. D-m-n-y decided. We returned in the evening to our lodgings where we ate some roast fowl. Mr. Custis had brought some cider and I some wine so that we fared well. Mr. Custis told me several things concerning managing the overseers which I resolved to remember. . . .

14. . . . I gave directions about everything and promised Tom Addison I would take him for my overseer next year for two of my plantations there. About 10 o'clock I got a man to show me the way across the country to the falls of James River. I took leave of Mr. Custis in about two hours. I got to my plantation called Shockoe about 12 o'clock, where I found all well, thank God. I went to my two other plantations on that side and found all things well, only little tobacco made. About 6 o'clock I returned to Shockoe and ate some boiled beef for supper. Allen [Bailey] had almost finished the storehouse there. I had not seen this place since the house was built and hardly knew it again. It was very pretty. . . .

15. I rose about 7 o'clock and said a short prayer and then gave Tom Osborne orders concerning what I would have done and then was set over the river to the Falls, where I found things in a bad way, but little tobacco, and that not well ordered, for which I reprimanded Tom Turpin. I ate some milk for breakfast and then I rode to Kensington and found the tobacco as ill managed as at the Falls at which I was angry with the overseer and with old Robin. Then I crossed the northeast way to Falling Creek which was about seven miles and almost all on my land. I found all things very well and Mr. Mumford was there who told me all was well at Appomattox. . . . We walked about and then went in the boat about three miles up the creek to look for a stone quarry and found several and it was late before we returned. . . .

16. . . . Captain Jefferson was at the sawmill and asked my advice concerning the dispute he is like to have about building a mill which I gave him as well as I could. I gave directions about everything and about 10 o'clock Mr. Mumford and I rode away to the Hundred where we got about one o'clock. I went to Isham Eppes'

house where I found the Colonel and Frank Eppes. I stayed with them about half an hour and then went over the river and found Mr. Anderson much better and learned that Dr. Cocke had been with him and that he was gone to my house. I ate some bacon for dinner and about 4 o'clock went home where I found the Doctor and all my family well except Redskin Peter who was very sick. The Doctor brought me several letters from England. I likewise found Tom Randolph and Tom Butts there; the first offered himself to be my general overseer. . . .

17. . . . We were very merry as we always are with the Doctor. At night we drank a bottle of wine and ate some bread and cheese. Mrs. Dunn was troubled with a toothache which abated our mirth a little. Colonel Harrison's brigantine arrived from the Madeiras full of wine and brought hopes of a peace. . . .

18. . . . James Bates came to buy Skimino Mill and at last agreed to take it for £248. He brought me a letter from Mr. Custis by which I learned that my sister had been ill. When Bates had secured his bargain he went away home, notwithstanding I would have had him stay to dinner. . . . I had a little of the piles and my wife was indisposed . . . .

19. . . . About 9 o'clock came an express to summon me to the Council which was to be the next day, which made me get ready to go with the Doctor notwithstanding my piles, which were a little better. About 11 o'clock I recommended my family and in particular the sick man to God and we rode away to my brother Duke's and from thence we went to the Colonel's, who we found very well by his own confession, and then I told him he was to go to Council the next day which made his back ache. Here we ate some milk and then proceeded to Queen's Creek, where we came about 6 o'clock and surprised the family who did not expect us. However they were pleased to see us. About 8 we ate some broiled turkey very heartily after which I grew so sleepy I could not hold open my eyes so that I was forced to go to bed. . . .

20. . . . My sister resolved to go to Williamsburg with us, which made us stay till 10 o'clock and then we all went together. When I had put myself in order I went with several gentlemen of the Council to wait on the Governor but he was not at home. However we saw the Doctor dissect a beaver and take out the castor

which is not the stones of the beaver but two glands just above the genitals. Then we returned to the capitol to Council where the Governor laid before us a petition from the people of Carolina to send them some assistance but we after some consultation thought it necessary to answer them with the assurance that we had made a treaty with the Indians in their favor. I told the Council there was a rumor that the people of South Carolina had hired 1,000 Indians to come and cut off the Indians who had committed the massacre, and this proved true for in the evening the Governor had a letter from Governor Hyde with an account that the Assembly of South Carolina had raised £4,000 and sent about 700 Indians and some white people and had destroyed about six towns of the Indians and were about to destroy the rest. . . .

21. I rose about 7 o'clock and read nothing because I settled some business with Mr. Clayton and desired him to draw conveyances for the land, etc., which I had bought of Mr. Custis. He told me Mrs. Brodnax demanded something to acknowledge her husband's sale of land to me which I refused with some indignation, but she sent to excuse it and pretended it to be only in jest. I ate boiled milk for breakfast. The Governor did me the honor of a visit this morning without any business and stayed about half an hour. Daniel Wilkinson came to tell me he was engaged to Mr. Page or else he would serve me as a general overseer. About 11 o'clock I went to see the Governor's avenue and his great house which pleased him. I stayed about an hour there and then took my leave of him and rode directly home, where I got about 6 o'clock and found all my family pretty well, thank God. . . .

· · ·

27. . . . My overseer brought a mustrat [sic] which I dissected and got out the musk which is in two glands not far from the anus. In the evening I could not walk and therefore danced my dance, and heard the guns of a ship come to Swinyards. At night I read some Latin in Milton. . . .

28. . . . About 11 o'clock came Tom Randolph to inquire about his place of general overseer and brought me a letter from his brother Will to which I wrote an answer. Tom Randolph and I talked about the business but I desired to stay a week more before I could promise him. . . .

· · ·

March, 1712

. . .

2. I rose about 7 o'clock and read a chapter in Hebrew but no Greek because Mr. Grills was here and I wished to talk with him. I ate boiled milk for breakfast and danced my dance. I reprimanded him for drawing so many notes on me. However I told him if he would let me know his debts I would pay them provided he would let a mulatto of mine that is his apprentice come to work at Falling Creek the last two years of his service, which he agreed. I had a terrible quarrel with my wife concerning Jenny that I took away from her when she was beating her with the tongs. She lifted up her hands to strike me but forbore to do it. She gave me abundance of bad words and endeavored to strangle herself, but I believe in jest only. However after acting a mad woman a long time she was passive again. I ate some roast beef for dinner. In the afternoon Mr. Grills went away and I took a walk about the plantation. At night we drank some cider by way of reconciliation and I read nothing. I said my prayers and had good health, good thoughts, and good humor, thank God Almighty. I sent Tom to Williamsburg with some fish to the Governor and my sister Custis. My daughter was indisposed with a small fever.

3. . . . My daughter was better this morning, thank God. I beat Billy Wilkins for telling a lie. . . . In the evening Tom returned from Williamsburg with letters from several persons containing some public [s-s] concerning the Duke of Marlborough being removed from all his places of honor and profit and that it was talked that he was also put into the Tower. . . .

. . .

8. . . . In the afternoon young John L-t came to ask my opinion concerning his wife who had lost the use of her hands and feet for which I advised her to bathe in cold water after taking two purges. . . .

9. . . . The man returned who came from my brother Duke's and promised to come about 14 days hence to work for me, he being a bricklayer. His name is Cornelius H-1, a man of above 80 years old and yet he walked from Mr. Duke's over. . . .

10. I rogered my wife this morning and rose about 7 o'clock but read nothing because Mr. Mumford was here and because they set

up a case for my clothes. . . . Mr. Mumford and I took a walk with our bows and then played at billiards and he beat me. . . . At night I read some news but found myself exceedingly sleepy and took a nap in the chair for about an hour and Mr. Mumford took a nap also but the women sang and were merry. . . .

11. . . . The weather was clear and cold; however I went over the river about 11 o'clock and then proceeded on my journey to Major Harrison's where I got about 3 o'clock and [found] him at home but he was indisposed in his breast, for which I persuaded him to enter into a milk diet. About 5 o'clock I ate some bacon and fowl for dinner. In the evening Peter Poythress came with 14 of the Tuscarora Indians whom he was going to conduct to the Governor. They told us the Carolina men had killed no more than about 20 old men and women of their people and had taken about 30 children prisoners when all the young men were not at home, that the Tuscaroras could [cut] them all off but that they saw some English among them which hindered them and their business with the Governor was to give the reason why they could not perform their articles and to inquire whether they might defend themselves in case they're attacked. . . .

12. . . . About 10 o'clock came Mr. Cargill the minister, who agreed to go with [us] on board the "Pelican," but Frank Lightfoot who had promised broke his word. We took a walk and I saw the Major's improvements about his [threshing]and his [c-l-g grass] and I saw him trim his vines. About 12 o'clock we went on board and were saluted with seven guns and a glass of canary. About 2 o'clock we went to dinner and I ate some of the beef that was preserved after the new manner and found it very juicy and not very salt. It is the best way of saving meat and will preserve it for several years free from taint and was found out by chance by a poor carpenter who keeps the secret to himself and gets abundance of money. We did not find Captain Thompson on board but we found his son who entertained us generously and gave us 32 guns in all. We stayed till about 10 o'clock and were merry and almost drunk. However we got well to Major Harrison's and behaved ourselves very discreetly. About 11 o'clock we went to bed where I was guilty of uncleanness and neglected to say my prayers but had good health, good humor, but unclean thoughts, for which I am sorry and hope God will please to forgive me.

13. I rose about 7 o'clock and found my head ached a little. I said my prayers and drank some chocolate for breakfast. This day

Major began his milk diet and resolved to continue it till the end of May next. About 9 o'clock I took my leave and the Major went to Colonel Harrison's and so rode some part of the way with me. He again protested to me he would keep strictly to his milk and I wished him good fortune. . . . Major Harrison told me he believed his father would never go more to Council. . . .

. . .

16. . . . In the afternoon Peter Poythress came over and told me the Governor received the Tuscaroras very coldly and ordered them to go and help the people of Carolina cut off Hancock town, which they said they would. . . .

. . .

19. . . . About 12 o'clock came John Randolph to see me. I desired him to go to Williamsburg to present a petition to the Governor as rector of the College that he might be usher and gave him some advice about it. He dined with us and I ate some partridge for dinner. In the afternoon I took him into the library and examined him and found him improved very much. . . .

. . .

21. . . . I found that my wife had an intermittent fever and therefore persuaded her to take the bark and got it ready for her accordingly and gave her the first dose about dinner. . . .

22. . . . My wife was ill of her fever, notwithstanding the bark, insomuch that I sent for Dr. Cocke for fear of the worst. I read some news and sold some rights before dinner. . . .

23. . . . Shockoe Billy came from the Falls and bore a letter from Tom Turpin which let me know all was well there. He desired me to provide myself with another overseer because I found fault with some of his management and I wrote him word I would do as he desired. . . . About 2 o'clock Tom Randolph came and was wet with a gust that happened about that time and soon after came Tom from Williamsburg and told me the Doctor was gone to Rappahannock with Mrs. Russell and would not be home before this night. . . .

24. I rose about 8 o'clock and found my wife much disordered with the bark. . . . In the afternoon we walked about to see the people work and then read some more English and endeavored to

217

please my wife but could not till the evening and then [the evil spirit] went off. . . .

25. . . . About 12 o'clock we ate some cold roast beef and then took horses. We called at Captain Drury Stith's but did not light and so proceeded to Charles Fleming's where we got about 5 o'clock. Charles was very courteous to us only he complained he had no good drink but found, however, three bottles of cider. . . .

26. . . . About 8 o'clock we took our leave and rode up to my plantation where I found all well, thank God, only a little backwards in their business. We rested ourselves a little and then took a walk on the other side the river to show Captain Randolph my land there. We walked about three miles and then returned and ate some bacon and eggs for dinner. I had some wine with me from home. In the afternoon we rode to the rest of the plantations and found everything well. The weather was very good and warm. After we had seen everything and given the necessary orders we rode away to Major Merriweather's but he was not at home. However his wife was very courteous to us and would have got a supper for us but we told her we did not want to eat. . . .

27. . . . About 8 o'clock we took leave and rode away to the wading place in order to go to Shockoe but the water was so high that we could not pass so we were obliged to go round by the great bridge and was so discouraged with that we were resolved to return home and by the way called at Drury Stith's and found him not [home]. Here we ate some cold beef for dinner. Here we stayed about two hours and rode away home where I found my wife better and Dr. Cocke with her and my sister Custis. My man John had had the beam of the tobacco press fall on his head but it only made his neck stiff, thank God. . . .

. . .

29. . . . My sister Custis made several complaints to Mrs. Dunn concerning the unhappy life she led by Mr. Custis' unkindness but I believe it is owing to her humor, which seems none of the best. However she seems so easy here that she could not have much at heart. At night we drank a bottle of wine and were merry. . . .

30. I rose about 6 o'clock and read a chapter in Hebrew and no Greek because I prepared to go with the Doctor to Major Harrison's. I said my prayers and ate boiled milk for breakfast. My wife

and all my sick people were better, thank God, which encouraged me to undertake my journey. About 11 o'clock came Colonel Hill to go with us. However I ate some roast beef before we went and then I recommended my family to heaven and took my leave and were set over the river in my boat and then proceeded on our journey notwithstanding it threatened rain but did not rain till we came near to Major Harrison's. The Major was gone to Williamsburg but we were courteously entertained by his lady. She told me the Major did not keep very strictly to his milk diet. I ate some boiled beef for dinner. In the evening it rained very much. However we were as merry as we could be without the Major. I neglected to say my prayers but had good health, good thoughts, and good humor, thank God Almighty. I lay with the Doctor. Poor Colonel Hill had the headache terribly.

31. . . . We were set over the river with our horses but then we lost our way above six miles and did not reach Green Spring till about 3 o'clock where we met a messenger to the Doctor from Colonel Bassett to go to his wife who was dangerously sick. The Doctor went, though he was much tired, and we proceeded to Williamsburg and found the governors of the College sitting. Colonel Hill was sworn one of the members. Several things were done concerning the tenants and then we chose the Commissary rector. Then we went to the coffeehouse and I ate some cold roast beef and Will Robinson gave me a bottle of wine. Then he and I played at piquet and I lost 50 shillings. About 11 I went home to my lodgings where I said a short prayer and had good health, good thoughts, and good humor, thank God Almighty. We have had abundance of rain this month and I never saw the roads so wet in my life as we found them today. Some of us endeavored to get John Randolph to be usher but it was rejected because there were but 22 boys which was not a number that required an usher.

April, 1712

1. . . . I ate some boiled milk for breakfast, and then went to wait on the Governor and settled several accounts with him and talked of several affairs and particularly about my Lord Orkney's business and then we drank some tea. The Governor asked us to come to dinner. Then I waited on the Governor to Council where it was considered how to assist the people of Carolina with 200 men

according to the petition of their Governor, Council, and Burgesses, and at last we agreed to do it and pay it out of the quitrents rather than let the Queen's subjects perish for want of help. Then I went with Colonel Hill to dine with the Governor and ate some fish for dinner. Mrs. Russell looked very coldly on me. After dinner we took our leave and rode away to Colonel Duke's but by the way met Dr. Cocke who told us Mrs. Bassett was better. About 7 o'clock we got to Colonel Duke's but he had no drink for us. However we were merry till about 9 o'clock and then I went to bed and committed uncleanness. I neglected to say my prayers but had good health, good humor, but foul thoughts, for which God forgive me.

2. . . . We could not persuade Colonel Duke to go with us to the club, and therefore we took our leave about 11 o'clock and got to the Brick House before one and found but little company but several more came soon after, among whom were Colonel Bassett and Mr. Holloway, but none of them could tell us any news. About 2 o'clock we went to dinner, about 17 of us, and I ate some roast beef for dinner which was very fat and good. In the evening I went home with Colonel Bassett and found his lady much better and Jimmy Burwell and his wife came there likewise and told us they heard several guns this afternoon. We had a supper but I ate only some milk. Colonel Hill lay with me and snored terribly so that I could not sleep and I wouldn't wake him for fear his head should ache. . . .

3. . . . The Colonel would have had us stay to the christening of his child but I excused myself because I had left my wife sick and wanted to see her. About 10 o'clock we took our leave and the Colonel went with us to the store, about two miles off, where I bought a maid to look after my spinners. Here we saw the salt works. About 12 Colonel Hill and I went away home and by the way I called at Drury Stith's and let him know that the Governor had promised his brother to be sheriff and my petition came too late for him. Then I went home and found everybody well there, thank God, only some were sick at my quarters above. I found Mr. Salle here. . . .

4. . . . I wrote two letters to the quarters and one to Williamsburg and sent the last by my sister Custis who would go, notwithstanding it was like to rain. About 11 o'clock Mr. Salle went away likewise. I settled several accounts and wrote in my journal till

dinner and then I ate some fish. In the afternoon I rogered my wife again. The weather was very bad and it rained almost all day so that my poor sister was terribly wet except she called at some house. My wife and I took a nap after dinner and after our roger. I settled several accounts and read some news. It rained till night so that I could not walk. At night came the master of a ship lately come from Lisbon. We gave him some supper and I ate some broiled turkey with him. He told me he would let me have eight dozen of bottles of Lisbon wine. . . .

5. . . . The captain only drank a dram with me and would not stay to eat any breakfast notwithstanding I asked him. . . . In the evening I took a walk about the plantation and found some of my boys going to burn some of my hogshead staves, for which I beat them. Colonel Bassett sent the maid that I bought and I wrote him my thanks for it. At night I wrote two letters to my officers to choose men to go to Carolina. . . .

6. . . . My wife was a little indisposed but I persuaded [her] to take a walk which made her better. I read some English. Then my wife and Mrs. Dunn and I took a walk to see the peach orchard and to get us a stomach. Mrs. Harrison came just as we sat to dinner and dined with us. I ate roast beef for my part. In the afternoon my wife went to take the air in the coach and Mrs. Harrison with her. I took a walk and when I returned I read some English. Billy Brayne came to tell me that my wife was at Mrs. Harrison's and desired me to come there, and I walked there and stayed about half an hour and then we returned in the coach. . . .

. . .

9. . . . The weather was clear and warm which tempted me to go to the general muster in Henrico and accordingly I went about 11 o'clock but when I got as far as Colonel Hill's it began to rain so that I resolved to return and send John Grills. About 2 o'clock we went to a very indifferent dinner and I ate some bacon and peas but the Colonel would give me no wine, notwithstanding he had it in the house. In the afternoon we went to see the ships that were building and stayed there about an hour. About 6 o'clock Grills returned and told me there were 26 volunteers had offered themselves on the south side of James River. Then I took my leave and went home and found all well. I said my prayers and had good health, good thoughts, and good humor, thank God Almighty. My

wife had caused Moll to be whipped for not letting the people have what was ordered them.

10. . . . At night I ate some bread and butter and drank some cider and my wife and I romped for half an hour till we went to bed. . . .

11. . . . Mr. C-k the wireman came and told me about 30 volunteers offered themselves yesterday to go to Carolina. He made an end of my wire. About 12 o'clock came Colonel Frank Eppes, Major Farrar and Captain Worsham, to return me a list of the volunteers of Henrico which were in all 39. Colonel Littlebury Eppes came also and all these gentlemen dined with me and I ate some boiled beef. In the afternoon all the company went away and I wrote some things to prepare to go to Williamsburg. . . .

12. . . . I was a little out of humor this morning and beat Anaka a little unjustly for which I was sorry afterwards. About 11 o'clock I went to Mrs. Harrison's to wait on her to Colonel Hill's to see his ship launched and found Major Burwell and Mrs. Berkeley there. We went all together to Colonel Hill's where we found abundance of company but it was about 3 o'clock before the ship went off and then it went very well. . . .

13. I rose about 6 o'clock but read nothing because I got ready for my journey to Williamsburg. However I said a short prayer and ate boiled milk for breakfast. About 9 o'clock came Frank Eppes who offered his services to command the men to be sent to Carolina and I promised to recommend him for that post to the Governor. Mr. Clayton had no news except that our men had taken some prizes and carried them to Barbados. . . . Soon after dinner we went away to Colonel Duke's and Major Burwell and Mr. Clayton to Williamsburg. Tom Randolph went with me and we got to Colonel Duke's about 8 o'clock. . . .

14. . . . About 9 o'clock I persuaded Colonel Duke to go and show us my land that lay near him. We went to both my [huts] and saw some of my land and then we took leave of the Colonel and rode away to Mount Folly where we found all well, thank God. Here we ate some fried chicken and bacon and gave the plantation into Tom Randolph's charge and ordered the overseer to follow his directions in everything. Then we went from there and got to Queen's Creek about 6 o'clock where we found my sister well but my brother was not yet come over the Bay. About 8 o'clock I ate

222

some turkey and received a letter from the Doctor to let me know he would send his coach for me next morning or else come himself and told me the news about what our men-of-war had done in taking the prizes. . . .

15. I rose about 7 o'clock and read a little in my commonplace. I ate some boiled milk for breakfast and said a short prayer. About 8 o'clock came the Doctor in his coach and kept me here till 10 o'clock and then we took leave of my sister and rode in great haste to Williamsburg. I had not time to wait on the Governor but went into court as soon as I had put myself in order, where we sat till about one o'clock. Then I went home to my lodgings and did some business till 3 o'clock and then we went to dinner and I ate some fried oysters. After dinner I took a walk to see the Governor's house where we found the Governor, who took us home to drink some French claret where I saw the Baron [Graffenriedt], who seems to be a good man. . . .

. . .

17. . . . After dinner I went to Mrs. [Whaley's] where I saw my sister Custis and my brother who is just returned. Here we drank some tea till the evening and then I took leave and went to the coffeehouse, where I played at cards and won 40 shillings but afterwards I played at dice and lost almost £10. This gave me a resolution to play no more at dice and so I went to my lodgings where I said a short prayer and had good health, good thoughts, and good humor, thank God Almighty.

18. . . . Mr. Curle came to my lodgings and told me our Indian hostages were all run away last night. Several other gentlemen came, with whom I settled some business and about 9 o'clock went to the capitol where we sat till about 11 and then went to church, this being Good Friday, and Mr. Commissary gave us a sermon. . . .

19. My brother Custis came this morning before I got up to tell me that my sister was resolved not to agree to our bargain concerning the selling of the land and negroes. I was surprised at it but thought it only a stratagem to prevail with her husband to live at Williamsburg. I rose about 8 o'clock and found it raining. Several persons came in to do business and so the Major went away in a very great rage with his wife. I had a letter from her with many things very foolish in it. . . . We went to Council where we

had several examinations of Indians taken by Major Harrison by which we learned that our Indians knew of the design of the Tuscaroras. . . . Several of our young gentlemen were before Mr. Bland this morning for a riot committed last night at Su Allen's and A-t-k-s-n's, but came off with paying 10 shillings apiece. The gentlemen were Mr. Page, Ralph Wormeley, John Grymes, Mr. Johnson, and Jimmy Burwell, though I understand the last was not much in fault.

20. . . . About 10 o'clock came the Doctor, to whom I told the quarrel with my brother and sister Custis. About 11 I went to visit the President and went with him to church, where Mr. Commissary gave us a good sermon. I took the Holy Sacrament and then went with Mr. President to dine with the Governor, where I ate some boiled mutton. In the afternoon there were four Tuscarora Indians who had been taken up by the rangers of Prince George and were put into prison. In the evening I went to the coffeehouse, and then it began to rain violently and thundered. Here I tarried till about 9 o'clock, and then returned to my lodgings where I said my prayers and had good health, good thoughts, and good humor, thank God Almighty. The Governor told me privately that he intended to take the militia and march to the Tuscaroras soon and charged me to let nobody know it.

21. . . . The Doctor came to see me and we talked about the unhappiness of my brother and sister Custis, and in the middle of our discourse my brother Custis came in and told me my sister would acknowledge conveyances on some articles agreed between them. . . . About 2 o'clock I went up to my chambers and read some Italian and then came down to court again and sat till about 4 o'clock and then we went to dinner and then I invited my brother Custis to dine with us and I ate boiled beef. About 6 my wife came and let me know all was well at home, thank God. I waited on her to Queen's Creek where I could not disguise my resentment to my sister. I neglected to say my prayers but had good health, good thoughts, and good humor, thank God Almighty. I rogered my wife.

22. I lay with my wife till about 7 o'clock and read nothing, nor did I say my prayers; however I ate boiled milk for breakfast. About 8 o'clock came Captain B-r-k-l-t who came with the fleet and let us know all the fleet was come in and among the rest those that had my goods, thank God. He told me that Mrs. Cocke also

was come in the Harrison and two of her children. I hastened to Williamsburg and went to the Governor with this news and was the first to tell him for certain of the fleet. About 11 o'clock I went to court where we sat till about 2 and then went to council concerning some cases of land and then concerning the Indians. About 6 o'clock I went home with the Governor to dinner and ate some roast beef. Several Nottoway Indians were brought in to examine. . . .

23. . . . About 9 o'clock came Captain Isham Randolph and Captain Posford and brought me some letters from England, by one of which I learned that Dr. Cocke was Secretary of this colony. About 11 o'clock I went to court where I sat till 12 and then learned that my wife was come to town and went to her and had several more letters by Captain Turner who brought my goods for Williamsburg to the value of 2,000 first cost. Then I returned again to court and sat about two hours and then we went into council about the Indians and sat there till night. . . .

24. . . . My wife was not well. I left her and her company preparing to go to visit Mrs. Cocke but much company came in and hindered them. About 10 o'clock I went to court where I sat till about 3 and then we went to Council where several things relating to the expedition to Carolina were considered, the officers appointed, and Major Eppes was to command them. It was almost dark before we had done and then we went to dinner and I ate roast beef. The Indian prisoners endeavored to burn the door of the prison and had nearly performed it. . . .

25. I rose about 6 o'clock and my brother and sister Custis came about 7 to perfect the deed between us. There were several little quarrels between my brother and his wife, and my wife could not forbear siding with her sister and they would fain make me believe that I had promised that my brother should make my sister [easy], which was wrong and gave me a bad opinion [of] my sister. However at last everything was agreed between us and we signed and sealed. About 9 o'clock came the Doctor and I gave him joy for his wife's arrival in this country. About 11 I went to court and about 2 came in the women to acknowledge their deed in court. Then I went away with them to my lodgings and returned to court again and sat till 3 and went to take leave of my wife and her sister who went to Queen's Creek. About 4 we went to dinner and I ate some boiled beef. Then Mr. President and I went to wait on

225

Mrs. Cocke who is a pretty sort of woman. Soon after us the two captains of the men-of-war came to the Governor's but had no news. . . .

26. . . . About 10 o'clock I went to court, where we sat till about 2 and then went to Council concerning the Indians. The hostages were brought back again and were taken up near the Nottoway town. Several men were examined about their trade with the Indians but nothing could be got from them. About 6 I went home with the Governor to dinner and ate some fricassee of veal. The Doctor was returned from Colonel Bassett's and told us his wife was better. . . .

27. . . . Colonel Duke was still sick and went out of town this morning without taking leave of anybody. It is to be feared he will be buried by his old woman who is more than 80 years old. Colonel Carter went also away yesterday for good and the rest went out of town so that I was the only councillor left in town. About 11 o'clock I walked to church and had a sermon from a new parson. After church the Governor asked me and my wife to go down with them but we were engaged to go to Queen's Creek because Colonel Custis was there. Accordingly we went there and found the Colonel and some other company. About 3 o'clock we went to dinner and I ate some boiled beef. After dinner we took a walk in the orchard and then because my wife was tired she and I went to loll on the bed. There I rogered her. At night we drank some syllabub. . . .

28. I rose about 7 o'clock and before I could dress me I learned the President was come. I neglected to say my prayers but ate boiled milk for breakfast. The weather was cold this morning. About 9 o'clock Mr. President and I went to Williamsburg in his coach and got there about 10. I did some business at my lodgings and then went to court and sat till 12. Then I went home and my brother and sister Custis passed conveyances to me for part of Colonel Parke's estate and then came and acknowledged them in court. At the same time I made over Skimino Mill to James Bates. We sat in court till about 3 o'clock and then went to dinner and I ate some fowl and bacon but my wife dined at the Governor's. . . .

29. I rose about 6 o'clock but could read nothing because of much business I had to do. I neglected to say my prayers but drank some

chocolate for breakfast. My wife prepared to go away to Green Spring, and about 9 o'clock I was sent for to court where we sat till about 3 when we finished all the business and then went to dinner about which time my wife went out of town. I received a letter from Frank Eppes by which I learned that his father would not let him go on the expedition notwithstanding he had engaged the Governor to give him that place. This made me very much out of humor. However I ate some broiled pork for dinner. After dinner I and several of the gentlemen of the Council went to wait on the Governor to let him know this disappointment. The Governor did not seem much moved but asked us to drink a bottle of claret with him. The President and they that stayed in town accepted his invitation. . . .

. . .

May, 1712

1. . . . Colonel Hill came about 7 o'clock and about [. . .] he and I took leave of Mrs. Bland and rode to Green Spring where we found Dr. Cocke and his wife and Mrs. Russell and about 12 came Captain Posford to let us know he had brought his boat to carry us home but we stayed to dinner and I ate some veal. After dinner I and my wife, Mrs. Dunn and the child, and Colonel Hill went to the boat, and [after] six hours we got home. . . .

2. I rose about 7 o'clock but read nothing because I was taken up with opening some of my goods. I said my prayers and ate boiled milk for breakfast. The weather was very warm. My wife was indisposed and had a sort of looseness. I had several boat-loads of goods come ashore from Captain Posford who had one of my flats of nine hogsheads. We opened several goods which proved very indifferent and particularly the saddle which was the worst I ever saw. . . . I rogered my wife in the morning and also wrote a letter to England and settled several accounts.

. . .

4. I rose about 6 o'clock and as I walked before the cellar window I heard something running, at which I went and called the boy and it was a vinegar barrel which had not been well stopped. . . .

5. . . . About 11 o'clock came Mr. T-l-r from Williamsburg with a letter from the Governor concerning the debt due to my Lord

Orkney. He also had orders to choose some walnut planks. I made him stay to dinner because I had several things to return to the Governor. . . .

6. . . . About 10 o'clock came Llewellyn Eppes and his wife. I entertained them courteously. About 12 o'clock came Colonel Littlebury Eppes and gave me a letter from the Governor by which I understood that the General of Carolina had made a peace with the Indians and that it would not be necessary to send any men to their assistance. . . .

.   .   .

8. . . . My people washed the sheep in order to clean them for shearing tomorrow. . . .

9. . . . My people sheared the sheep this day till noon. I ate some boiled mutton for dinner. In the afternoon it began to rain and grew very cold so that all my people went to plant the tobacco and planted 4,000 plants. . . .

10. . . . It rained a cold rain, the wind northeast. However my people went to plant tobacco again and planted about 26,000 this day. . . . I gave all the people a dram after planting in the rain. At night we ate some bread and buttter and drank some Lisbon wine. . . .

11. . . . My clothes were brought ashore but when I opened the box I found half the clothes taken out of the box. I sent immediately on board the ship commanded by Turner to let him know I had been robbed and Mr. Randolph was so kind as to go aboard and all the men were searched and their cabins but nothing was found. About 11 we went to church where I saw a man who told us he had read in a gazette that the King of France was dead. Mr. Anderson gave us a good sermon and after church he and several others came to dine with me. . . .

12. . . . Redskin Peter was again sick in pretence but I tied him up by the leg to cure him and it did cure him. My people planted tobacco again. I settled several matters till dinner, and then I ate some dried beef. Just before dinner came Mr. Custis and told me all was well at Queen's Creek. He came in order to go with Tom Randolph to share the tobacco at the quarters in King William. In the afternoon we took a walk about the plantation and got some

cherries. In the evening my brother Custis complained his head ached and he would not drink anything. . . .

13. I rose about 6 o'clock but read nothing because I prepared to go with my brother to Falling Creek. I said my prayers and ate boiled milk for breakfast. The weather threatened rain but did not discourage us from going but before we went came several masters of ships and Colonel Hill and Mr. Bland who told me all was well at Williamsburg. These were going to Prince George court. About 11 o'clock my brother Custis and I set out and rode to Colonel Hill's where we found Mr. Anderson, who gave us some cherries. We stayed till our horses got over the river and then rode to Falling Creek, where we found two negroes sick and some other things out of order for which I scolded at Mr. Grills. My brother was pleased with the sawmill. . . .

14. . . . About 9 o'clock I gave the necessary orders and then took my leave of my brother Custis and delivered him into Tom Randolph's hands and returned home and the weather began to clear up again. There was a great noise in the wood made by certain flies by some called drouth flies. About 12 o'clock I got home and found all well, thank God, but my wife was out of humor; that made me so likewise. Mrs. Harrison and Mrs. Hamlin came and dined with us and I ate some broiled shoat. In the evening I took a walk about the plantation and was a little out of humor because my wife was not so kind as I thought she should be. . . .

. . .

19. . . . The weather was clear and cold. I ordered my colt to be branded. There were abundant flies like locusts in the wood which make a shrill noise but do no visible mischief, and the birds eat them so that we saved our cherries and other fruit from them. . . .

. . .

21. . . . At night I received a letter from Dr. Cocke, who desired me to persuade Captain Posford to send his boat to Green Spring for him and his lady. . . .

22. . . . My wife caused Prue to be whipped violently notwithstanding I desired not, which provoked me to have Anaka whipped likewise who had deserved it much more, on which my wife flew into such a passion that she hoped she would be revenged of me.

I was moved very much at this but only thanked her for the present lest I should say things foolish in my passion. I wrote more accounts to go to England. My wife was sorry for what she had said and came to ask my pardon and I forgave her in my heart but seemed to resent, that she might be the more sorry for her folly. She ate no dinner nor appeared the whole day. . . . I said my prayers and was reconciled to my wife and gave her a flourish in token of it. I had good health, good thoughts, but was a little out of humor, for which God forgive me.

23. . . . My wife and I were very good friends again. Captain Posford sent his boat to Green Spring for Dr. Cocke and his family. I ate bacon fraise for dinner. In the afternoon I put several things in order and then wrote another account but committed so many mistakes that I was forced to write it over again. . . .

24. . . . By 12 o'clock there came the Doctor and his wife and Mr. Catesby and the Doctor's daughter. I received them very courteously and gave them a glass of canary and some cakes to stay their stomachs. There was no news but only that L-r-n T-y had found a silvermine. About 3 o'clock we went to dinner and I ate some beans and bacon for dinner. In the afternoon the daughter, Mr. Catesby, and I went into the swamp to see the nest of a humming bird and the Doctor followed along. However we found a nest with one young and one egg in it. . . .

25. . . . About 11 o'clock we went to church where Mr. Anderson gave us a good sermon. The two Mrs. Thomsons were come up to see Mrs. Eppes and I invited them to come and see us. I took three of the masters of ships home with us to dinner and I ate some dried beef. In the afternoon the masters went away very early and we went to take a walk in the evening. At night we drank a bottle and the women went upstairs by themselves. I said my prayers and was out of humor that my wife did not come to bed soon. . . .

26. . . . I wrote several letters to send by the Doctor to Williamsburg who threatened to go tomorrow. I did nothing but write out another account to send to England before dinner. I ate some boiled pork. In the afternoon I wrote more letters till the evening and then took a walk about the plantation with the ladies and afterwards Mr. Catesby and I walked in the garden. . . .

27. . . . In the afternoon we went into the library to see some prints. We spent the afternoon in conversation and in the evening

we took a walk and ate some cherries. At night we had a syllabub and drank a bottle and were merry. . . .

. . .

31. . . . In the afternoon came Mr. Salle from Manakin town and Phil W-b-r to renew his bill of exchange. I wrote another account and then my wife and the ladies went out in the coach and in the evening the men and I walked out to meet them. They all ate some supper at night except me who did not find myself very well. . . . I was out of humor with my wife for her foolish passions, of which she is often guilty, for which God forgive her and make her repent and amend.

June, 1712

1. . . . I said my prayers and ate nothing for breakfast because I was indisposed and feared an ague which I had [favorably], thank God, but my wife took no notice of my complaint. Mrs. Cocke had a letter from her husband with an account of two prizes condemned. The weather was cloudy. I grew so ill that about 10 o'clock I was forced to go to bed and soon after had a most violent fever and sore throat. My fever continued with great violence till about 6 o'clock and then it began to abate and then I took the bark, very willingly, to avoid having another fit. Mrs. Cocke had the goodness to come and sit above an hour with me. Mrs. Dunn gave me the bark in the night. I slept indifferently but had no command of my thoughts nor humor, God's will be done.

2. I rose not in the morning but took the bark in bed and sweated much and ate nothing but two eggs all day. I began my two ounces of bark and did not rise till the afternoon for about two hours and then went to bed again. I said a short prayer and found neither my strength nor looks much altered. Mrs. Cocke made me a short visit this day while I lay abed. I endeavored to eat some minced veal but could not eat but very little or nothing. . . .

3. . . . The stonecutter came from Williamsburg to put up my marble chimney piece.

4. I rose about 8 o'clock and found myself pretty well, thank God. . . . Colonel Frank Eppes came to account with me and I

gave him a wipe about hindering his son from going to Carolina. We had 11 people at dinner and Mr. Clayton among them but I ate nothing but bread and butter. In the afternoon most of the company went away and Mr. Mumford came and told me all was well at Appomattox. At night I went early to bed but the ladies talked so loud I could not sleep a great while, which made me uneasy. I said my prayers and had indifferent health, no thoughts, and bad humor. God's will be done. The stone[cutter] got some irons made for the marble.

5. I rose about 9 o'clock and found myself not well for want of sleep. I said my prayers and had tea and bread and butter for breakfast. The stonecutter began to work in the library chimney. I wrote in my journal all that happened since I was sick. . . . I ate some boiled mutton for dinner but did not dine with the rest of the company because they would not have the window shut where it rained in. This made me a little out of humor. After dinner I found myself better and walked about the garden all the evening, and Mr. Catesby directed how I should mend my garden and put it into a better fashion than it is at present. I ate two poached eggs for supper and did not go to bed till the rest of the company. . . .

6. . . . I was very lazy and did only settle some accounts before dinner. In the afternoon walked about very much and read nothing. About 4 o'clock came Tom [Howlett] and I settled accounts with him. Then I took a walk about the plantation and returned some time before it was dark out of pure discretion, and found Prue with a candle by daylight, for which I gave her a salute with my foot. . . .

7. . . . In the afternoon I read a little English till the evening and then Mr. Catesby and I took a walk about the plantation and I ventured to eat six cherries. I ate two poached eggs for supper. I took the bark four times this day. I said a short prayer and had good health, good thoughts, and good humor, thank God Almighty. I rogered my wife with vigor.

8. I rose about 8 o'clock and took the bark. I said my prayers and had tea and bread and butter for breakfast. I found myself pretty well this morning. The weather was cool. I took four doses of bark today to make an end. We prepared to go to church where we had a good sermon by Mr. Anderson. It was very hot at church.

We stayed to receive the Sacrament which I did devoutly. Nobody came to dine with us. I ate some roast pigeon for dinner. In the afternoon came the Doctor very much fatigued but brought no news. . . .

9. . . . I prepared to go to Williamsburg with the Doctor and my sister Custis. The weather was very hot and the boat came not so soon as we expected so that we ate again about 12 o'clock and I ate some roast chicken. The boat came not till almost 3 o'clock and then we took leave and went first on board the "Harrison" where we drank some strong beer and then proceeded in our voyage with a fair wind but it was late before we got to Green Spring. Tom was not at the landing with the horses but we soon met him. We found all well at Green Spring and drank some canary. The weather was exceedingly hot so that I dreaded going to bed. . . .

10. I rose about 4 o'clock with design to go away to Williamsburg but our horses were not ready till 6 and then the Doctor and I rode to Williamsburg. When I got there I lay down and took a nap for two hours and then went to the coffeehouse and drank six dishes of tea and then intended to go wait on the Governor but he prevented us by coming to the coffeehouse; however we made him the compliment that we were just coming to wait on him. About 12 o'clock we went to the capitol to Council where we agreed that for the future there should always [exist] a commission of oyer and terminer whether there were any criminals or not, but were content to go without pay for this time because no commission had [existed]. The Governor exposed an anxiety about his double dealing with the Doctor about his commission of secretary. About 5 o'clock we went to dine with the Governor and when we got there happened a terrible gust. I ate some boiled beef for dinner. At night the Doctor was sworn secretary. About 11 o'clock the President set me home in his coach where I neglected to say my prayers but had good humor, good thoughts, but indifferent health, thank God Almighty. The gust this evening split the mizzen mast of the "Harrison" and had like to burned the ship.

11. . . . About 9 o'clock I went to the coffeehouse and drank some tea and stayed there till 12 o'clock and then went to the capitol where Colonel Ludwell and I were to determine the difference between the two Burwells and their sisters and we had the good fortune to do it to their entire satisfaction. About 4 o'clock the

Doctor and I went in his coach to the Commissary's where we dined and I ate some fowl and bacon. About 6 we went in the Doctor's coach to Green Spring where we found several people. Here we went to bed for two hours and then rose and went to the landing in the Doctor's coach and there went into the boat in order to return home and we slept in the boat. . . .

12. About 5 o'clock in the morning we went ashore at Major H-n-t where we slept about three hours on beds where there were abundance of chinches. About 11 o'clock we had an indifferent breakfast of bacon and peas and water to drink. About 12 o'clock we got into the boat again and about 3 got on board the "Harrison" where I heard the damage the gust and [. . .] had done her. We ate some [anchovies] and drank some wine and strong beer. About 6 o'clock we proceeded to Westover where we found all well, thank God. We drank some syllabub and talked till about 9 o'clock and then retired. I said a short prayer and had good health, good thoughts, and good humor, thank God Almighty. I rogered my wife with vigor. My sloop went this morning to Williamsburg.

13. . . . In the afternoon I put things again in order in the library and then walked in the garden. I had a small quarrel with my wife concerning the [nastiness] of the nursery but I would not be provoked. In the evening Mr. Catesby and I took a walk about the plantation and I drank some warm milk at the cowpen and there discovered that one of the wenches had stolen some apples. . . .

14. . . . It rained this morning and was pretty cold; however we kept our purpose to go aboard ship; about 12 o'clock the boat came for us and about one we went with a fair wind to Swinyards. All the ships there had their ornaments out and we were received with 11 guns by the "Harrison." About 2 o'clock came Captain Randolph and Captain Turner and then we went to dinner and I ate some ship's beef. We had abundance of guns all day long so that in all we had about 120 from all the ships. Tom Randolph came in the afternoon and told me all was well everywhere. The rain kept us till 10 o'clock and then we returned home and were so merry that Mr. Catesby sang. . . .

· · ·

21. . . . My wife was out of order but three hours' sleep recovered her. Mrs. Dunn had her face swelled very much. I ate some cold

beef and sallet for dinner. In the afternoon I settled several accounts and then read more Latin in Sallust. Mrs. Harvey came to see my wife, who is exceedingly altered from a very pretty woman. There was a little gust in the evening but it rained but little and did not hinder me from walking about the plantation. I drank some warm milk from the cow. . . .

22. . . . I heard this day that Captain Llewellyn died on Thursday last which surprised me because I knew not that he had been sick. . . .

23. I rose about 6 o'clock and found Mr. Grills here and the Dutch joiner. I settled accounts with the last and I got the first to put up the glass in the library. Mr. Hardiman came here about the horse that killed his father. . . . It was cold weather. My [wife] was sick with being with child.

24. . . . I had a letter from Colonel Eppes to invite me to Captain Llewellyn's funeral. There was a gust and thunder but it did not reach us, thank God, for my people continued to cut oats. . . .

. . .

July, 1712

. . .

10. . . . My wife was still indisposed but would not be bled till after an hour's trying. . . . This day Mr. Page was married to Judy Wormeley. . . .

11. . . . I said my prayers and drank milk from the cow. Our house Jenny was taken very sick, for which I caused her to be bled and gave her a vomit. The weather was cloudy and hot. My wife continued weak. I wrote a letter to England and several other matters till about 12 o'clock and then came Colonel Hill to settle accounts with me and gave me bills for the balance. He stayed to dinner with us, and I ate some boiled beef. My wife longed for small beer and I sent to Mrs. Harrison's for some but she had none, so that she drank a bottle of strong almost herself. . . .

. . .

13. . . . I received a letter from Dr. Cocke in which he desired me to pay Posford £25 but in my answer I excused myself. The

weather was cloudy and very hot. My wife was a little better, thank God. I read some news till dinner and then I ate some roast shoat. In the afternoon I took a nap and then my wife and I had a small dispute which put her into a foolish passion and she continued out of humor all day and would not speak to me. Then I read some news again till the evening and then I took a walk about the plantation. When I returned I spoke kindly to my wife but she would not answer me; however I considered her weakness and bore it. . . .

. . .

15. . . . This was the hottest day we have had this year. I ate some roast shoat for dinner. In the afternoon I settled some things in the library. My wife had the headache violently. I wrote more letters to England till the evening and then took a walk about the planta-tion. I have had three calves die in three days. Mrs. P-l-n-t [Pleasants?] had hallooed a great while for the ferry but could not be heard. Therefore I desired [her] to go home with me and a boy set her over the river which she did. She told me that Colonel Hill had the gout. . . .

. . .

17. . . . I had invited John Eppes and Mr. Dennis to come and dine with me but they came not till after dinner. My wife wished to seal an instrument before two justices and she did it before them. They stayed all afternoon and went away in the evening and then I and my wife took a little walk in the orchard. . . .

. . .

20. I rose about 4 o'clock and got myself ready and then took my leave of my wife that was abed, and of Mrs. Dunn who was up, and went over the creek in my boat and then proceeded to Wil-liamsburg. The weather was very cool and favored my journey much. By the way I said my prayers. I got to Williamsburg before church and after I had made myself ready I went to church with Mr. Bland. I found Mr. M-s-t-n, a mad person, in our pew, who behaved himself oddly. After church the Governor asked me to go home with him to dinner. I ate some tongue and udder. Mrs. Russell was very much out of humor with me. Colonel Quarry and Captain Smith, commander of our man-of-war, dined with us and we stayed till late and then went home in the Governor's coach. . . .

21. I rose about 5 o'clock and wrote several things and prepared my public accounts in order for passing this day. I ate some boiled

milk for breakfast but neglected to say my prayers. About 9 o'clock came Colonel Ludwell to examine my accounts and then we went to Council where my accounts were passed. Mr. Jeffrys, the surveyor of James County, was accused of having used the Governor's name to several unjust things, [and] was obliged to ask his pardon on his knees before his accusers. The Governor proposed the dispute there was between him and the President whether he should have the salary from the day of his arrival in the country or from his being sworn, but the President would not submit to our judgment. About 4 o'clock we went home to dine with the Governor, and I ate beans and bacon. . . .

22. I rose about 5 o'clock and wrote several letters and accounted with the Commissary and several others and paid them their money. I ate boiled milk for breakfast but neglected again to say my prayers because I was very busy. I wrote several letters and took leave of the masters of ships who went away this morning. I accounted with several of the naval officers and then went to the Governor's and paid him £1000 and then took my leave of him and returned to my lodgings where I continued to write all the rest of the day till the evening and then went to visit Mrs. Bland and ate some minced veal and then took a walk and met Mr. Blackamore, who was drunk. Then I returned to my lodgings where the Doctor came to see me to tell me I was mistaken about his note. . . .

23. I rose about 5 o'clock with intent to go to Queen's Creek, but the rain prevented me. I wrote another letter and then went to visit the Doctor and drank tea with him and his wife. Here I stayed till about 9 o'clock and then took leave of them and Mr. Bland and rode to Queen's Creek where I found everybody well. Here I wrote several notes wherein I promised to give £5 for each of my negroes run away. About 12 o'clock came the Doctor and his lady. We were very merry together and about 2 o'clock we went to dinner and I ate some salt fish, which would have been good if we had had butter to them. About 5 o'clock I took leave and rode to Colonel Duke's whom I found sick of a fever. Here I drank some good ale. In the evening I wrote a letter to the Governor to let him know the Colonel was really sick. . . .

24. I rose about 5 o'clock and took leave of the Colonel and rode over to Mr. Duke's where I found all pretty well. Here I ate some milk and stayed about an hour and then proceeded on my journey

and on the road said my prayers. About 11 o'clock I got home where I found everybody pretty well, thank God, and the sloop come from Falling Creek with the rest of the granary. . . . My wife was better, thank God, than when I went away. There fell a hail this afternoon that damaged abundance of tobacco. I could not walk in the evening because it was very wet. . . .

25. I rose about 5 o'clock and had a letter from Colonel Ludwell to send a statement of the 2 shillings per hogshead, which I did. I read a chapter in Hebrew and also in Greek. I said my prayers and drank some milk from the cow. I danced my dance. My wife was pretty well. The weather was cloudy and hot. I settled several accounts and caused Billy Wilkins to be whipped for not writing well. I ate fish for dinner. In the afternoon I read some news and then went into the library and read some Latin till the evening and then I took a walk to see the carpenter at work. I had a letter from Colonel Hill which I answered. . . .

. . .

29. . . . My wife was much indisposed again. I read some law and wrote the most remarkable part of it in a book till dinner and then I ate some roast mutton. In the afternoon I put several things in order and then read some news and afterwards read more law till the evening and then I took a walk about the plantation and saw the carpenter work. . . .

. . .

August, 1712

1. . . . I read some law and abridged it in a book. My wife resolved to take the bark. I ate some broiled pork for dinner. Parson Goodwin came just before dinner but would not stay. In the afternoon I took a nap in the library and then read more law till the evening. . . .

. . .

4. . . . In the afternoon I took a walk in the garden, it being very cool and then I read more law till the evening and then I took a walk to see the house, now the roof was put up this day, notwithstanding the rain which fell often today. . . .

5. . . . Mr. Bland's shallop brought me up some things and some books among the rest, which I looked over, which hindered me

from reading the law. Colonel Frank Eppes came just before dinner. I ate some roast pork. After dinner the Colonel and I took a walk to see the granary. . . .

· · ·

7. . . . Mr. Bland told us the Governor, Dr. Cocke, and his wife, and my sister Custis had been sick but were all better again. In the evening my wife and I had a dispute about her taking the bark which put her out of humor. . . .

8. . . . I wrote a letter to the Governor and sent Bannister to Williamsburg to inquire how the Governor did. I also wrote to the Doctor to consult him concerning my wife, who was pretty well this morning. The wind was northwest and very cold. I read some law till dinner and then I ate some roast lamb. . . .

· · ·

10. . . . My wife was better, thank God, and began to [take] a decoction of the bark with mint water to keep it from coming up. The weather was cloudy and cool, which made us resolve to go visit Drury Stith in the coach and about 11 we ate some apple pudding and then Mr. Grills came and told us all was well at Falling Creek. About 12 we got into the coach and about 3 we got to Drury Stith's where we ate some good mutton and were made welcome and returned home in the evening and the horses performed well. This journey agreed well with my wife. . . .

11. . . . My wife was pretty well and continued to take the decoction of the bark with much reluctance. I read some law and abridged it till dinner and then I ate some boiled beef for dinner. In the afternoon I went to the granary to see the people work. . . .

12. . . . I had a letter from Colonel Ludwell concerning our [representation]. I read some law till about 12 o'clock and then came Mr. Dennis to get some Jesuit's bark for Mrs. Irby which I gave him. He stayed to dinner and I ate some fried pork. In the afternoon we took a walk to the house to see the workmen and then he went away. I read law again till the evening and then I took a walk about the plantation. At night I read in the *Tatler*. . . .

· · ·

14. . . . About 8 o'clock came Mr. Bland on his way to Williamsburg and I wrote two letters by him. I read no law before dinner. I ate some boiled pork and in the afternoon put several things in

239

order in the library and then read some Latin. I rogered my wife in the library, who was pretty well again. In the evening I took a walk about the plantation and saw a ship come up to buy wheat. At night I read in the *Tatler*. . . .

15. . . . Captain M-r-l, commander of the prize, came ashore and I lent him a horse to ride to Colonel Hill's to enter. Just as he was gone came Mrs. Harrison and Colonel Eppes and stayed here to dinner. In the afternoon we spent our time in conversation. Captain Eppes went away sooner than Mrs. Harrison, who stayed till the evening. One of Captain M-r-l's seamen showed us some feats of activity in tumbling. . . .

. . .

17. I rose about 5 o'clock and read nothing because I prepared to go to Colonel Duke's [church]. I said my prayers and ate milk and hominy for breakfast. I ordered my horses over the creek and about 7 o'clock was set across myself. The weather was cooler and cloudy. However in about two hours I got to my brother Duke's where I found them all well, though they had lately been sick. Here I stayed till 11 o'clock and then was set over the river and got to Colonel Duke's about 12 where I found Colonel Hill. . . . Colonel Duke was well and resolved to go with me next day to Council. About 2 o'clock I ate some boiled beef for dinner. Colonel Duke gave us the best he had and we were very merry. In the evening we took a walk in the orchard and ate some peaches. . . .

18. I rose about 5 o'clock and resolved to go early but was forced to stay for the two colonels till almost 6 o'clock. I said my prayers and had some milk from the cow. Colonel Duke rode a new horse which he had of Colonel Eppes. We rode together as far as the ordinary and there Colonel Hill parted with us and went to Queen's Creek but Colonel Duke and I proceeded to Williamsburg, where we got about 9 o'clock, and when we were dressed we waited on the Governor with Colonel Carter and Colonel Smith who told me the Commissary was sick. We found the Governor well and Colonel Ludwell with him. We sat at council in the Governor's house and had the Indians before us, who offered to bring in Hancock to show us their sincere intentions to make peace. We also agreed to have an Assembly the 22nd of October. About 4 o'clock we went to dinner and I ate some boiled beef. Mrs. Russell and I were [g-r] civil. At night we drank two bottles each of good claret and went to our lodgings [at] 11 o'clock in the

Governor's coach because it rained. I neglected to say my prayers and committed uncleanness, but had good health and good humor, thank God Almighty.

19. I rose about 5 o'clock and found myself disordered with the claret I drank last night but not so much as Colonel Carter, who was very sick. I neglected to say my prayers. About 7 o'clock I went to Mr. Bland's where I drank tea till about 9 and then rode to my brother Custis' where I found all well but heard nothing of my negroes. Here I stayed till dinner and ate some roast veal. After dinner came Mr. Catesby and told us the Doctor was sick again and very [amiss] or else I would have visited him. In the evening I rode to Green Spring where I found everybody well. Colonel Hill came there also in the evening and we ate some fruit and drank drams and other drinks. The dram was a remedy for the heartburn which the claret I had drunk the night before had given me. I said my prayers and had good health, good thoughts, and good humor, thank God Almighty. In the night Colonel Hill was taken very sick and I rose to his assistance but when he had vomited he was easy.

20. I rose about 4 o'clock and drank some tea and ate bread and butter and at break of day rode away and passed the ferry about sunrise and paid what I owed to the ferryman. The weather was very hot; however before 9 o'clock I got to Captain John Stith's where I ate some quince and milk for breakfast and then took a nap on the couch for about an hour and about 11 o'clock my wife and Mrs. Dunn came there with the child in the coach. She told me she had lost her fits and that our people were well at home. About 3 o'clock we went to dinner and I ate some fowl and bacon. In the afternoon we sat and talked till about 5 o'clock and then took leave and returned and got home before dark. I found all well, thank God, and because we were all weary we went early to bed. . . . Mrs. Dunn received a letter from Major Custis about borrowing money of his wife.

. . .

23. . . . I took a walk about my plantation, and then walked with my wife in the garden, where she quarreled with me about Mrs. Dunn. I spoke my mind with calmness. At night I read in the *Tatler*. . . .

. . .

25. . . . My wife had a bad rest last night and a fever for which she resolved to take the bark in powder. I read some law till dinner and then I ate some pork and peas. My wife was disappointed in her dinner for which she cried and I thought would have miscarried but it went off again. . . .

26. . . . The weather was cold but my wife was not well; however she resolved to go to Colonel Eppes's and to strengthen ourselves we ate some fried mutton pie before we went. About 10 o'clock we got into the coach and got to Colonel Eppes's before 12. He was abroad but she was at home. We sent to Colonel Hill and Mr. Anderson who came to us with Drury Stith and Colonel Eppes came soon after. I persuaded Colonel Hill, Colonel Eppes, and Drury Stith to draw lots which two should stand burgesses and the lots fell upon Colonel Hill and Colonel Eppes. About 5 o'clock we had dinner and I ate some roast mutton. In the evening we went to Colonel Hill's. . . . We spent the evening in conversation till about 9 o'clock and then we went to bed. I rogered my wife and neglected to say my prayers but had good health, good thoughts, and good humor, thank God Almighty.

27. . . . Mr. Anderson and Mrs. Dunn went to fish and caught some fish and they were dressed for us about 11 o'clock and I ate some fish. Here we stayed till about 2 o'clock and then we all went to Llewellyn Eppes's, where the mistress of the house spent all her time in getting victuals and we hardly saw her. We ate abundance of fruit and were very merry till dinner which came about 4 o'clock. I ate roast mutton again, and poor Mrs. Eppes ate nothing with us. We stayed till near 6 o'clock and then took leave of the company and returned home where we got about 7 o'clock and found all well, thank God. When we had inquired into all the affairs of the family I said my prayers and had good health, good thoughts, and good humor, thank God Almighty. It rained in the night. I rogered my wife.

.   .   .

September, 1712

1. . . . I sent Billy Brayne to Williamsburg with Tom in order to go to the College and desired Mr. Bland to take care of him. My wife was very well, thank God. . . .

2. . . . In the afternoon I gave my wife some lawn to make her shifts. Then I read some Latin till the evening and afterwards took a walk about the plantation. At night I read in the *Tatler* and Tom returned and brought me some letters from Williamsburg. My head ached very much this afternoon. . . .

3. . . . My wife was pretty well and and gave Prue a great whipping for several misdemeanors. I read some Latin till 12 o'clock and then walked to court and invited Colonel Hill and several gentlemen to dinner. I ate some roast beef. There was no news. In the afternoon I went to court to hear a case between Colonel Hill and Mrs. Harrison where Will Randolph behaved himself rudely and so did Colonel Hill, for which I told them both they ought to be put into the stocks. . . .

4. . . . Colonel Ludwell's man called here and told me that Colonel Harrison and Colonel Ludwell were sick. About 12 o'clock came Frank Lightfoot and his brother and dined with us, and I ate some roast beef. In the afternoon we went and played at billiards and [I?] won most games. . . .

. . .

6. . . . In the afternoon I was shaved and cleaned my teeth and then read a little Latin till the evening and afterwards took a walk about the plantation and found several things out of order, for which I reproved the overseer at night. I settled the time of the boys so that they might have leisure to improve themselves at night. . . .

. . .

8. . . . In the afternoon we went to billiards and I lost a bit. My wife had an hysteric fit pretty violently which lasted about an hour. In the evening we took a walk about the plantation and at night drank a bottle of brandy punch which rejoiced us very much. . . .

9. . . . I gave the necessary orders and prepared for my journey to Falling Creek. Mr. Mumford went away to Prince George court and I went towards Falling Creek about 11 o'clock. I got to Colonel Hill's about 12 but found nobody at home but Mr. T-r-t-n who thanked me for the physic I had sent him and said I had saved his life. I went over the river and got to Falling Creek about 3 where I found all well, thank God, and learned that Mr. Randolph was better. He came soon after himself and looked very indifferent but had lost his fever. He told me that my prescription had done

him much service. About 6 o'clock I ate some mutton for supper and about 7 o'clock Mr. Curle came from his sloop. I gave him a bottle of wine. . . .

10. I rose about 6 o'clock and said a short prayer and then walked to the mill where I discoursed Mr. Grills about everything. About 7 o'clock Mr. Curle came to me again and offered to go with me to Captain Webb's where we got about 8 o'clock and Mr. Randolph brought three men there who had robbed my orchard but when they plead guilty I forgave them on condition they would find security for their good behavior. Here I ate some bread and butter and then took leave and went with Mr. Curle to the Falls where I found everything in good order. About 12 o'clock we went over the river and saw the quarters on that side. We returned to the Falls about 5 o'clock and I ate some roast shoat. About 6 o'clock we returned to Falling Creek. . . .

11. I rose about 6 o'clock and said my prayers and then went to the mill with Mr. Randolph and Captain Soane came to me. I discoursed with them about the quarters and then ate some milk for breakfast. About 9 o'clock I took leave and returned home and came to Colonel Hill's about 12 where I found a sick family and learned that Colonel Eppes was sick likewise. I stayed to dinner and ate some boiled beef. After dinner it thundered and rained a little but soon held up and I went home where I got about 6 o'clock and found my wife with a [. . .] headache and two or three people sick but on recovery, thank God. Mr. Bland was just going away but had no news at all. . . .

12. . . . My wife had a good a great [*sic*] quarrel with her maid Prue and with good reason; she is growing a most notable girl for stealing and laziness and lying and everything that is bad. I settled several accounts till dinner and then I ate some roast veal. In the afternoon I settled several things in the library and then read some Latin till the evening. Afterwards I took a walk about the plantation. I gave the bark to Moll and Jenny but Tom had a fever again. At night I read in the *Tatler*. I said a short prayer and had good thoughts, good health, and good humor, thank God Almighty. I rogered my wife with vigor.

13. . . . About 5 o'clock one of my negroes came from Falling Creek with the coach horses and brought a letter from Mr. Grills that told me all was well, thank God. In the evening I took a walk

about the plantation and at night read in the *Tatler,* after having examined my boys. I said my prayers and had good health, good thoughts, and good humor, thank God Almighty. I rogered my wife again.

14. . . . About 11 o'clock I went to church and heard a good sermon from Mr. Anderson, who with Colonel Hill and Mrs. Harrison and her daughter came to dine with us. I ate some boiled beef for dinner. I told Mrs. Harrison people said she was going to be married and she could not deny it. The company went away about 5 o'clock between which and dinner there was abundance of rain. . . .

. . .

16. . . . This morning I sent Tony to Falling Creek with two horses in the room of the two horses I had thence for the coach. The weather was clear and cool and my wife was a little out of order with scolding at the people. I settled some accounts and walked to see the carpenter at work. . . .

17. . . . Soon after dinner came Mr. Catesby from Williamsburg and brought me a letter from Dr. Cocke by which I learned that there was great likelihood of peace and that we had possession of Dunkirk and that several of Colonel Parke's murderers were taken and some sent to England in irons. We gave him some victuals. Then we took a walk about the plantation. At night we drank some punch and were merry. . . .

18. . . . My man John was incommoded still with the piles. Mr. Catesby and I took a walk and I found Eugene asleep instead of being at work, for which I beat him severely. This is the first day we had a fire in the hall. I settled several accounts and then ate some hog's haslet. In the afternoon came Sam Good and bought two negroes of me for £60 towards paying for the land which I had of him. . . .

. . .

20. . . . I settled my accounts till dinner and then ate some fricassee of possum. . . .

21. . . . In the evening my brother Custis' boy brought me letters from the Doctor to desire me to meet the Governor and come to Pamunkey Town with Mr. Catesby because Mrs. Russell had told

him I only gave myself an air in pretending to wait on the Governor. At night I wrote two letters to send by the boy. . . .

22. I rose about 6 o'clock and read a little Hebrew and nothing in Greek because I prepared to go to Mr. Lightfoot's on the Pamunkey River in order to meet the Governor next day at the Pamunkey Indian town. I said my prayers and ate some boiled milk for breakfast. About 11 o'clock I left my orders with Bannister concerning the sloop and everything else and took leave of my wife and with Mr. Catesby rode to Drury Stith's were we drank some persico and then proceeded to Mr. Sherwood Lightfoot's where we arrived about 5 o'clock. He received us very courteously and gave us some boiled beef for supper of which I ate heartily. He lives in a good plantation and seems to be very industrious. About 9 o'clock we retired to bed. I said a short prayer and had good health, good thoughts, and good humor, thank God Almighty. Riding cured my cold, thank God.

23. I rose about 7 o'clock and shaved myself. I said a short prayer and about 9 ate some roast beef for breakfast. The weather was cloudy and threatened rain; however about 10 o'clock we rode to Mr. Goodrich Lightfoot's who lives about a mile from thence. It rained as soon as we got on our horses. There we stayed till the Governor and all the company came in by the man-of-war boat. About 12 o'clock they came by and then notwithstanding the rain was violent we went over the river where the Governor received me very kindly and so did all the rest of the company, except Mrs. Russell. It rained violently all day so that the company could see nothing and the Governor's cook could scarcely get the dinner. However he did get one about 2 o'clock and I ate some boiled mutton. We were merry but were forced to stay in one of the Indian cabins all day and about 5 o'clock the company were forced to return in the rain to Captain Littlepage's but Mr. Catesby and I returned to Mr. Lightfoot's. Abundance of people came to the Indian town to see the Governor but were very wet and indeed the rain disappointed us all. There is an Indian called P-t W-l who has now his 20 wives. There was also an Indian who was ill of a bite of a rattlesnake but was on the recovery having taken some snakeroot. About 9 o'clock we ate some blue wing and then retired to bed. . . .

24. I rose about 7 o'clock and we prepared to go to the election of burgesses in New Kent. I said my prayers and ate some beef for

breakfast. About 10 o'clock we took leave and Mr. Lightfoot went with us to the courthouse where abundance of people were assembled and about 12 o'clock they chose Major Merriweather and Captain Stanhope their burgesses without opposition. Captain Littlepage told me the Governor resolved to reach home this night. However I resolved to go to Colonel Bassett's because I had promised to meet the Governor there. Accordingly we rode there and arrived about 5 o'clock. The Colonel had been sick but was better but his son was sick. We had some fish for supper. The Colonel and his wife received us kindly. . . .

25. I rose about 7 o'clock and found the weather cloudy which made us resolve to stay here this day. I said a short prayer and drank milk tea and ate plum cake for breakfast. Then Mr. Catesby and I took a walk about the plantation and found it inclosed by marsh and therefore must be very unwholesome. Mr. Catesby killed two snakes in the pasture. About 3 o'clock we went to dinner and I ate some boiled mutton. In the afternoon Mr. Catesby and I took another walk but the Colonel was not well enough to walk with us. He complained he wanted bark and therefore I promised to give him some if he would send. . . .

26. . . . The Colonel's [godson] was very sick which put them into a fright. About 10 o'clock we took leave and rode home but stopped at the Brick [House] where we learned that Colonel Eppes and Captain Harwood were chosen burgesses and that Dick O-n had 33 votes. Here we ate some plumcake that Mrs. Bassett had given Tom to bring for us. Then we proceeded to Drury Stith's where we drank some persico. Then we took leave and rode home where we got about 5 o'clock and found everybody pretty well, thank God, only somebody had stolen one of my great flats out of the creek. We ate some cold roast beef for supper. I was dead weary and therefore we went soon to bed where I rogered my wife but I neglected to say my prayers. . . .

27. . . . In the afternoon I found myself a little out of order but did not much regard it. I put several things in order in the library and then I took a walk with Mr. Catesby who was likewise disordered. The women also walked with [. . .]. When I returned I was much worse. However at night I drank more strong drink than usual. When I went to bed I had an ague which was followed by the fever, which continued most of the night, and I slept very indifferently. . . .

28. I was pretty well again this morning but did not rise till about 8 o'clock and then I went into the river to prevent another fit of the ague and found myself much better after it. I ate boiled milk for breakfast. Mr. Catesby went in the river with me and had a violent looseness which carried away his fever. . . .

29. I rose about 7 o'clock and went again into the river against my ague. I read a chapter in Hebrew and some Greek in Lucian. I said my prayers and ate boiled milk for breakfast. I danced my dance. I continued very well, thank God. The weather was cold, the wind northeast. My wife was pretty well. About 11 o'clock I was a little fevered and my head ached a little; however I would not give way to it. I had not much stomach to dinner; however I ate some broiled beef. In the afternoon I put several things in order in the library and at night Mr. Catesby came and told me he had seen a bear. I took Tom L-s-n and went with a gun and Mr. Catesby shot him. It was only a cub and he sat on a tree to eat grapes. I was better with this diversion and we were merry in the evening. I said my prayers and had good health, good thoughts, and good humor, thank God Almighty.

[1]*Mary Eppes*: Probably the daughter of William Eppes, sheriff of Prince George County in 1705. See *The Virginia Magazine of History and Biography*, III, 394.

[2]*Grills*: Byrd mentions three persons named Grills. One generally referred to as "Mr. Grills," was overseer at Falling Creek. Another, simply called "Grills," was brother of the overseer and was employed in some capacity by Byrd. A third Grills, John, was employed at Westover probably as an apprentice or secretary. Byrd does not say whether John was related to the overseer. It is frequently difficult in the context to distinguish between these three persons.

[3]*Manakin Town*: an Indian settlement on the south side of the James River, twenty miles above the falls, settled by French Huguenots about 1701.

[4]*Fast day*: fast days and days of prayer to ask divine intercession in times of calamity were not unusual in colonial America.

[5]*Stupe*: a piece of tow, flannel, or other cloth, wrung out in a hot liquid and applied to wounds or ailing parts.

[6]*Whisk*: whist.

[7]*Burning coals*: a folk game, not a dramatic production.

[8]*Shot in a bow*: this probably means that the marksmen were standing in a semi-circle rather than that they were using bows and arrows.

[9]*Sell by inch of candle*: the instructions to the governors of Virginia specified that the quitrents should be sold "by inch of candle"—*i.e.*, at public auction, bidding to stop at the burning out of an inch-long candle (*The Virginia Magazine of History and Biography*, IV, 53; XXI, 356.) However, this method was now being given up, and the quitrents sold by the auditor and the receiver general themselves (*Executive Journals of the Council of Colonial Virginia*, ed. by H. R. McIlwaine (Richmond, 1925-1930), III, 248.)

[10]*Stone horse*: stallion.

[11]Mrs. Mary Byrd's will was admitted to probate, June 1, 1710, on petition of her son by an earlier marriage, Thomas Howlett. Mary Howlett is mentioned in 1685 as administratrix of Thomas Howlett (*Henrico County Records*, 1667-1692, pp. 211, 356-357). Perhaps Mary Byrd was the wife of Thomas Byrd, who predeceased her by three days.

[12]*Settled my closet*: the meaning is obscure. Perhaps he means that he or someone on his orders arranged his belongings in his closet, or in a small room; *closet* had both meanings in the early 18th century.

DATE DUE

OCT 13 '64	FE 8'84		
FEB 28 '67	SE 19'84		
MAR 14 '69	OC 10'84		
DEC 2 '69	MAR 21 '89		
FEB 25 '70			
JUN 21 '71			
OCT 6 '71			
NOV 22 '76			
SE 27 '77			
OC 7'77			
MR 6'78			
OC 8 '78			
NO 22'78			
SE 2 5 '79			
SE 3 0 '81			
SE 27'82			
OC 12'82			
OC 5 '83			
GAYLORD			PRINTED IN U.S.A.